THE OBSERVER REVISITED

HARO

THE
OBSERVER
REVISITED
1963-64

Compiled by
CYRIL DUNN

HODDER AND STOUGHTON

FOREWORD

This new collection of pieces and drawings from *The Observer* is presented as a recording of the year. It is not a direct, consecutive or complete account of what happened. It shows instead how the paper responded to certain events, some of them important and some trivial, some of them sombre and some funny, as events in any year are apt to be. Each piece has been chosen for its quality and may be absorbed separately. Where necessary the setting has been lightly sketched in, to make things intelligible not simply to those who have lived through this stretch of time but also years hence to people for whom the Beatles, the Fourteenth Earl, the Boss Men of Dallas and the tall Watutsi will be the haziest of figures. In other words, we have tried to make this a book worth keeping.

As source material for an enduring record, newspapers have severe limitations. The people who write for them work inside the events they describe and brush against the characters they try to weigh up. The fashions of the time are their own. They respond to the arts in a context of novelty. They are themselves involved in the social debate. But there is a sense in which this closeness can be an advantage. As privileged spectators, newspaper people see things happen and hear what is said, often noting peculiarities rarely thought significant or dignified enough for the official record. They sense, too, the emotions of the moment, which do not survive.

What we have tried to preserve in this book is not history in the academic sense, but some of the detail with which history is capable of being enriched. We hope the technique we have used will commend itself from the first pages, where the assassination of Kennedy is covered. It may be years before the real significance of this event can be established. Meanwhile, you will find overleaf the immediate reaction of a leader-writer to the overwhelming news of Kennedy's death, followed by an almost light-hearted account of how the President talked and behaved in private, written by a reporter who had spent hours in his company. Both of them are moving to read—and neither could be written hereafter. It seemed wasteful to bury them— and the others like them rescued by this book—in a basement under Blackfriars.

A newspaper book of this kind can present the character and style of a year. It also discloses the nature of the paper itself, largely created by the nature of the people who work for it, their common attitude to life. This book has been put rather loosely together, but we hope its readers will find the same thread running through Anthony Sampson's record of his night as Nkrumah's prisoner, Patrick O'Donovan's story of Pope Paul's journey into the Holy Land, Nigel Gosling's vision of Leningrad, the notebook Maurice Richardson kept in Crockford's Club, and John Gale's version of the cheetah-hunt on Shooter's Hill.

CONTENTS

7

Illustrations

Cartoons by Haro appear as Frontispiece, and on pages 103 and 212
Cartoons by Feiffer appear on pages 106 and 200.
Cartoons by Abu appear on pages 23, 71 and 83.

The Killing of Kennedy

A Life-enhancing President

On November 22, 1963, in Dallas, Texas, President John Kennedy was assassinated—shot for no immediately obvious reason by someone who was not at once identified. This leading article was written about him the day after he died.

When great men of State die, it is their achievements which come to mind. The tragedy of Kennedy's death is that we have also to mourn the achievements to come. There is a feeling that the future has been betrayed.

When John Kennedy became President, he not only symbolised youth in a world dominated by older men. He brought with him a sense of intellectual adventure. Suddenly, new prospects seemed possible. Life itself seemed more exciting. He seemed to be not so much the heir to an existing political situation as the herald of a new one.

But Kennedy was no visionary driven on by dreams. He was a cool-headed politician with a great regard for facts. Indeed, the intellectual detachment which allowed him to see, more clearly than most men, what needed to be done, also at times prevented him from mobilising the emotional fervour necessary to overcome opposition and to carry his policies through.

This was most true of his domestic policies. He had the courage to challenge deep American prejudices about public spending, socialised medicine and foreign aid. He saw the supreme importance of the Civil Rights issue. And he fought hard to get his views accepted. But his success in these fields was limited. He was thwarted by the cumbersome American system of government, and did not always succeed in overcoming his weakness in the Congress by appealing to the people over their heads, as Roosevelt so frequently did.

Perhaps his greatest successes were in the crucial issues of world affairs. Not that his policies were entirely free of ambiguity. He was, after all, elected after a campaign in which he attacked Eisenhower for failing to deal with Cuba and stressed what subsequently proved to be a mythical missile gap. But, once in office, he began an intensive study of the facts that never slackened.

The importance of the disastrous invasion of the Bay of Pigs lay in Kennedy's ability to learn from mistakes. He quickly perceived the folly of one of his campaign promises and in subsequent crises—Berlin and Cuba again—he showed a rare combination of caution and daring. The risks he took were based on a cool assessment of the situation. And in his moments of epic success, he resisted all temptation to crow—thus turning victory into constructive achievement.

For Kennedy was quick to see the implications of the Cuban crisis. He realised that it showed not so much the supremacy of American power but the dependence of the United States and Russia on each other. The lesson he drew was that it was necessary for the two Powers to establish a working relationship with each other: that in a situation dominated by nuclear physics, the real enemy was not Communism but instability and chaos.

For the first time, it seemed just possible that America and Russia would pursue a limited common aim, modifying their rivalry to meet the need to prevent nuclear proliferation. In the event, only the test ban treaty materialised. But the perception that a new era could be opened, that there were tremendous opportunities ahead for constructive initiative, had been gained.

While Kennedy lived, there was hope that these opportunities would be exploited. With his death at the hands of a crazed assassin, that hope has been lessened, though not entirely destroyed. The new President, Mr. Lyndon Johnson, is an able, perhaps a very able, politician, but a man of a more ordinary mould. And while it is improbable that there will be any dramatic changes in policy—indeed, the new President may be more successful than his predecessor in persuading Congress to accept existing policies—it is difficult to see these policies being further developed to create a new order in our disordered world society.

But as the example of Truman showed, the office of President can bring out unexpected qualities in those who hold it. The men who helped to shape the Kennedy policies—McNamara, Rusk, Robert Kennedy and others—are still at hand. Even more important, the world realities which determined these policies remain the same.

It would therefore be wrong to assume that the new President will change the purpose or intention of American policy. But the effectiveness of Kennedy's Administration lay as much in its *style* as in its actions—the way policies were carried out was as important as their actual content. They were characterised by the President's keen respect for intellect, ideas and knowledge.

It was his style which also gave him his unique personal prestige outside America. His intellectual, somewhat princely, yet keenly professional approach to his tasks had an appeal beyond the shores of America: the sense of excitement which he conveyed quickened the tempo of political life everywhere. He communicated his own

sense of adventure to others. Here was a man who saw himself a
world leader, heir not only to America's political legacy, but to
Europe's intellectual tradition and, through his Irish ancestry, to
the hopes and aspirations of the underprivileged everywhere. The
final irony is that the most rational of present-day statesmen
should have met his death as the result of an apparently irrational
act.

In the end, Kennedy's qualities as a man command as much affection as respect. In him, the private man was never lost in the public
figure. The friends he made before he became President were the
friends he kept while in office. We mourn a man who—with his
beautiful wife, his respect for ideas and the arts, his humour, his
informality and modesty in the face of the tremendous responsibilities, which he fully understood—represented something vital, life-
enhancing. His death diminishes us all.

Kennedy in Private

by Joseph Kraft

This personal study was written for us by a former New
York Times *reporter who worked for Kennedy as a speech-
writer in the 1960 election campaign.*

John F. Kennedy was to the manner born. Nothing became him so
much as the White House. His true *metier* was to be President of the
United States.

The proof of it was in the flowering of his wit. During the 1960
campaign, when I came to know him, he constantly bit back jests or
offered them tentatively as if people might not catch on. But in the
White House the comic spirit gushed forth and usually in the form
of some wry sally at his own expense. It was typical of him that
after extolling the Presidency he added: ". . . and besides, the pay is
pretty good."

In the middle of the crisis that followed the discovery of Soviet
missiles in Cuba, he said of a garrulous, hard-line Senator from the
Mid-West: "This will make Homer Capehart look like the Churchill
of the Sixties."

When the two leading Republicans happened to visit Denmark
in the space of a week, he sent to the American Ambassador there
a letter saying: "All I see of you is pictures with Eisenhower and
Nixon. Do you know something I don't know?"

When Britain dragged her heels on the project for a ship-based multilateral force, he said to a backer of the M.L.F.: "How does it feel to be an admiral without a fleet?"

Most of his life he worked against the grain of the obvious. Of his chief political handicap—his religion—he made an asset. The profile of courage that emerges from his own book is a profile of leaders at odds with colleagues and constituents. His most famous gesture— the short chop of the hand, close to the body—found its true meaning against the background of expansive arm-waving native to the American politico.

Out of the tension of opposites, he drew his force as a speaker: "Let us never negotiate out of fear. But let us never fear to negotiate." Though a close family man, he was neither socially nor politically a joiner. As a young Congressman he was chiefly impressive as a model of what the typical Boston politician did not have—financial probity. He never made the Senate "club"; nor did he want to. As a candidate, he said of the kind of speeches he sought: "I need something distinctive. I can't just sound like any Senator."

During his time as President the greatest progress came on an issue he did not force—Civil Rights. Even in the crazy circumstances that made him, allegedly, a victim of the extreme Left in the city of the extreme Right, there was, thus, an inner logic.

His strength was in adversity. A bad back put him in pain, or on the threshold of it, for most of his last years. But he never showed it, or spoke of it. Above all things he hated what he called "whiners" —which is one reason he never established *rapport* with the liberal wing of the Democratic Party. His war-time struggle for survival in the South Pacific was part of a national legend long before he became President. No one who saw him face the Protestant Ministers in Houston, Texas, during the campaign could forget the gallantry of his performance, or the restraint under provocation.

It is said, and perhaps rightly (though I have a different candidate), that his finest hour came when the two worlds were eyeball to eyeball in the Cuban missile crisis. He never kidded himself, or others, that things were rosy. Perhaps alone among American Presidents he insistently called attention to unsolved economic problems during a period of great boom. When his popularity rose after the Bay of Pigs, he said: "My God, it's worse than Eisenhower." Burke Marshall, the Assistant Attorney-General for Civil Rights, and one of the many fine persons brought into government by the Kennedy regime, once said of him: "Whenever I went to see him there was trouble. I always had bad news. But he always asked what should be done next. He met trouble moving forward."

The last time I saw him was several hours after the most recent stoppage on the Berlin autobahn. I knew nothing of the matter, not even that it had happened. But he seemed especially grave, and I

14

asked what was wrong. He said: "I guess I'd complain if it would do any good."

Perhaps because of the tension between what he was and what people expected him to be, he was a restless man—and impatient. At all times he was in motion, smoothing his hair, adjusting his tie, fiddling with his belt, clicking a pen against his teeth, slipping his hands in and out of his pockets. During Press conferences he had visibly to restrain himself from answering questions before they were asked. The hallmark of his closest associates—of Bundy, Sorensen, O'Donnell and his brother—was crispness.

Connected with the restlessness was an insatiable appetite for detail. There were large areas of national life with which he could bring himself to grapple only with great effort—agriculture, for instance, and almost anything to do with making money. But in areas that engaged his interest, he could never have enough of facts and figures. He fired questions as if he had only a minute to understand the whole universe.

One, and perhaps the only, telephone conversation he had with de Gaulle broke down because he had so little French. There was a translator, of course, but before one sentence could be communicated, the interpreter was being swamped with new ones: tell him this, tell him that, and so on.

No matter was too small for his attention; he once called personally to check on the almost petty expenses incurred by an Under-Secretary of State on a trip abroad. When someone complained about the surface of the White House tennis court, he strolled down, examined it himself, and declared it to be satisfactory.

The continual repetition of only slightly different phrases—"We shall pay any price, bear any burden, meet any hardship, support any friend, oppose any foe"—was equally an expression of restlessness: normally his mind moved so rapidly that for the sake of clarity he deliberately said the same thing many times over. It was the same with his frequent use of numbers and statistics: they were a way of making the same point over and over again in short, staccato punches.

Otherwise, he was not in the slightest mathematical. As much as most men he was apt to mix up millions and billions. The order of things in their places, just so, was alien to his soul. His office and desk were rarely neat; his secretary used to have to pick up behind him. His associates at the White House never held a formal staff meeting and assignments fell into place rather than being parcelled out. Speaking of the State Department, he once said that when everything was in perfect array it meant that nothing much was going on. It is remarkable that the only known case of a missing document was the case of the Staff paper that fell into Diefenbaker's hands in Ottawa.

To his younger brother, Bobby, the Attorney-General, he was

15

bound by ties of blood, shared experience and a similar grimness of outlook and underlying gaiety. But what the Attorney-General most contributed was a feeling for organisation. He could shape things up in a way comfortable to his brother. Even so, no one associated with the 1960 campaign could place credence in the stories of the well-oiled machine. In a deep sense, the Kennedy method was the method of disorder.

The characteristic approach was to fill the air with possibilities—or "options" as they came to be called—many of them different, and some even contradictory. To these free rein would be given: the President, indeed, once sent the State Department a series of questions about relations with France, with a request that no one giving the answers was to know the source of the questions. He would allow events to play over possibilities, forcing the outlook now one way, now another. Then, just as events seemed about to force his hand, he would step in and make his move with a characteristic twist of his own that, ideally, anyway, left him master of the situation.

That is what happened during the Cuba missile crisis—which is one reason why the Administration glowed in the success of the exercise. It seemed to be happening a few weeks later in the meeting with Macmillan at Nassau—which is why that conference was followed by a false afterglow. It happened pre-eminently this summer. On June 10, after a season of wavering that evoked from the President himself a reference to the "winter of our discontent", he set his hand simultaneously to the issues of Civil Rights and a *détente* with the Soviet Union. In the morning, at the American University, he delivered a speech on disarmament that opened the way to the test ban treaty. In the evening, in a nation-wide television address, he set out his Civil Rights programme. To my mind, that was his finest hour.

By nature, he was cautious. He made decisions at the margin, committing himself little, and leaving room for escape. He had *par excellence* the ability to separate things out—the analytical capacity. Politically, he tended to court the opposition and ignore his friends. He gave high office to many Republicans, and always clothed soft-line sentiments in hard-line dress. His motto might have been: No enemies to the right. One thing his advisers could never quite get into their heads was that he really believed in pinching pennies—both for himself and the Government. Like most cautious men, his real difficulty was not in saying "yes" (which could always be tempered); but in saying "no" (which was final).

After the cancellation of Skybolt, he went against the whole logic of his Nato nuclear policy to do the Polaris deal with Macmillan. He once asked me why his foreign policy was being criticised even in responsible circles; I cited Nassau and softness towards Britain. He did not deny it, but said something like: "If you were in that kind of trouble, you would want a friend."

16

The true explanation of the Bay of Pigs fiasco lies here, too. He was suspicious of the invasion project as soon as he came to know of it, and whittled it down considerably; but he did not know how to dispose of it entirely, and he let it go through after assurances that if it failed it could be written off as a minor incident. Still, he learned the lesson, and applied it in Laos—and not in the sentimentally tough way supposed by the *realpolitikers*. "If it hadn't been for Cuba," he told an aide in the summer of 1961, "we would be fighting in Laos today."

Politics was the only profession he ever practised seriously. He was the son of an office-holder, and the grandson of elected officials, and he was political to the core. He knew the workings of the wards, and his hunches were often better than those of his pollsters. I once asked him why the Governor of Oklahoma was campaigning for him in the State of California. He said: "Read Steinbeck and you'll discover that California is full of Okies. Besides, we're not going to take Oklahoma, anyhow."

Yet for all his savvy, there was in him a streak of naive incredulity, and it showed itself particularly with his family. During the 1960 campaign a well-known Republican woman declared for Nixon. Practically no one was surprised. But he said: "How could she do such a thing? She knew my mother; she knew my father. She knew me when I was a child."

Most of his adult life he lived in the nation's capital. In the sense that Truman's Administration came from Missouri, Roosevelt's from New York and Harding's from Ohio, his was a Washington Administration. He cared for the city, which he worked to beautify, and if he could be said to represent any single interest, it was the Federal interest. It seems fit that he is buried, unlike other Presidents, across the river in the Arlington National Cemetery.

What was distinct in his approach to foreign policy was the political content. He was probably the first American President to understand that other countries did things prejudicial to the U.S. not because they had un-American ideals, but because they had domestic problems.

His affinity with Harold Macmillan was based on their fellowship as political animals. "With Uncle Harold," a White House staff member once said, "he can sit down and talk easily of what this silly game of running countries is all about." Because he understood their political problems he had a personal *rapport* with most of the leaders of the uncommitted world: and the harmony he established between American policy and their aspirations is one of the important achievements of his Administration.

Connected with his political bent was his fascination with the Press. He read all the papers—the news accounts, the editorials and the columns. He paid them too much attention, and he knew it. Once he passed a self-denying ordinance against the reading of a certain column. Next day his staff came upon him reading the column. Perhaps he could not resist it because of concern for his image, as some suppose. More likely, it was because he regarded the Press as the essential means of political communication. It had power over him, and he could not manipulate it in the way dear to politicians. He saw in the papers not just accounts of what had happened, but stories written or planted for political purposes.

Reporters were to him friends, and sometimes foes; but never neutral chroniclers of the passing scene. Editors and publishers, even as they preened themselves on having his attention, protested, or affected to protest, at his meddling. In fact, he knew their business far better than any of them. Had he outlived his time in the White House, it is probable that, in some way, he would have turned to journalism.

Because he masked his political purposes, the Press picked out as his salient characteristic, style. The public was pleased to believe it. It is true that he had charm to burn, and was almost too good-looking to be true: a veritable cover boy. Women he always appreciated; and with them he was by turns humorous and gallant. One journalist he admired was Mary McGrory, a Washington reporter. Once she was shut out from her turn in the rotating pool of reporters by his side. When she protested, he said: "You and I will never be apart, Mary."

There was taste in everything he did, but not that artificial creature, style. His enthusiasms were simple. He liked the sea and the sun, sailing, swimming, soup, steak and Scotch whisky. His friends were not complicated—swells from New York who abounded in gaiety, and a few of the Boston Irish. Best of all, perhaps, he could relax with Dave Powers, a friend whom he made door-keeper at the White House, and who once uttered a famous tribute to the ruler of Iran: "You're my kind of Shah." Of showiness he had a positive horror. "Not too spectacular," he said in assenting to a White House fireworks display for a foreign guest who liked that kind of thing. He went occasionally to the horse country of Virginia, but it held no appeal for him. Once at the British Embassy when he was about to bite into some fancy whitish dessert, the Ambassador, Sir David Ormsby-Gore, who knew him very well, warned him that it was not ice-cream. The President pushed the dish away.

Distinction in many fields he recognised, and more than any past President he worked to foster it. The woman he chose as his wife was a living testament to excellence in woman. He had a weakness for great men—even de Gaulle—and he peppered his talk, as well as his formal speeches, with their sayings. He brought to government, quite literally, the best minds of his generation. He personally took a hand in the design for a civilian medal of honour which he instituted primarily to celebrate intellectual achievement. At his insistence, the foremost American critic, Edmund Wilson, though he had just written a silly book attacking income-tax and the Administration, was included in the first honours list.

It was said against him that he lacked heart, and emotional commitment. Perhaps. But his mission was to be an antidote to Eisenhowerism—to identify and meet problems that resisted sentimentality and required grain. It was also said against him that he failed to stir the masses. Perhaps, though, the millions who waited hours to pay final respect do not bear that witness. But he had an undoubted kinship with the best this country has to offer—with men of high purpose and intelligence, public conscience and true accomplishment. These will remember him long after his face has passed from the magazine covers, long after his initials are gone from the headlines, long after his name has ceased to cross the public lips. For them, he quickened aspirations into reality. He began to make dreams come true.

"Yesterday a Shaft of Light . . ."

One of the things Kennedy had time to bring about was a nuclear test ban treaty—four months before he was shot. We printed in full the speech he made about it to the American people and these are extracts.

"I speak to you tonight in a spirit of hope.

"Eighteen years ago the advent of nuclear weapons changed the course of the world. Since that time, all mankind has been struggling to escape from the darkening prospects of mass destruction on earth.

"In an age when both sides have come to possess enough nuclear power to destroy the human race, the world of Communism and the world of free choice have been caught up in a vicious circle of conflicting ideology and interests. Each increase of tension has produced an increase in arms: each increase in arms has produced an increase in tension.

"In these years, the United States and the Soviet Union have frequently communicated suspicions and warnings to each other, but very rarely hope. Our representatives have met at the summit and at the brink; they have met in Washington and Moscow, at the United Nations and in Geneva. But too often these meetings have produced only darkness, discord and disillusion.

"Yesterday a shaft of light cut into the darkness. Negotiations were concluded in Moscow on a treaty to ban all nuclear tests in the atmosphere, in outer space and under water. For the first time, an agreement has been reached on bringing the forces of nuclear destruction under international control. . .

"Now, for the first time in many years, the path of peace may be open. No one can be certain what the future will bring. No one can say whether the time has come for an easing of the struggle. But history and our own conscience will judge us harsher if we do not now make every effort to test our hopes by action, and this is the place to begin. According to the ancient Chinese proverb: 'A journey of a thousand miles must begin with a single step.'

"My fellow Americans, let us take that first step. Let us, if we can, get back from the shadows of war and seek out the way of peace. And if that journey is one thousand miles, or even more, let history record that we, in this land, at this time, took the first step."

Her Reticence

If I could send him only
One sleeve with my hand in it,
Disembodied, unbloody.
For him to kiss or caress
As he would or would not—
But never the full look of my eyes,
Nor the whole heart of my thought,
Nor the soul haunting my body,
Nor my lips, my breasts, my thighs
That shiver in the wind
When the wind sighs.

THEODORE ROETHKE

The Great Communist Quarrel

The Shattered Monolith

by Edward Crankshaw

*The year brought out into the open a massive dispute be-
tween Russia and China about world Communist strategy
and the pursuit of national interests. In this article our
Soviet expert argued against jumping to simple conclusions
about the nature of the quarrel.*

Fifteen years ago the Western world deployed itself to meet a very
real menace. This was the menace of Russia under Stalin, but it was
called, confusingly, the Communist challenge.

When Stalin died, in 1953, that menace died with him—but it has
taken 10 years for this fact to be brought home to us. Three years
later Stalin and Stalinism were denounced by Khrushchev, who, at
the same time, rejected Lenin's teaching about the inevitability of
war and violent revolution. At that point the international Communist movement, which had been held together only by Muscovite
single-mindedness, began to fall apart at the seams.

The idea of the Communist monolith was always a simplification.
It distorted, perhaps stultified, political thinking in the West for a
decade and a half. Now we show every sign of oversimplifying the
Sino-Soviet quarrel as we once oversimplified the Communist menace
itself. Already, people who, until a few months ago, refused to believe
that there was a rupture of any kind are busily dividing the Communist world into pro-Russian and pro-Chinese factions, and totting
up the scores: the French Communists, we are told, are 100 per cent
pro-Russian; the Malayans, 100 per cent pro-Chinese; the Brazilians,
all 50,000 of them, 50 per cent pro-Chinese, 50 per cent pro-Russian.
And so on.

The assumption underlying these statistics appears to be that the
pro-Russian and pro-Chinese parties, or factions, are being used as
passive instruments for the furtherance of the aims of Moscow and
Peking. In fact, long before the Sino-Soviet quarrel began, at least
some of the fraternal parties were using Moscow to further their own
private aims; now they are using both Moscow and Peking.

One simple example, to set the tone. The Rumanian comrades have lately been making inviting gestures in the direction of China, which is a long way away, and defiant gestures in the direction of Russia, which is just across the border. Nobody in his senses would believe for one moment that Mr. Gheorghiu Dej and his colleagues, desperately trying to make the Rumanian economy work, are eager to join with the Chinese in a militant revolutionary crusade, conducted in the teeth of Soviet disapproval, to shatter the last bastions of imperialism and capture Asia, Africa, Latin America for the cause.

Like all Eastern or Central European Communists, the Rumanians want, and need, a quiet life, not a nuclear holocaust. They are not interested in the outer world, except as an outlet for trade. Their object in appearing to flirt with Peking has no other purpose than to warn the Russians of the present limits of Moscow's authority.

The Communist world, they are saying in effect, is not what it was. This is no time for you, Nikita Sergeievich, to start bulldozing our legitimate national aspirations. You could do this once upon a time because you had all power; we lay in your shadow, and there was nowhere else for us to go. Now there is somewhere else for us to go.

Moscow lost its virtue as the headquarters of a coherent and disciplined international movement when, with the death of Stalin, it lost the will and the strength to conduct itself imperially. When it comes to imposing an alien system on weak neighbours, there is no stable halfway house between ruthless discipline and confusion. The public defection of China from the Muscovite cause (in which she was never seriously joined) merely highlights confusion.

The first thing the West has to do is to start looking at the world as it is and to think of it in terms of peoples, races, nations (ancient and newly emergent) instead of in terms of blocs. Communism means one thing in Italy, another in East Germany, another in Poland, another in Sweden; something quite else in Indonesia, in Venezuela, in Syria.

Stalin ruled by rigid discipline. In the interests of the Soviet Union, Russian power and Russian gold were used to subvert idealists, rebels and intellectual thugs all over the world and to discipline them into fifth columnists active in the cause of Moscow. Those who queried Stalin's orders or produced ideas of their own were expelled from the brotherhood, or killed.

Of course the idea of international Communism, of the dynamic of world revolution, existed. It burned with a smoky flame in innumerable souls, some noble, some envious, some power-seeking, some merely destructive, all conspiratorial by nature. Some of these were Russians, a rapidly decreasing band; but Stalin and his functionaries were not among them.

This is not to say that their way of thinking was not heavily conditioned by ideas received from Lenin. It was. But the ends to

22

which they applied this way of thinking were not Leninist ends; their assumption of absolute power inside the Soviet Union was facilitated by the almost schizoid dualism of the Russian people.

Lenin himself was driven by dreams of international brotherhood —until, with the responsibilities and harassments of power upon him, he was forced increasingly to identify himself with Russian ends and to adapt himself to Russian, as distinct from Marxist, methods. But the dream was real enough, and for a long time it had nothing to do with nationalism or Russian power. All the peoples of the world

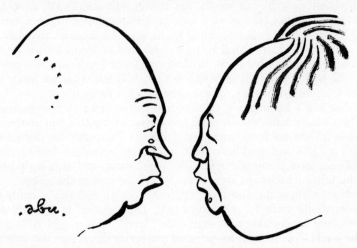

were to advance on lines exposed in a clear-cut historical formula, involving violent revolution and the temporary dictatorship of the proletariat. After that (here the vision was hazy, but all the more exciting for it) they were to dwell together in concord, according to their different national habits, each for each and all for all. In this dream, which did not last long in the Soviet Union, there was indeed a Communist menace—not a Russian menace as later, under Stalin, but a world-wide series of linked internal menaces to the then ruling classes of all lands.

The Leninist dream still lingers on in some quarters (not Russia; not, one would say, China; and not noticeably among the leading cadres of the 89 fraternal parties), but it does not cut much ice. The remarkable thing is that it survived Stalin at all.

Khrushchev discourses upon it with warmth, enthusiasm and, sometimes, wit. "We shall bury you!" he cheerfully exclaims. But this prophecy is full of semantic pitfalls. Who are "we"? And who are "you"? If by "you" Khrushchev means a whole range of entrepreneurs, from the late Mr. Rachman up to quite a height, symbolising the seamier side of what we optimistically call the capitalist system, then how right he is: but then "we" includes all the rest of us.

If by "we" he means the Soviet bloc—the Warsaw Pact Powers—and by "you" the Western Alliance, then he is asking for trouble and he knows it. But if he means by "we" Moscow Communism and by "you" everything against it, then the West has an imposing new comrade in arms disposing of 650 million souls, increasing at the rate of 30 million a year.

It is more to the point to ask what Khrushchev means by Communism, and only he can supply the answer. His statements, as so far delivered, do not take us very far. Lenin's apocalyptic dream appears in his mind to have been reduced to the quest for material abundance, leisure, and culture to fill in time: the kind of thing British Prime Ministers are rebuked for in the leader-pages of *The Times*. A menace to the higher values it may well be; but it is not what we mean by the Communist menace, or even the Russian menace.

Nor is it what many of the fraternal parties mean by Communism. The Chinese have shown themselves especially bitter and contemptuous of Khrushchev's unexpressed slogan: Prosperity for the Soviet Union first—and good luck to the rest of the comrades! And Chinese criticism here is sharply echoed by poor, weak, and aspiring people who inhabit backward areas over the greater part of the globe.

Not for them the dream of "catching up with America": many of them would settle for a loaf of bread. The spectacle of Khrushchev presiding comfortably over one of the "have" Powers, and arranging the world to fit in with his personal prosperity drive, does not appeal. To the have-nots, Chinese methods seem to have more to offer. But this is not to say that the fraternal comrades wish to exchange regimentation in the interests of Soviet prosperity and power for regimentation in the interests of Chinese imperial ambition.

If the Communist monolith never really existed, the current image of two rival Communist Romes is equally misleading. There is now no Rome at all.

The focus of interest has shifted from Moscow and Peking to the individual fraternal parties all over the world, with more to come. Each has to be studied in the context of its own historical and geographical setting and tackled accordingly. But we know little about them.

For example, we know that the Brazilian party which, though small, used to be so brilliantly organised under that most intelligent and perceptive of Communist leaders, Prestes, is now split right down the middle. We know that his rivals are leading a militant, pro-Chinese wing, which has now captured half the party, on a rabidly anti-American ticket.

But we do not know to what extent these men are genuine fanatics, convinced believers in Mao's Road, recoiling in righteous indignation from the sophisticated gradualism of Prestes and looking for support from the angry, the impatient, the desperate, who see their only hope in violent action soon—or whether they are using China as a stalking-horse in a personal bid to steal power from Prestes.

If it comes to that, we do not know whether Prestes himself, so skilfully arguing Khrushchev's line, regards the Russian comrades as the guardians of the true faith, or as Gringo barbarians useful to Brazilian or Latin-American Communism because they have money to burn and an armament that frightens the Americans. The gentleness and sophistication of Preste's speech at the Moscow conference of November, 1960, warmly supporting Khrushchev against the Chinese, was in itself a reproach to the crudity of Russian methods.

At the same meeting, Jesu Faria of Venezuela, who also supported the Russians, nevertheless indicated clearly that his respect for Khrushchev stopped well this side of idolatry. He supported Moscow because he thought Khrushchev's policies more intelligent in the atomic age than Mao's, and particularly because the Chinese had been actively engaged in trying to undermine his own authority over the Venezuelan party (oil again?). But he thought that many of the speakers at that meeting had been altogether too uncritical of the Soviet comrades, who, he said, had themselves committed many errors. He hoped that the Russians would be clever enough in future to devise a system that would put an end to inter-party quarrelling and prevent future schisms.

These remarks were a foretaste of more to come. The Cuban adventure last autumn did not at all redound to Khrushchev's credit. If the Chinese had been more subtle and had made at least some attempt to present their invasion of India as anything but old-fashioned power-politics, had disguised their eagerness to do a *Real-politik* deal with Pakistan, had shown more concern for the fraternal comrades in South East Asia and less for Chinese nationals in that area, and had resisted the temptation to boast of their contempt for the nuclear threat, which frightens most comrades, like all of us, out of their wits, they might have made much more headway.

It is probably not too much to say that for a whole variety of reasons the general feeling among Communists, in most countries, about Russia and China is "A plague on both your houses!" Dismay, exasperation, sometimes contempt—in face of the imbecilities and crudities displayed by the heirs of Ivan the Terrible and of Confucius —are felt by many Communist leaders who were not privileged to be born Russian or Chinese.

In purely practical terms this quarrel, or the way it has been conducted, has alienated fellow-travellers and the eager members of "front" organisations all over the world, has bored to distraction the faithful who are trying to get on with the march towards the millenium, has caused neophytes in darkest Africa to raise their eyebrows. In intellectual terms, it has plumbed depths of mental squalor which make the flesh of the more intelligent Communists creep. In political terms it has indicated that the senior partners of the Socialist camp are more interested in their own power struggle than in the future of the movement.

In the last resort, and for the time being, Russia will win when it comes to commanding the allegiance of the party as a whole. She has the money, the power and the prestige. It has yet to be proved that Mao's solicitude for the weaker brethren is any deeper than Khrushchev's: it is easy to appear solicitous when you have nothing much to give.

Khrushchev, though an inferior dialectician to Mao and his worshippers, has much more good sense. He is closer to the age we live in, and he is being dragged ever closer by the demands of fraternal comrades, such as Togliatti of Italy, who actually live in it.

With his very vivid sense of the calamitous nature of nuclear war (no doubt the Chinese are just as afraid, but they dare not say so), he appeals directly to all those good comrades who do not want to be blown up. On a lower level, he is beloved by many smaller parties, who know that their only hope of survival is to lie low for some time to come.

He is one, also, with those parties who either rule or inhabit countries with comparatively advanced economies, which, though they may diligently beaver away (as in Britain) to make things difficult for their present masters, would nevertheless prefer to live as destructive minorities in a comfortable land than inherit a ruin. More than this, Russia really has the last word, if she cares to say it, with parties which would naturally gravitate, one would say, to China: she has, for example, more to give to Laos (if she cares to give it) than the Chinese.

But what does it all amount to? And where is the central leadership on the march to revolution? Khrushchev may reassure himself with Leninist slogans, but he knows very well that for the foreseeable future he is interested above all in consolidating Soviet power and security, avoiding war, and augmenting the prosperity of his country. There is no ideological dynamism here.

China cannot begin to pretend to leadership of a world that embraces Europe and North America. Other parties, though they may value Moscow's support, have their own problems. When the Swedish Communist leader, Hagberg, announces to the Moscow Conference that the concept of the dictatorship of the proletariat is outdated and that Swedish Communists are determined to co-operate with the Swedish Social Democrats, whom they see as a true workers' party, the writing is on the wall (this was a secret speech among Communists, not an essay in propaganda).

When Mr. Gollan, of London, at the same meeting, reads the

Chinese a lecture explaining that they have no conception of British ways and no true appreciation of the strength of the British Labour movement, he is also warning the Russians.

As for Italy, Togliatti and Longo are already far out in a deeply heretical move towards "reformism". They are meeting with opposition within their own party, but it is not at all clear whether the "Chinese" wings in Padua and elsewhere are motivated by admiration for Mao or dislike of Signor Togliatti.

These uncertainties are legion. The only certain thing is that the proper way to approach the Communist menace is to pay less attention to Russia and China and a great deal more to the problems of the separate countries of the "Socialist camp" and to the discontents in our own midst. Each country that feels it can produce a better solution than the Communist solution should strain itself to the utmost to *prove* that it can—and help, even at a sacrifice, the weaker brethren.

China After the Split

by Dennis Bloodworth

Our Far East Correspondent looked at the implications for
Asia of the schism between Moscow and Peking.

It is a fundamental Chinese teaching that the best generals win their campaigns without losing an arrow. And it would be a mistake to expect a spectacularly aggressive policy from Peking as a result of the rift with Moscow.

The Chinese, whatever Mr. Khrushchev may say, do not believe in a nuclear holocaust as a means to world revolution—though they do think that, on a planet obsessed by the fear of atomic war, modest insurrections may sometimes be risked with impunity. Their main reply to Russia's assertion of Soviet supremacy in the world Communist movement is likely to be an exploitation of China's appeal to the underdeveloped countries of Africa and Asia.

The Chinese, who look upon the underdeveloped continents as their rightful zones of influence and South East Asia as a backyard over which their lapsed sovereignty should be reasserted, are already preparing their arguments: they are fellow Asians whose pigmentation is their passport. Russians are hated whites, first cousins to colonialists. Caucasians from Manhattan or Moscow give aid with the cold eye of an investor, and only the Chinese opens his purse in the friendly spirit of an elder brother.

China does her lobbying in the Afro-Asian club, and her object is to get the Russians blackballed. At a meeting of Afro-Asian journalists in Jakarta earlier this year China triumphed and the Soviet were ignominiously refused full participation. They were not Afro-Asians. A get-together of Afro-Asian trade unionists is also to be held in Jakarta shortly; once more the Indonesians will be hosts and the Chinese, it is thought, will gladly foot most of the bills.

On the ideological plane the Chinese take more tricks. They attract because they have carried through a peasant revolution in Asia; equally, they are purists who urge active support for revolutionary movements in a region where insurrection holds out a hope of power that cold constitutional procedure withholds. Struggling for ascendancy, Vietnamese Communists, North Koreans and Pathet Lao are pro-Chinese. Exiled or downtrodden, Malayan and Thai Marxists look to Peking.

Communist sympathy often coincides with nationalist aspirations : Japanese Marxists who are pro-Chinese find themselves in harmony with non-Communists who resent Russia's acquisitive grasp on South Sakhalin and who believe that Japanese big business could still take a lion's share of the legendary (if illusory) market of 700,000,000 Chinese customers. The Burmese are swayed by nagging awareness of their 1,200-mile frontier with China, and for similar geopolitical reasons accord China suitably timorous favour.

But if the Russians are regarded as whites, whose leader has not reconditioned but betrayed Marxist-Leninism, the Chinese are no better loved. Their ill-concealed sense of racial superiority has been acutely resented in Africa, and in Asia their imperial disdain and their hateful business acumen have, on different planes at different times provoked enmity, bitter envy, and hurt national pride.

The Chinese Communist struggle for domination in Afro-Asia can be expected to be marked by the more intensive manipulation of some 14 million overseas Chinese. In this respect the new Federation of Malaysia may turn out to be the test-case. For the Chinese will constitute the biggest single ethnic minority in the Federation and already there are armed men in the Sarawak jungle.

Meanwhile in Indonesia the three-million Chinese community, predominantly pro-Peking, still dominates the economy of the country. One consequence is that the Chinese Embassy in Jakarta disposes of £20 million in local currency for immediate political purposes, according to estimates of worried Indonesian experts.

The Indonesian Communist Party might well be persuaded, therefore, to play a key role in China's new design for Asia, however reluctantly. A purely Chinese movement in Malaysia would risk political isolation, but the backing of Indonesia's Communists might make the subversion of Malays possible.

There are further snags, however. The Indonesian Communists

cannot afford to be branded as the henchmen of China. Peking cannot provide emergent countries of Asia with aid on a scale to which they have now become accustomed from Washington and Moscow. Moreover, possibilities of creating purely Afro-Asian organisations are limited. Peking cannot hope to build up effective rivals to existing international mass organisations, and must set out to capture them instead.

The Chinese will not try to slash through this confused and problematical tangle with a sword, but will pick it patiently apart. They may intensify local conflicts in Laos and Vietnam where the ultimate aim is Communist control of China's neighbours and where the immediate achievement is to get Americans bogged down in futile Asian culs-de-sac.

But the Chinese will not invite full-scale war on their doorstep, and if they can gain their ends by tricking the West at another Geneva Conference which might produce a "neutralist solution" for South Vietnam also, they will jump at the chance.

China's hardening enmities may be felt most strongly in India, for India is anathema on all the main counts. New Delhi offers the principal democratic challenge to China's claim to leadership of Asia. Pandit Nehru is, *par excellence*, the seemingly durable bourgeois nationalist leader who obstructs rather than furthers the cause of Socialist revolution. Confronted by fellow Asians in Peking, Indians turn for support to the imperialist West. Khrushchev fails to back his Socialist partner in the Sino-Indian border quarrel, and perfidiously sympathises with the enemy.

It is in India, therefore, that China may try to discredit all her adversaries in Asia. For the more threatening Mao Tse-tung becomes towards India, the more incongruous Khrushchev's position on the wrong side of the fence can be made to look. The propaganda campaign against Delhi is likely to be intensified, and Peking will show temporary readiness to negotiate only in order to make Indian rearmament and Western military assistance appear unnecessary and compromising luxuries.

China is reported to be strengthening her position in Himalayan States, and building up forces in Tibet. Although she is ready to provoke major military incidents this year, she will do so, however, only if Russia can be further embarrassed and India made to look small in Asia without fear of violent reprisals.

China's haughty, intransigent words are in fact ill-matched by pragmatic acts. Chinese Communists are exponents of revolution, but they do not encourage Indonesia's Communists to try to seize control in Indonesia in the face of the National Army. They are suspicious and distrustful of bourgeois nationalists, yet they woo the Afro-Asian bloc.

Everywhere they can be trusted to feel their way along the lines of least resistance. In Malaysia their principal method will not be to foster insurgency but rather to undermine Tengku Abdul Rahman's anti-Communist regime in favour of something left-wing, suitably penetrated but ostensibly democratic.

There will, on the other hand, be no kotowing to the Soviet Union. Until 1959 China was heavily dependent on Moscow for economic aid on the gigantic scale needed to assemble the infrastructure of a modern Chinese Socialist State. But since then she has endured three terrible years of acute shortages, under-nourishment and economic atrophy during which the Russians added to the effect of calamitous weather and administrative muddle by withdrawing their technicians and suspending their assistance.

China and the Communist regime, which has dragged her through these years of trial, both survived. Today China is self-reliant and the Communists know they can probably demand great sacrifices of the millions without risking counter-revolution. The Soviet Union's ability to apply economic pressure is drastically reduced.

The Chinese will no longer put all their eggs in the Russian basket. As the recent visit to Britain of their Minister for Trade indicated, they will try to diversify their foreign commercial relations—and incidentally exploit "capitalist contradictions" in the West by tempting America's allies in Europe and the Commonwealth into a net of profitable trade agreements.

Today China wants Sino-Soviet solidarity on her own terms or not at all. None the less, it would be foolish to assume that the door to reconciliation between Moscow and Peking has been irrevocably slammed. The customer may have refused the offer, be out of the shop and half-way up the street. But in Asia that is only the beginning of serious bargaining.

The Change at the Vatican

The True Legacy of Pope John

by Barbara Ward Jackson

Almost his last words were "Let them be one" when Pope John died in Rome on June 3, 1963. Here Lady Jackson discusses the work of this remarkable Sovereign Pontiff.

Pope John XXIII reigned so short a time, yet made such profound changes in the direction of Catholic policy that, inevitably, the first question after his death is: can his influence endure? And the question is not altogether easy to answer. At least a part of his astonishing impact on his fellow-men sprang from something potentially evanescent—the irresistible attraction of his personality.

With each month of his reign, the sense of an unusually vital, wise and touching human personality gained strength. For every visitor, there was, it seems, an appropriate and personal welcome. Kings or children, Anglican archbishops or Orthodox patriarchs, Nobel prizewinners, visiting journalists, workers, peasants—all left him with a sense of having encountered a profound, paternal affection which was theirs not for this or that distinction or achievement but simply because in each of them he saw a child of God.

It is easy to sentimentalise such an impression, to confuse it with the surface benevolence of our public relations age. But paternal affection is the precise opposite of superficial sentiment. It is rooted, it is reliable and resistant, it lies beyond all play of circumstance; its great biblical image is the father's welcome to the prodigal son. In an epoch much given to talk of the "father figure", John XXIII offered something more consoling—the image of fatherly love.

One can, I think, argue that this paternal aspect of the Pope's personality offered a clue to some of the major purposes and emphases of his short but astonishingly fruitful reign. If a man's deepest convictions underline for him the fact of mankind's substantial unity, if the phrases which recur and recur in his writings and allocutions are "the human family", "the unity of mankind", "the sons of God", "the brotherly unity of all," then the likelihood is that he will underline what unites rather than what divides, will stress the common themes, not the disruptive quarrels, and will seek with all his energy to find ways in which men of diverse beliefs may, without compromising principle, come to understanding, mutual respect and, if possible, agreement.

This is the spirit which informs his great encyclicals *Mater et Magistra* and *Pacem in Terris*. This is the spirit which inspired every aspect of his constant work for human reconciliation.

But now the man who projected this image of fatherhood in the single human family is dead. Will the work which sprang from his moving dedication to unity survive his loss? His greatest effort of spiritual reconciliation lay, of course, in the calling of the ecumenical council. His chief aim in calling such a General Council of the Church was to enable Catholics, by seeking a profound renovation in their own corporate life, to become more worthy and effective participants in the great ecumenical dialogue between the Christian communions.

Moreover, he invited non-Catholic observers from many different communions to take the closest possible part in the Council's deliberations. The aim of reconciliation through charity dominated all else and in his discourse opening the Council, the Pope squarely included non-Catholic Christians in his reference to "the entire Christian family"—once again, the image of the family—and "exulted greatly . . . at the efficacy" of their prayers for a reunited Church.

Yet the Council is now, by the fact of his death, automatically disbanded with its labours no more than begun. One cannot doubt that it will be recalled by his successor. But will the earlier *élan* survive?

A darker question-mark hangs over his work of secular reconciliation. For those who would see the Vatican as a fighting champion of the West in the cold war, the Pope must have often seemed a singularly unresponsive ally. There has, of course, been no compromise in the Church's essential opposition to Marxism. It is, after all, difficult to reach a middle position between denying and affirming the existence of God. Yet the last four years have brought changes in emphasis.

One has the impression, for instance, that the Pope was wary of seeing Catholicism put to political uses as, say, an official rallying point for anti-Communism in a country like Poland. The special emphasis given to the invitation of Russian Orthodox representatives to the General Council is not without significance, given their subservience to the Soviet Government. The Vatican's caution in denouncing "Godless atheism" in other than very general terms is in sharp contrast to the pointedly anti-Russian eloquence of so many pro-Western crusaders.

To a certain extent, no doubt, this restraint was largely prudential. Millions of Catholics in the Eastern bloc live under Communism and the Pope would not, it seems, lay on them a heavier burden than they could bear. He clearly hoped, in return for a less intransigent tone, to secure a minimum freedom of action for Catholics in countries such as the Ukraine, or Czechoslovakia or Hungary in which the old hostility entailed the imprisonment of leading Catholic churchmen.

Yet the policy of *détente* did not spring wholly from a tactical desire to work out a *modus vivendi*. John XXIII avoided all over-simple distinction between a wholly virtuous West and a monstrous conspiracy on the other side.

He grew up in one of the first Italian dioceses to react seriously to the challenge of modern industrialism. His whole thinking was in-fluenced by the liberal tendency in French social Catholicism. He could see that man can lose his way, not only by the false doctrines of Communism, but equally by the West's besetting temptation— that of seeking a "well-being based exclusively on the comforts of life". He won the devotion of the Socialists in Venice by his constant concern for the poor and the unemployed, and not every anti-Communist enthusiast could take comfort from his constant re-minders that wealth is given for one overriding purpose—not "to balance the books" but for "the advantage of the human family".

There is no denying that the Pope's approach roused profound misgivings in some Catholic ecclesiastical and political circles. Con-servative Italians accused him of making Communism respectable and thereby adding a million votes to the Communists in Italy's recent general elections. Right-wing Germans stonily attacked him for "selling out" German interest to the Poles and the Russians. A few American leaders clearly preferred the old black-white simpli-cities of the cold war. Mr. Khrushchev's condolences and flags at half-mast in Havana hardly reassured them.

It seems highly probable, therefore, that there will be a counter-attack in favour of more cautious policies. In the case of the *modus vivendi* with Communism it could have some effect. Uncertainty does in fact cloud the question of what the Pope's efforts would actually have achieved. The doctrinal gap remains unbridgeable, and compromise is also under attack from Communism's Chinese and Stalinistic extremists. If neither side can afford concessions, a dialogue may indeed be maintained. But it may well come to resemble the nuclear stalemate at Geneva.

One can be far more confident over the work of religious reconcilia-tion. The Vatican Council may not have completed much work but it demonstrated clearly the extent and vitality of the Church's modernis-ing tendencies. The bishops, assembled from the ends of the earth, took a more liberal view of their opportunities than the Rome-bound *Curia*. They were not only encouraged by the Pope. They were en-couraged by one another. Thus he helped to articulate and dramatise the growing readiness for more liberal policies. But he did not create it and it will therefore survive him.

Nor is this greater freedom a matter only of sanctions and movements within the Church. The moods which he projected go beyond any single group or interest. Pope John contrived with the utmost simplicity to speak to the human condition, to give mankind a glimpse, however fleeting, of how their world might look if it were under the governance of love.

With undimmed confidence, Pope John looked beyond the crises of our day towards a profounder movement of gathering unity, towards the creation of an "earthly city" which would in the fullness of time mirror that heavenly city "where truth reigns, love is the law and whose extent is eternity".

And since the aspiration towards a world-wide society in which a moral community can take the place of the present community of potential destruction is confined to no one communion, nation or race, one can believe that in a profound sense the Pope's work and influence will not slacken in the years ahead. On the contrary, he could do so much in so short a time just because he was moving with a great tide of history. Those who mourn him now can therefore try to share his serene confidence that the tide still moves towards the flood.

A Brave Priest

This was our own Comment on the Pope's death and on what he had tried to do.

"I come to bury Caesar," said Antony, "not to praise him." But it is possible to bury a man with praise, and there is some danger that this fate may be reserved for Pope John. For the Pope was not simply a good old man but a brave old man who was trying quite deliberately to transform the Roman Catholic Church in important ways. There will be a strong temptation among those Catholic cardinals and bishops who did not agree with him to pay lavish tributes to his memory—and then modify what he was trying to do.

Seen from outside the Church, Pope John had three missions: to nudge the Church into a quite new tolerance of other Christians and of non-Christians whom Rome has for centuries harshly regarded as beyond the pale; to disentangle the Church from its alliance with reactionary politics in Italy and other countries; and, most important of all, to remind Catholics that Christ's message was to love your neighbour—not only your Catholic neighbour or even your Christian neighbour, but your Communist neighbour, too. In his famous last

34

Encyclical he went some way to applying Christianity to the problem of co-existence between the West and the Communist world.

It seems probable that the movement towards Christian unity is now too strong to be reversed; but the "opening to the Left" is still highly precarious, and the Pope's message that "there are no political communities which are superior by nature and none which are inferior by nature" is still so revolutionary as to seem shocking to many Western minds. Yet Pope John's words, like Christ's Sermon on the Mount, spoke to the heart of every man because they expressed simple but vital truths. A Catholic Church which has accepted tolerance as a virtue and which preached this message could be a living influence for good in a world which is still bitterly divided into warring tribes.

Pope Paul in the Holy Land

by Patrick O'Donovan

Cardinal Montini, Archbishop of Milan and a declared disciple of "the incomparable John," was chosen to succeed the dead Pope. He assumed the name of Paul VI. In January this year he made a brief tour of the Holy Land and was the first Pope to be seen there since Peter. Patrick O'Donovan followed him throughout his journey and when it was over sent us this despatch from Jerusalem.

It has long been the practice of the Roman Church to proclaim her position still more strictly. To condemn in a terrible way. Or to promulgate a relevant dogma in the face of new threats. Under the new dispensation she has reinterpreted the custom. In the face of a series of societies indifferent to or hostile to the spiritual life, the head of the Church goes off on the most public possible act of prayer.

The visit of the Pope to the Holy Places is clearly a part of the process of opening up the Church of Rome. Traditions that were once sacred begin to look unnecessary. Her claim to universality begins to include a universal charity. Her claim to authority is unchanged, but there is a new emphasis on the measure of truth held by others.

Tolerance is being slowly reinstated as a virtue, and humility practised on the part of the whole Roman Church.

At present these are tendencies only, and it is probable that the expression of all this in symbolic form was quite secondary to Pope Paul's private purpose.

His primary purpose was almost certainly to be a pilgrim. And, with the Church beginning to rethink her origins and organisation, to go to the Holy Land was natural and right.

There is no doubt that it was an act of prayer. There was, for once, no discernible cynicism in the huge corps of Pressmen following a public figure. He is a startling figure, made more impressive by the uniforms of his office, which here by Papal standards were kept simple.

He is a slight, recollected figure, upon which a fierce self-discipline has been imposed. His gestures are austere except when he greets in public, and then they are wide, baroque and rather beautiful.

There are no violent gestures. His steps are small and sure even on rock roads, so that he seems to glide along in his cassock. And he projects himself as well as any public figure, though in a different way. He accepts the necessary technical importunities of photographers. He pauses and lifts his arms to please crowds hungry with loyalty or curiosity. There is nothing theatrical in this. There is a slightly frightening authority about him. He lacks the physical beauty of Pius XII or the disarming humanity of Pope John. He can combine spirituality with a tycoon's efficiency. He has something of his own which has yet to be defined.

No one anticipated how difficult and dangerous this tour would be. There were disorders at several places, before altars, in public squares, along the Via Dolorosa. They would perhaps be more scandalous to a man of Anglo-Saxon origin than to any other. They were born largely of sheer religious fervour and of an overwhelming loyalty to the person in St. Peter's Chair. For the Pope is a tremendous reality to Catholics. They in fact believe he is the Vicar of Christ on earth. And to Catholics and Christians isolated among Arabs or Jews and feeling inferior as a tolerated minority or as accepting Government favours that they have not won in history, the fact of the visit of a Pope in their town was overwhelming.

There was an element of pressing forward to touch the hem of his garment, which intellectually and by any standards of good manners was indefensible. But it could be understood. As an Italian friar recovering his breath after a buffeting on the Via Dolorosa put it—with pardonable inaccuracy—"After all, this is only the second Entry into Jerusalem."

The most famous incidents occurred at the Damascus Gate and along the Via Dolorosa. There was the first terrifying sight of the Pope being carried along like a leaf in the midst of fervour that turned into panic. One was frightened not only for the Pope but also for oneself.

After a little, some order was restored to the procession.

The silver patriarchal cross went on, the altar boys tottered over the cobbles, the friars, who had been singing "Surge Jerusalem", still went by, two by two. The Pope still existed in a knot of soldiery.

36

One or two prelates managed to follow. The interlopers in front and behind him still mindlessly heaved and fought. He stopped to pray at a Station of the Cross, and the priests turned back to see what he was doing and the riot began again.

The soldiers hesitated to strike at the priests, though one of them was sent reeling with a blow on the face from one of the Pope's men. From then on it was a slow, deadly fight to the Sepulchre.

It was hardly better inside. The Pope arrived, grey in the face and gleaming with sweat in the bitter cold evening. Even here his Mass, said at a portable altar before the little Russian aedicule that is the Sepulchre, was the still centre of turbulence. The rotunda, the adjacent aisles, were crowded and heaving, roaring with comment and expostulation. Cardinal Tisserant, his beard awry, was locked outside.

Despite previous apparent agreement, at the last moment the Franciscans, who have the official custody of the Latin holy places, insisted that they alone should command all entry to the Sepulchre. They could not cope. The Jordanians, who had previously issued a calculated number of passes, were ignored. In rueful apology, the Franciscan's spokesman said. "That's always our trouble: religion."

This sort of unnecessary confusion was the fruit of the sort of jealousy for which the Pope, one evening, subtly reproved the Catholic leaders. It is old-fashioned and ugly. In the past, perhaps, it meant survival. It meant faith and loyalty. Now it seems almost like a crusader mentality.

The Pope was the Latins' treasure, like the third lamp from the left over that shrine or the right to clean the outside of this window in the other. The Latins at least are likely to be a little more humble in the future.

But apart from the attempt at a personal and symbolic pilgrimage by the Pope—in which everyone who saw it seems to believe there were obvious other implications—has it changed or advanced anything?

The Pope, whoever he is, is now probably the most important V.I.P. in the world. This is far from meaning that he is, therefore, the most powerful or the most interesting man. This is an odd phenomenon to occur at a time when religion appears to many as a dying concept. There has always been interest in the office since its establishment, even among those who detested it. There are the awe and splendour that surround it. There is the idea that it is a fascinating survival from a dead past, which gives it a connoisseur's curiosity value.

But the interest has lately been dramatically increased. And with the increase goes a tendency to exaggerate its political power. The increase came with Pope John. His political actions were based on the simplicity of good will. He tried to practise what he preached and he tended to leave the Roman virtue of prudence go hang itself.

He made Christianity in action exciting for Christians in a new way, and respectable to non-believers. From the outside it looked like a revolution and it caught the imagination of the world. Pope Paul is still riding on this reputation. He is a cooler, less intuitive man. He decides after ratiocination. In Milan he was referred to as a priest who could not weep. He wept in the Holy City.

After this trip to Jerusalem, it does not look as if he has chosen the middle of the road, though it is impossible yet to be sure. He has not shown, and probably never will, the headlong progress of Pope John, whose brief reign can now be seen as a feverish attempt to catch up with the times, to speed up the changes that the Church does make from time to time in the light of new conditions and new thought.

But for the moment more people than ever before have hopes of the political side of the Papacy. When it says peace, it means just that and not the triumph of an ideology. When it talks ecumenically, it now means an honest dialogue and not a new way to save souls in the Roman Catholic manner. He has become more than the leader of the largest religious sect.

Because of this almost top-heavy prestige, Pope Paul in Jordan received the greatest welcome the country could afford. The King, an experienced pilot, himself went up into the control tower at Amman Airport to talk the Italian plane in through the low clouds and poor visibility. And the whole population of Amman, the male part anyway, seemed to be standing in the streets to see this famous stranger. Indeed the Jordanian soldiers, whose reputation is the highest in the Arab world, found it difficult to maintain their discipline before this illustrious, though only vaguely identified, Mufti. They, too, had a tendency to kiss his hand or touch his clothing.

As part of this respect and awe, they attempted openly to enlist him on their side in their aching quarrel with Israel. There was a demonstration of dispossessed Arab refugees as he crossed the Jordanian frontier. There were frequent Press suggestions that as a man of peace and truth he must be on their side. King Hussein gave a Press conference in a cinema before the Pope arrived, in which he stressed the common origins of his and his visitor's religion. He also insisted that the Christian conscience could not ignore the living injustice of the fact of the refugees and of the aggression his people had suffered.

It would be wrong to expect any lessening of tension as a result of the visit. The Jordan Press and radio even stepped up their verbal assaults on Israel. The Pope was in an awkward position. The Muslim leaders were exquisitely courteous. But he can leave only a slight disappointment, heightened perhaps by the marring disorders.

38

The case in Israel was somewhat different. There was a certain emotional restraint in their welcome.

Perhaps dominant was the fear of an assassination. It seemed a perfect opportunity for an *agent provocateur* to recreate the old Christian anti-semitism. Like a cloud, the memory of Dallas in Texas hung over the visit.

Then their previous experience of Christianity, and indeed of the Papacy, had not been encouraging. The Israeli President in his farewell speech said: "Let every nation walk in the name of its own God." This is the traditional rabbinical answer to would-be proselytisers. I do not think it was meant that way. But it had a truth in it. A friend said in private that they had learnt all they wanted to about Christianity at Auschwitz. And when Pope Paul defended the war-time policy of Pius XII there was a ripple of surprise among those journalists who could understand his Vatican French.

The Israelis admitted his courage and left it at that.

The interest in and the courtesy for the visit were the more remarkable because in a way it had offended them. After their 16 years as a sovereign nation, the Vatican does not recognise them. And the Vatican's private excuse that this would make the plight of the many Christians in Arab countries still more difficult impresses them about as much as do the arguments for Pius XII's cautious war-time policy.

The Pope did not cross into Israel via the Jerusalem crossing lest it be taken as a recognition of Jerusalem as the capital of Israel—under the 1947 General Assembly decision it is a *corpus separatum*. He came as a private person from an unrecognised country, and the Israelis made a special gate for him at Megiddo (Armageddon) and the President and Government greeted him and said farewell, which in protocol was a considerable concession. The Pope's cable of gratitude to the President was addressed from his plane to Tel Aviv, the old capital.

And yet the Israelis seem now profoundly gratified. There is first the sigh of relief that no incident occurred. The refusal of the oriental Chief Rabbi to meet him is generally dismissed as unfortunate, or politics. The idea that the first Pope since Peter visited the Holy Land only after the ingathering of the Jews is important to them. And the face-to-face courtesies that were exchanged were eloquent and real, and pregnant with change. In retrospect, the Israelis seem to believe that something good has happened.

Perhaps historically the most important thing was the meeting between Paul and Athenagoras. He of Constantinople is the senior Patriarch of the Orthodox Church, though he cannot command all his prelates and faithful as the Pope does his.

It has been suggested here that in fact the pilgrimage was hardly more than a cover for a meeting, previously agreed upon in secret. There is no evidence for this. It is far more likely that the Patriarch

39

seized the opportunity to fulfil his former offer to meet the Pope on neutral ground and as an equal. There was even something curiously haphazard about their two comparatively brief meetings.

Athenagoras and the other Orthodox Patriarchs of Jerusalem, Antioch, Alexandria and Moscow regard themselves as the equals of the Pope, though they accord him a primacy of honour as the occupant of the Apostolic See of St. Peter.

The Catholics freely admit that the Orthodox have all the sacraments and the Apostolic Succession. The two wings of the Church broke apart 900 years ago, largely for political reasons, and the Orthodox have hardly developed since that break, admitting none of the subsequent councils nor any of the pronouncements of Popes, who they believe have usurped to themselves the authority and infallibility that properly belong to the whole Church. Since the break they have, however, developed a distrust, even a hatred in some places, for the Franks or Latins, based largely upon undimmed memories of pillage, betrayal and contempt.

In this meeting, then, the Patriarch did a brave thing. There is no great longing in his scattered Church for this sort of meeting.

The autocephalous Church of Greece was openly suspicious and hostile. While the two prelates met upstairs, the Orthodox Patriarch of Jerusalem was downstairs urging a reporter not to take it all too seriously. A local Greek monastery started a vigil of prayer to avert the meeting.

When he spoke before the manger in Bethlehem, the Pope laid down the difficulties in the path of reunion, which tend often to be underestimated. He said of the hope for reunion, "Even on this very special occasion we must say that such a result is not to be obtained at the expense of the truths of faith. We cannot be false to Christ's heritage; it is not ours but His, we are no more than stewards, teachers and interpreters."

No fundamental concessions: the Church is still built on a rock. But there is change. He went on: "We shall take pains to keep alive the desire for understanding and union, and we shall put our trust in prayer, which, even though it is not yet united prayer, rises up nevertheless simultaneously from ourselves and from Christians separated from us, like two parallel columns which meet on high to form an arch, in the God of unity." It is an image that he had used before in a private talk with Pastor Niemöller.

But what has been changed and what has been advanced? In religious terms about as much as the test ban treaty. An Orthodox delegation from this part of the world is likely to attend the next session of the council, and theological negotiation of the most protracted sort is probable.

In political terms little has been changed. Neither Israel nor Jordan will change an iota of her policies. The part of the Council Schema

40

that deals with Jews and the Christian attitude to Jewry is likely to have an easier passage. But the Pope has had no temptation to dabble in Middle Eastern politics.

There is still left the conviction that the few small things started here may have unimaginable consequences. The Pope, if his speeches mean anything, has been profoundly moved, and it could only happen here.

This is the place, the Levant it used to be called, where it all began. Every sort of Christianity, however eccentric, has a root in this place. The Mohammedans regard it as more immediately theirs. This rough land is inseparable from the Jewish religion.

For a Christian in the new frame of mind, the bare rock crevices and caves, which are most of the holy places, emphasise his faith's essentially uncomplicated origins. And the poverty of these places, the small Christian communities struggling to survive in a largely unsympathetic or indifferent community, encourage humility. The terrible jealous sharpness of the difference between the sects in a place like this makes the ancient disunity still more scandalous.

The Pope has made a gesture in the tradition of his predecessor. Gestures are sometimes as valuable as positive actions. And a large part of the world paused to watch these inconclusive three days, not because of the riots, but because the Pope of Rome went back on the ugliness of history.

High Argument

Our Image of God Must Go

by the Bishop of Woolwich

When we published this article by Dr. John Robinson on March 17, 1963, a controversy began not only among learned theologians but in society at large. It disclosed a remarkably general concern about the condition of our religious life. The article is re-printed here together with two of the immediate rejoinders.

Few people realise that we are in the middle of one of the most exciting theological ferments of the century. Some theologians have sensed this for years; but now, quite suddenly, new ideas about God and religion, many of them with disturbing revolutionary implications, are breaking surface.

If Christianity is to survive it must be relevant to modern secular man, not just to the dwindling number of the religious. But the supernaturalist framework within which traditionally it has been preached is making this increasingly impossible. Men can no longer credit the existence of "gods", or of a God as a supernatural Person, such as religion has always posited.

Not infrequently, as I watch or listen to a broadcast discussion between a Christian and a humanist, I catch myself realising that most of my sympathies are on the humanist's side. This is not in the least because my faith or commitment is in doubt, but because I instinctively share with him his inability to accept the "religious frame" within which alone that faith is being offered to him. I feel that as a secular man he is *right* to rebel against it, and I am increasingly uncomfortable that "orthodoxy" should be identified with it, when it is simply an out-moded view of the world.

The new ideas were first put on record by a German pastor in a Nazi prison in 1944: "Our whole 1,900-year-old Christian preaching and theology rests upon the 'religious premise' of man. What we call Christianity has always been a pattern—perhaps a true pattern—of religion. But if one day it becomes apparent that this *a priori* 'premise' simply does not exist, but was an historical and temporary form of human self-expression, i.e., if we reach the stage of being radically without religion—and I think this is more or less the case already— what does that mean for 'Christianity'?

"It means that the linchpin is removed from the whole structure of our Christianity to date."

Those words were written on April 30, 1944. It is a date that may yet prove a turning-point in the history of Christianity. For on it Dietrich Bonhoeffer first broached the subject of "religionless Christianity" in a smuggled correspondence with his friend Eberhard Bethge, who subsequently edited his *Letters and Papers from Prison*.

Bonhoeffer was a Lutheran pastor of very traditional upbringing. Had he lived, he would now be in his late fifties. From 1933-35 he was in charge of the German congregation in Forest Hill, South London—where the church, rebuilt out of British war-damage money, is now dedicated to his name. In the inner circle of the German Resistance, he was privy to the plot on Hitler's life, and within a year of penning that letter he had been hanged by the S.S., on the eve of liberation by the Americans.

When his letters were first published—a bare ten years ago—one felt at once that the Church was not ready for what Bonhoeffer was saying. Indeed, it might properly be understood only 100 years hence. But it seemed one of those trickles that must one day split rocks.

The speed with which his ideas have became current coin is not, I think, the result solely of the quickening pace of communication and change. It is the result of one of those mysteries of human history whereby, apparently without interconnection, similar ideas start bubbling up all over the place at the same time. Without this, I suspect, Bonhoeffer might have remained a voice in the wilderness for decades like Kierkegaard a century earlier.

Perhaps at this point I may be personal. A year ago I was laid up for three months with a slipped disc. I determined to use the opportunity to allow their head to ideas that had been submerged by pressure of work for some time past. Over the years convictions had been gathering—from my reading and experiences—which I knew I couldn't with integrity ignore, however disturbing they might seem.

But I wrote my book* shut up in my room. What has astonished me since is the way in which within the last six months similar ideas have broken surface in articles and conversations in the most unlikely places—as far apart as Africa and Texas. However inarticulate one may be, one detects an immediate glance of recognition and what the editor of *Prism* has called "an almost audible gasp of relief" when these things are said openly.

It is not easy to put one's finger on the common factor. I suppose it is *the glad acceptance of secularisation as a God-given fact*. For we

---

* *Honest to God*, by the Bishop of Woolwich (S.C.M. Press).

of our generation are secular men. And our question, as Christians, is: How can Christ be Lord of a genuinely secular world?

Hitherto, says Bonhoeffer, Christianity has been based on the premise that man is naturally religious; and it has been presented as the best and highest religion. The corollary has been that to the non-religious it has nothing to say. A person had to become religious first —to have, or be induced to have, a religious sense of sin or need for God: then Christ could come to him as the answer.

Modern man has opted for a secular world: he has become increasingly non-religious. The Churches have deplored this as the great defection from God, and the more they write it off, the more this movement has seen itself as anti-Christian.

But, claims Bonhoeffer boldly, the period of religion is over. Man is growing out of it: he is "coming of age". By that he doesn't mean that he is getting better (a prisoner of the Gestapo had few illusions about human nature), but that for good or for ill he is putting the religious world-view behind him as childish and pre-scientific.

Bonhoeffer would accept Freud's analysis of the God of religion as a projection. Till now man has felt the need for a God as a child feels the need for his father. He must be "there" to explain the universe, to protect him in his loneliness, to fill the gaps in his science, to provide the sanction for his morality.

But now man is discovering that he can manage quite happily by himself. He finds no necessity to bring God into his science, his morals, his political speeches. Only in the private world of the individual's psychological need and insecurity—in that last corner of "the sardine-tin of life"—is room apparently left for the God who has been elbowed out of every other sphere. And so the religious evangelist works on men to coerce them at their weakest point into feeling that they cannot get on without the tutelage of God.

But "God is teaching us that we must live as men who can get along very well without him." And this, says Bonhoeffer, is the God Jesus shows us, the God who refuses to be a *Deus ex machina*, who allows himself to be edged out of the world on to the Cross. Our God is the God who forsakes us—only to meet with us on the Emmaus road, if we are really prepared to abandon him as a long-stop and find him not at the boundaries of life where human powers fail, but at the centre, in the secular, as "the 'beyond' in our midst".

Another way of putting this is to say that our whole mental image of God must undergo a revolution. This is nothing new in Christianity. The men of the Bible thought of God as "up there", seated upon a throne in a localised heaven above the earth, and it was this God to whom Jesus "ascended".

But with the development of scientific knowledge, the image of the God "up there" made it harder rather than easier to believe. And so, very boldly, Christians discarded it. I say very boldly, for in order

44

to do so they had to go against the literal language of the Bible.

For it they substituted another mental image—of a God "out there", metaphysically if not literally. Somewhere beyond this universe was a Being, a centre of personal will and purpose, who created it and who sustains it, who loves it and who "visited" it in Jesus Christ. But I need not go on, for this is "our" God. Theism means being convinced that this Being exists: atheism means denying that He does.

But I suspect we have reached the point where this mental image of God is also more of a hindrance than a help. There are many who feel instinctively that the space-age has put paid to belief in God. The theologian may properly think them naive. But what they are rebelling against is this image of a Being out beyond the range of the farthest rocket and the probe of the largest telescope. They no longer find such an entity credible.

To the religious, the idea of a supreme Being out there may seem as necessary for their thinking as was once the idea of a Being up there. They can hardly even picture God without it. If there wasn't really someone "there", then the atheists would be right.

But any image can become an idol; and I believe that Christians must go through the agonising process in this generation of detaching themselves from this idol. For to twentieth-century man the "old man in the sky" and the whole supernaturalist scheme seem as fanciful as the man in the moon.

Sir Julian Huxley has spent much time in his deeply moving book, *Religion Without Revelation*, and in subsequent articles in this paper, dismantling this construction. He constantly echoes Bonhoeffer's sentiments, and I heartily agree with him when he says, "The sense of spiritual relief which comes from rejecting the idea of God as a superhuman being is enormous."

For the real question of belief is not the *existence* of God, as a person. For God *is* ultimate reality (that's what we mean by the word), and ultimate reality must exist. The only question is what ultimate reality is like. And the Christian affirmation is that reality ultimately, deep down, in the last analysis, is *personal*: the world, incredible as it may seem, is built in such a way that in the end personal values will out.

Professor Bondi, commenting in the B.B.C. television programme, *The Cosmologists*, on Sir James Jeans's assertion that, "God is a great mathematician," stated quite correctly that what he should have said is "Mathematics is God". Reality, in other words, can finally be reduced to mathematical formulae. What the Christian says is that in, with and under these regularities, and giving ultimate significance to them, is the yet deeper reliability of an utterly personal love.

That, in the world of the H-bomb, is a desperate act of faith. On purely humanistic grounds I could have no basis for believing it as more than wishful thinking. Huxley ends his book with the words, "My faith is in the possibilities of man." It is significant that he was able to reissue it in 1957 without even a mention of the possibility, not to say probability, that there might not, within his frame of reference, be any prospects for humanity at all.

The belief that personality is of ultimate significance is for me frankly incredible *unless* what we see in Jesus of Nazareth is a window through the surface of things into the very ground of our being. That is why, in traditional categories, the survival of Christianity turned upon the assertion that He was "of one substance with the Father". For unless the substance, the being, of things deep down *is* Love, of the quality disclosed in the life, death and resurrection of Jesus Christ, then we could have no confidence in affirming that reality at its very deepest level is personal. And that is what is meant by asserting that God is personal.

This has nothing necessarily to do with positing the existence of a Person, an almighty Individual, "up there" or "out there". Indeed, as Paul Tillich, the great American theologian, also from Germany, has said: "The protest of atheism against such a highest person is correct."

Tillich has shown that it is just as possible to speak of God in terms of "depth" as of "height". Such language is equally symbolic. But it may speak more "profoundly" to modern man brought up on "depth psychology". Indeed, I believe that this transposition can bring fresh meaning to much traditional religious symbolism. Tillich talks of what is most deeply true about us and for us, and goes on:

"That depth is what the word God means. And if that word has not much meaning to you, translate it, and speak of the depths of your life, of the source of your being, of your ultimate concern, of what you take seriously without any reservation. Perhaps, in order to do so, you must forget everything traditional you have learned about God, perhaps even that word itself. For if you know that God means depth, you know much about him. You cannot then call yourself an atheist or unbeliever. For you cannot think or say: Life has no depth! Life itself is shallow. Being itself is surface only. If you could say this in complete seriousness, you would be an atheist, but otherwise you are not."

Those words from his *Shaking of the Foundations* (now published as a Pelican) had a strangely moving effect on me when I first read them fourteen years ago. They spoke of God with a new and indestructible relevance, which made the traditional language about a God that came in from outside both remote and artificial. And yet they preserved his "profound" mystery and transcendence.

The ultimate Christian conviction is that at the heart of things there is "nothing, in death or life . . . in the world as it is or the world as it shall be, in the forces of the universe, in heights or depths—

nothing in all creation that can separate us from the love of God in Christ Jesus our Lord." That I believe passionately. As for the rest, as for the images of God, whether metal or mental, I am prepared to be an agnostic with the agnostics, even an atheist with the atheists.

Indeed, though we shall not of course be able to do it, I can understand those who urge that we should give up using the word "God" for a generation, so impregnated has it become with a way of thinking we may have to discard if the Gospel is to signify anything.

I am well aware that what I have said involves radical reformulations for the Church in almost every field—of doctrine, worship, ethics and evangelism. This is a dangerous process, but immensely exhilarating; and the exciting thing is that it is not being forced upon the Church from outside but is welling up from within.

*

Rejoinders

1. By the Most Reverend Doctor Edwin Morris, the Archbishop of Wales.

I have not yet read the Bishop of Woolwich's book, *Honest to God*, but no doubt his own summary of it (*The Observer*, March 17) fairly represents his views. With the Bishop's wish to shock people into thinking afresh about their religious beliefs I have much sympathy; but unless this is accompanied by constructive guidance, the shock leads only to bewilderment.

I am bound to say that the Bishop's article fails to give constructive guidance. In fact, he looks forward to "radical reformulations for the Church in almost every field—of doctrine, worship, ethics and evangelism", and he regards this as "a dangerous process, but immensely exhilarating". How the hungry sheep of Christ are to be fed while the next two or three generations of theologians are enjoying these intellectual exercises he does not say.

The Bishop makes a great show of clearing the ground. Christianity must become relevant to modern secular man, and as its "supernaturalist framework" is not acceptable, the Bishop will help destroy it. Men no longer believe in God as a supernatural Person, so the Church must change the image of God. Bonhoeffer's "religionless Christianity" is on the right lines, though how there could be any reality which this verbal contradiction would fit the Bishop does not explain.

The Bishop refers to "the religious" as a tiny minority of mankind, rather as Professor Hoyle refers to "the Christians" as if they are a curious sub-species. Indeed, the Bishop seems to support Bonhoeffer's view that man no longer needs religion; he is "growing out of it".

Like Laplace, modern secular man has no need of the hypothesis of God. Being now master of his fate, he does not require a "Father-projection" to give him a sense of security. Like Sir Julian Huxley, all that man needs is "faith in the possibilities of man".

We are even invited to believe that "God is teaching us that we must live as men who can get along very well without him." It would be interesting to know how the Bishop knows this. Those oddly religious people who are said to cling to the notion of a God who is "out there" are merely a pathetic survival from a childish age.

There may be some simple souls whose picture of God deserves the Bishop's destructive criticism, but the Church has always combined belief in God's transcendence with belief in His immanence. "Thus saith the high and lofty One that inhabiteth eternity, whose name is Holy: I dwell in the high and holy place, with him also that is of a contrite and humble spirit," was an Old Testament insight that finds repeated expression in the New Testament and in the Church's services.

The picture of God on a throne, high and lifted up, was combined in the mind of Isaiah with the picture of God in personal control of human history, which is the biblical view as a whole. If modern secular man no longer believes it, his disbelief does not make it untrue.

The idea that modern man has outgrown religion seems to me to be completely false. Religion expresses itself in worship, and modern man worships gods many and lords many. The vast majority worship the god called Money, using Stock Exchange lists, football pools coupons, bingo cards or betting slips as prayer books. Many worship the transient gods and goddesses of the film world, or the current pop singers. Sex is another popular goddess, with a whole range of pornography as the bible of her devotees. A few worship the god called Humanism.

There is nothing new in all this. Only the outward form of the idols has changed, and we shall not get rid of these idols by changing the image of the true God.

In particular, the statement that "Mathematics is God", which the Bishop approves, is a poor substitute. When I read that "In the beginning God created the heavens and the earth," I can easily think of God as "a great Mathematician", giving eternal principles of order to His universe, and I can bow in adoration and wonder before such a God. But the statement that "Mathematics is God" leaves me stone cold. In fact it seems to me to be meaningless.

I should like to know how the Bishop performs the verbal gymnastics needed, say, when celebrating the Holy Communion, to translate the Prayer Book into language expressive of his present views. It must be very exhausting. Fortunately he does not have to do it audibly.

Tillich's view that God is to be found in the depths of our own being, which fascinates the Bishop, is as old as Psalm 139, combined there, however, with belief in God's transcendence. As for Huxley's faith in the possibilities of man, the Bishop allows that it was "significant" that Huxley could reaffirm this in 1957 without a mention of the H-bomb. Significant of what? Of a blind spot in Huxley's thinking? Man's possibilities (or actualities) include not only the H-bomb, but also the napalm bomb, the gas chamber, bacteriological warfare, nerve gas, and so on. It is arbitrary to have faith only in man's finer possibilities when we know of these other possibilities.

The Bishop makes no mention of man's need of grace, redemption, salvation. Modern man, it seems, has become not only the measure of things but also the measure of God. I see no Gospel in this doctrine.

The notion of modern man as self-sufficient is only the old British heresy of Pelagianism, and the view that man can get along quite well without God in the world is only a rehash of seventeenth-eighteenth-century Deism. The very title of Toland's book *Christianity not Mysterious*, would serve as a heading for the Bishop's article. Perhaps one of our enterprising publishers will seize the profitable chance to issue Bishop Butler's *Analogy of Religion* as a paperback.

2. By Canon T. R. Milford, Master of the Temple.

A hundred years ago it was Oxford clergymen who made the pace and took the knock. Now it is the turn of Cambridge men, of whom Dr. Robinson is one, to say in public what many clergy and dons for many years have been saying among themselves. We must admire his courage and honesty.

It is a fact that in spite of all our talk about God and religion and their supreme importance, "God" and "religion" are almost completely ignored where the interests of contemporary man are vitally engaged. All the main departments of human activity have escaped in the last 300 years from theological control, and have expanded by freely following their own internal principles.

Art and history, science and technology no longer submit to authoritative principles laid down in advance or revealed from above. They have taken to the experimental inductive method: they work by trial and error and appeal to experience to justify their tentative conclusions; and they have grown and flourished exceedingly. The case is the same with psychology, and is becoming so with morals as well.

This is the central source of that "secularisation" which is transforming not only Christendom but also the ancient civilisations of the East and the tribal traditions of Africa. It is a world-wide, irreversible fact which must be wholeheartedly and gladly accepted. This is the "coming of age" of which Bonhoeffer speaks.

Enter a Church, and the whole atmosphere is different. Actually, it is unorthodox to describe God as "a Person". But the impression one inevitably gathers from the way He is spoken of and addressed is that He is just that. Yet the commands which He issues, the punishments which He is asked to remit, and the blessings He is asked to bestow are nowhere identifiable in what goes on outside the Church.

To expose this is surely evidence of a genuine pastoral concern and not of a donnish remoteness from life as it is lived in the parishes. For the Church cannot "save the world" from triviality, superficiality, materialistic hedonism, cynicism and despair if it keeps itself safe by repeating the traditional formulas without question.

Is the really important point the one flagged by *The Observer* headline OUR IMAGE OF GOD MUST GO? Say, rather, any image of God taken by itself may become an idol. We need "out there" and "down there" as well as "up there" and "in here" and "all around" as well. We must find God in research, God in technology, God in mutual care; and *also* (this is the important positive point in the article) in the depths of our own souls, as psychology is beginning to explore them, in the mysterious depths where our consciousnesses are linked with one another and with the whole evolving process of life.

The Church has always known this, you say? To which the world may well reply, "Don't talk of Love—show me."

Life on the Island

Political Aspect

The Struggle for Labour Power

Already named as the next Labour Prime Minister, Hugh Gaitskell died on January 18, 1963, when he was 56. This unexpected tragedy caught the Party ill-prepared for the leadership struggle which followed, here examined in DAYLIGHT by our Political Staff.

There are times in the life of a political party when a few days suddenly light up, with a relentless glare, the real workings of power and ambition.

Such have been the last four weeks for the Labour Party. A month after Hugh Gaitskell died, they elected the man who had been Gaitskell's most conspicuous opponent: during that interval, in the knowledge that they might well be choosing the next Prime Minister, the whole party were caught up in the agonising choices, reappraisals and shifts of loyalty which led, last Thursday, to the election of James Harold Wilson.

This weekend, Wilson faces the ugly fact that, in spite of his majority, only a minority of his close colleagues in the Shadow Cabinet voted for him.

The man who, at the beginning of the month, seemed so shadowy and aloof still seems, this weekend, a bland enigma. His voice, his pipe, his home and surroundings, all add to the general impression of impenetrable greyness.

He lives in a small brick house (burgled when he was at the last Labour Party conference) with a white face and new pale-green paint in Southway, Hampstead Garden Suburb, a modest road of beech and privet hedges, and small, grotesquely pollarded trees. In the mornings he can look across a playground and netball pitch and hear small children singing hymns in the Henrietta Barnett Junior School, a low building with a rocking-horse in the window.

It has been no part of the Wilson plan to make his home into part of his political life. Gaitskell might entertain large gay parties of middle-class intellectuals, in a fashionable part of Hampstead, but

51

the Wilsons, farther out in the less fashionable Suburb, have scarcely even seen the Gordon Walkers, just across the fence.

"He's been in my house times without number in the past few years," said one of his closest associates, "but I can't have been inside his front door more than twice." "If we overdo the social side," said Mrs. Wilson not long ago, "Harold doesn't get his work done."

In the battle for the leadership, it was this baffling seclusion that was to prove Wilson's greatest asset.

Only a month before his election, Harold Wilson had flown back from America, on January 19, the day after Gaitskell's death, into the midst of the most crucial political battle of his career. Throughout Gaitskell's illness Wilson had been lecturing in the United States, hearing news of the worsening situation. Ten times he rang up Transport House to ask about his chief.

When Wilson's grey, stocky shape came down the gangway from the Boeing 707, flight BA 538, he looked pink-eyed from lack of sleep, dazed and withdrawn into private thought. A bitterly cold wind whipped across the tarmac. Wilson, as usual, wore his ominous Gannex raincoat with the tartan lining. The newspapers at the airport bookstall, below the news GAITSKELL DEAD, had headlines asking WHO WILL BE THE NEXT LEADER? WHO TAKES HIS PLACE? WHO LEADS NOW? Most papers mentioned Wilson's name as the most likely, but without much conviction or enthusiasm.

In the meantime, George Brown, the party's Deputy Leader, had been touring depressed areas in the North. The contrast between the two men could not then have been more pointed: they seemed quite irreconcilable. Only two months ago Brown had defeated Wilson for the Deputy Leadership, by 133 to 103; they were proclaimed and obvious rivals.

In the struggles within the party, Wilson had always been inclined to seek compromises. Brown, on the other hand, had wanted to make the party face issues squarely, even if it meant a stand-up fight. There was little love lost. Brown talked openly of Harold and his tricks; Wilson was more inclined to drop little remarks obliquely aimed at George. Their temperaments as well as their political attitudes were opposed. Brown was direct, outgoing, ebullient, impetuous; Wilson was sidelong, watchful, contained, calculating.

As Gaitskell's end drew near, Brown had been in two minds whether to carry on in the North or to call the whole thing off. He was in a highly emotional state, for his relationship with Gaitskell, though sometimes stormy, was close and intimate, one of the most stimulating of his life. Finally, at Manchester, he abruptly ended a television interview, telling the viewers that he had to rush out to the airport to catch a special R.A.F. plane to London. There were, in fact, three hours to wait; which he spent drinking miserably with aides and Pressmen.

Like Wilson, Brown knew when Gaitskell died that he faced his decisive political battle and could not afford to be dilatory. He had to turn his thoughts, quickly and realistically, away from the tragic week behind, and towards the struggle for the future.

Both Brown and Wilson maintained a display of unity, but neither could conceal his rivalry. Brownites and Wilsonites began to assess their strength.

This was the calculation.

Wilson, it was reckoned, could count on the support of the left-wing M.P.s, the unilateralists and neutralists, and the left-centre: perhaps seventy or eighty all told. Brown should have the backing of a large slice of the union-sponsored members, plus at least some Gaitskellites. These were reckoned to total about eighty.

Here, it seemed, as the opening shots were fired, were the bases from which each had to advance towards the 125 votes needed for victory. But either man was going to find his last forty recruits hard to come by, because each was disliked more fervently than he was liked.

It was Wilson who made the first, quiet move. Three days after Gaitskell's death, during the regular eve-of-reassembly meeting of the Labour Shadow Cabinet, he suggested to Brown that they should meet afterwards to establish some ground-rules for the inevitable contest. Alone, in a corridor outside the chamber, they reached a secret agreement.

According to accounts which appeared in three national newspapers two days later, they agreed that each would accept the position if the other won and serve as Deputy Leader. They also agreed that each would do his best to restrain his supporters from denigrating the other principal, on the grounds that the reputation of the future Leader and Deputy Leader must not suffer damage during the contest.

But there is still some mystery about this "pact". As soon as he read the reports of it, Brown denied in an interview with the local paper serving his constituency, the *Derby Evening Telegraph*, that he had ever agreed to be Deputy if defeated for the leadership. His impression was that his corridor encounter with Wilson had been nothing more than an informal chat, lasting about two minutes: the upshot of it had been that both of them agreed to keep off personalities. According to Brown, there was no truth in, or even foundation for, the sort of detailed pact that had looked in the Press as if it had been drawn up in a solicitor's office.

Wilson certainly took responsibility for the leak, which occurred, he said, through a misunderstanding with a lobby correspondent. He took the blame for this misunderstanding and apologised to Brown at the meeting of the National Executive the next day, though he never repeated his apology in public. Brown thought the whole story was designed to demonstrate Wilson's loyalty and to cast doubts on Brown's faith in his own chances. Whatever the rights or wrongs of the incident, Wilson certainly considered Brown made a mistake in issuing his denial.

Already confused by the pact, Brown next learned on Wednesday, January 23, that Callaghan was probably going to run. Looking back, it is easy to see that this was the first body-blow of the campaign.

For Brown thought that Wilson would be his only real opponent. Since they were the strongest candidates, why should anyone try to challenge them? Most Labour M.P.s were agreed that the intervention of a third man could only delay the result, prolong the uncertainty, and engender still more disunity. Brown had already seen Callaghan to try to ensure that only one of them would stand.

Accounts of their meeting differ, but Callaghan came away convinced that they had agreed on the need to beat Wilson, and that Brown might be ready to stand down if Callaghan ran. Brown's recollection was that Callaghan might stand down or would not be running.

But Brown had left one vital group of people out of account. These men were a minority; but there were enough of them to deny either Brown or Wilson an outright victory, and they included such influential figures as Denis Healey, Douglas Jay and Michael Stewart. They did not fancy the thought of either Wilson or Brown. As one mourning Gaitskell lieutenant put it later: "It's like a child being asked which step-mother he would prefer."

In this group's view, Wilson's record of equivocal loyalty to Gaitskell over Clause Four, his unclarity over nuclear disarmament, his reluctance ever to state a view until he saw which way the cat was going to jump—all these made him unfit, they thought, to wear the mantle of their dead leader. Beyond that, they told one another that Wilson was a small man, lacking vision, generosity of mind and steadfastness of purpose.

But these same men were equally reluctant to back George Brown. They had been on his side through the bitter party controversies of the past. They admired his courage and loyalty. They even suspected that he had more capacity for leadership than Wilson. But there were fatal flaws in his character. He flew off the handle; he was too unpredictable; he was too tactless. His long connexion with the *Daily Mirror*, suddenly disclosed last year, had dismayed some of his friends.

Some of the trade union M.P.s were unhappy, curiously enough, about his working-class background. Everyone recalled his clash with Khrushchev at the famous Labour Party dinner, an incident that displayed Brown's warmth of heart and pluck, but also gave an alarming glimpse of his lack of self-control. Would he behave himself at Number 10? Could George possibly be trusted, if he ever got into a room alone with Kennedy and Khrushchev?

So began the most embarrassing, painful and decisive phase of the election: the emergence of a group, whom Brown might have expected to back him, but who now instead began looking for a third man to beat Harold Wilson.

Those looking included some of the most active, ardent Gaitskellites. On the Monday after Gaitskell's death, in the roomy top-floor flat in The Boltons belonging to Gaitskell's close friend, Anthony Crosland, some of the leading figures in the old grass-roots Gaitskellite Campaign for Democratic Socialism, Bill Rodgers, Dick Taverne, Denis Howell, Douglas Jay, were gathered with a few other prominent Gaitskellites. Who could beat Wilson? Crosland was for Callaghan. Howell as strongly for Brown. Jay was for Callaghan. Rodgers and Taverne, two of last year's crop of young by-election winners, were at first uncertain, though they soon plumped for Brown.

Later that week two other meetings of M.P.s were held in a smallish flat in a modern block in Greycoat Place, Westminster, filled with good, rather austere, modern furniture. It belonged to the quietly wealthy, dapper Jack Diamond. In the chair was the senior man present, John Strachey, and a couple of dozen Gaitskellites. Argument on the claims of Callaghan versus Brown was keen but inconclusive.

By the end of the second meeting they had to confess defeat. It was a sad moment: Gaitskell's closest supporters could not agree who should succeed him. The ranks were neatly split. So, in a last attempt to reach some agreement, it was decided to organise a straw poll of the whole Parliamentary party. The result was put before a further meeting of the group after the weekend: 105 for Harold Wilson; 95 for George Brown; 45 for Jim Callaghan.

But having got the figures, what on earth did they mean? They didn't prove that all Callaghan men would vote for Brown or all Brown men for Callaghan on the second ballot; so it was still wholly obscure which one was the better to run against Wilson.

While these wrangles went on, an initiative had been taken elsewhere. On the day before Gaitskell's funeral two senior right-centre front-benchers, Denis Healey and another member of the Shadow Cabinet, waited on Callaghan in his office in Bridge Street, just across the road from the Houses of Parliament. Neither had been involved in the private talks at Diamond's flat. They were both unhappy about George Brown and wanted to tell Callaghan that he ought to stand. (Healey's companion very shortly switched to Brown.)

Personable, intelligent without being clever, naval in background, classless in appearance, Callaghan seemed to have the right white-collar-union experience which, together with his glassy contemporary house at Blackheath, made up an image calculated to appeal to rising young marginal voters. Never disloyal to Gaitskell, yet cleaving a central path through the conflicts of the previous decade, would Callaghan not prove acceptable to both wings of the party?

Callaghan at first was reluctant. Then, in the House that afternoon,

Douglas Jay, in his slightly patronising way, told him it was his duty to run. Even then Callaghan hesitated; his chances of success, or even of avoiding humiliation seemed obviously slight. His wife was against it. It was only when he heard that Patrick Gordon Walker, the Shadow Defence Minister, was about to throw his hat in the ring that he finally agreed to stand.

Nor was Gordon Walker the only name being canvassed at this time. In their desperate desire to avoid Wilson, M.P.s were talking of Sir Frank Soskice and even Michael Stewart as dark horses ready, if goaded, to enter the race.

Some people argued that Gordon Walker would have been Gaitskell's own choice. Comfy, pipe-smoking, one of nature's housemasters, Gordon Walker would deliver a nice fireside chat, but he was too far to the right ever to make a wide appeal to Labour M.P.s. He soon withdrew. So did Stewart.

Soskice, from the beginning a fancied outsider, never got started. He stubbornly refused to let his name go forward. In any case there were few people who could envisage this retiring, selfless advocate, with his crab-like tread and treacly voice, wielding effective power.

So Callaghan's name went forward. Wilsonites were overjoyed. All they now had to do was sit quiet and muster all the support they could. Their opponents were split and likely to fall out.

By the same token, Brown men were cast down. Even if Callaghan did not come second, his intervention must mean a second ballot with Wilson out ahead on the first, and thus able to present that irresistible political spectacle of a bandwagon nearing home.

As for Brown, he was furious. As nomination day drew nearer, the signs of his fury so multiplied that it was difficult to sift fact from rumour. It was even whispered that he had already appointed five law officers. Word went round that he had described Callaghan as little better than an inferior Wilson. What if he were to be pipped at the post by this man, if his and not Callaghan's votes were eliminated! In that special chagrin which comes on those who see lesser men preferred, Brown made it clear that in no circumstances would he be prepared to serve under Callaghan.

It was a shrewd stroke. In politics it is not just the consequences which have to be measured but the consequences of those consequences. If the consequence of voting for Callaghan was to put Brown at the bottom of the poll, and if the consequence of *that* was the loss of Brown from the leading counsels of the party, then any M.P. wondering whether to vote Callaghan might well feel that was too high a price to pay, and be thrown back on Brown.

Gerry Reynolds, a tough and not exactly kid-gloved trade unionist, was now flat out in action on Brown's behalf, busily seeking votes by telling everyone the big men behind his champion.

Again, this was an effective move, for Brown's backers made an impressive roll-call: Sir Frank Soskice, Patrick Gordon Walker, James Griffiths—three revered elder statesmen—Alice Bacon, a devoted friend of Gaitskell, John Strachey and Tom Fraser. In face of this list Wilsonites could be relied on to lie low. With the exception of Dick Crossman and Tony Greenwood they had no prominent backers.

Brown went further. He began to carpet men who he felt had forgotten their duty. Tony Crosland was hauled over the coals. Reg Prentice, an able, rosy-cheeked young M.P. from Brown's own union, was summoned and denounced as a deserter.

Wilson's men were delighted to see such fun. All the energy of their opponents was now being devoted, not to keeping out Wilson but to doing down Callaghan. Successfully, too. The fear of reprisals if Brown won whipped some into line, so much so that one shrewd observer was reminded of Jan Masaryk, the great Czech democrat, who, when asked why he was inclining to the Russians, said he preferred to be taken prisoner by the Americans.

At this stage political connoisseurs watched with especial pleasure the performance of the extraordinary George Wigg. Wigg is one of the most exotic men in politics: an old N.C.O., a fanatical racing man, a great patriot and expert on defence. It was Wigg's task now, as Wilson's campaign manager, to keep an exact tally of Wilson's voting strength, to drop an encouraging word here, to rally a doubter there.

It was unobtrusiveness with which he worked that helped to unnerve Brown's supporters, and encouraged them to acts of imprudence. While they were pushing and shoving, Wigg merely stood, as it were, in the paddock marking his card. Wilson, meanwhile, proclaimed that he would offer a pound to anyone who could prove that he personally had sought the vote of any Member. It was noticed, however, that throughout the battle Wilson was obtrusively friendly to his potential electors.

So, on February 7, the party moved to the first ballot.

Its result was declared to the Parliamentary Party, meeting in an upstairs committee room, at 6.30 on that day. The figures were spectacular: Wilson 115, Brown 88, Callaghan 41. Wilson had failed by a margin of only eight votes to get an absolute majority and win the contest outright first time round. Callaghan did better than either of the other camps had expected. A bare third went to Brown. Five Members abstained (One of them, 91-year-old Davie Logan, hastened to explain that he had been moving house and that he would certainly vote for Wilson in the second ballot.

All three factions agreed that the results pointed to a likely Wilson victory at the second ballot. After the ballot, Wilson went to dine quietly at Richard Crossman's strategically placed house in Vincent Square. The Brownites put on brave faces. The Callaghan faction soon realised that they had become, temporarily, the real king-makers.

They did not, however, enjoy this status for long. Wilson needed only eight more votes to win and by 10.30, when the House adjourned, at least twelve Callaghan men had chosen Wilson and his victory seemed assured.

Brown now had only one card left to play: an open challenge to Wilson to state his policies, in a last attempt to scare off Wilson's reluctant middle-of-the-road supporters. Two days after the first ballot, he implied publicly that he and Wilson differed in their "attitudes on vital issues". That night, at a Press conference in Huddersfield, Brown was asked to specify those "vital issues"; but he had evidently reflected that if he raked up the old embers he himself might be one of the first to go up in flames, and so declined to take the matter further.

Puzzled Wilson supporters, expecting an assault, concluded that the issue would remain to the end, as it had begun, a contest between personalities and not between policies. Their man was safe.

Thereafter, as the Wilson victory was confirmed on the second ballot (Wilson, 144; Brown, 103), there occurred that convenient forgetfulness of earlier bitterness which helps to make politics tolerable. As the television interviewers multiplied, Wilson the cheeky opportunist politician began mysteriously to change into Wilson the statesman and thinker. Even the Brownites were as satisfied as could be expected, believing that their hero would still be needed.

The aura of Downing Street was already working its magic. As one Labour Member put it, "I'm trying to forget that I ever voted for Brown."

Talking to Harold Wilson

Some of the motives, ideas and idealism of the new Labour Party leader emerged from a long conversation he had in the early summer with Kenneth Harris. Here are a few extracts.

Harris: Some men go into politics almost as a matter of course and some go in because of some personal Damascus. Why are *you* in politics?

Wilson: I suppose the short answer is because politics are in me, as far back as I can remember. Farther than that: they were in my family for generations before me, as they were in the families of dozens of members of the Labour Party. The first time I can remember thinking systematically about politics was when I was seven. I was in hospital with appendicitis. My parents came in to see me the night after my operation and I told them not to stay too long or they'd be too late to vote—for Philip Snowden.

Harris: Why was your family so politically minded?

Wilson: They were nonconformist by religion and radical by temperament. The Lib.-Lab. tradition. The day after the 1906 election results came out in Manchester, my grandfather—he was a Sunday school superintendent—chose for the hymn "Sound the loud timbrel o'er Egypt's dark sea! Jehovah hath triumphed, his people are free." It's the old story of the pursuit of religious freedom and indignation with social injustice combining to conflict with the established political order. My other grandfather, too, was a deeply religious man who believed that politics represented the nation's application of religious principles.

In my boyhood it was Chapel and the Scout movement, that kind of pattern. My wife's the daughter of a Congregationalist minister—I met her at a sports club. So I was impregnated with nonconformity. It was the soil out of which the Labour Party grew.

Harris: Does the religious side of the inheritance mean anything to you today? Are you a religious man?

Wilson: I have religious beliefs, yes, and they have very much affected my political views.

Politics seems to me to be applying values which we take for granted in personal life, such as being good to neighbours, to the bigger broader problems of group, and national, and international relationships. In my early twenties I got a bit rebellious and had a dreadful row in the *Christian World*. I felt the Church was too obsessed with personal vices such as drink, and not concerned enough with social evils such as unemployment and poverty.

A belief which doesn't express itself in service seems pretty dubious to me.

* * *

Harris: How much has Marx influenced you?

Wilson: Not at all. I've studied the subject as history; you can't begin to understand the Russians without it. But quite honestly, I've never read *Das Kapital*. I got only as far as page two—that's where the footnote is nearly a page long.

Harris: Who has influenced you?

Wilson: Well, my parents and the Scout movement. The Fourth Scout Law "A Scout is a friend to all and a brother to every other Scout". When I was twelve the *Yorkshire Post* ran a competition. You had to say who your hero was, and why, in fewer than 100 words. I won—if you can imagine me saying anything in under 100 words. Baden-Powell.

But that was indirect influence. The two men who influenced me

59

most, directly, were schoolmasters. One of them is still alive—in his eighties—I hear from him from time to time. A lifelong socialist. Not by argument, but by example. He was a great teacher—unselfish and unstinting.

The other was a much younger man. He died very young. He was killed on Scafell. It was a great blow when he died. He was a first-class teacher—classics scholar—and a natural athlete. He used to take us to hear any interesting man who was speaking in reasonable distance.

Harris: What was your father?

Wilson: You might describe him as a white coat worker. He was an industrial chemist working in a laboratory in a long white coat.

Harris: I read somewhere you had inherited a remarkable memory from him? Apparently you never forget anything you have read. Photographic memory?

Wilson: I wish it were true. In some ways my memory is hopeless. I could never learn poetry, never memorise any kind of prose text, in fact, anything visual at all, such as maps. Remembering faces is supposed to be a must for politicians, I'm afraid I'm not very good at faces, either. But I have got this peculiar memory—it's nothing to do with intelligence—just a matter of facts sticking in my mind— for dates and figures.

> *Among others who had helped to shape him Mr. Wilson mentioned his tutors at Oxford and, of course, Beveridge, with whom he worked as a research assistant for a couple of years before the war. In particular, said Mr. Wilson, "Beveridge reinforced my own puritan attitude to work"*

Harris: When you say puritan . . .

Wilson: It's not until very recently—a year or so ago, perhaps— that I haven't always been driven by a feeling that there is something to be done and I really ought to be doing it. I think it's the old puritan inheritance. I don't make any claims for it. But not until a year or so ago could I sit down on a Sunday night, say, pick up a book, a biography or some historical essays, and sit back without feeling that I *oughtn't* to be doing it.

Harris: Are you a puritan in the more general sense?

Wilson: Not in the least. I use the word "puritan" as a kind of shorthand. I can't say I admire conventional puritan morality. I think there's too much truth in the crack that Puritans were against bear-baiting not because it caused pain to the bear but because it gave pleasure to the spectators. I put tolerance and group morality above abstinence and a preoccupation with personal shortcomings

> *Mr. Wilson named Stafford Cripps and Clem Attlee as*

politicians who had especially impressed him and—as a great
personal influence—Aneurin Bevan. He was asked how this
influence had worked.

Wilson: It's very difficult to abstract from Nye's influence on one. It was the whole man, you see. He taught me the power of the public platform. I wish I had a tenth of his power on the public platform. And he corrected my interest in detail. Nye always took the broad view.

In many things he was lazy, and avoided detail, if he could, anyway, but he had the gift of instinctively seeing the horizon. He never failed to see the wood for the trees. I regard him as the best-educated man I have ever met, particularly in philosophy, but he could see everyday political issues in their deep human perspective and he could communicate them simply and instantly—to anybody. He never forgave me for having been an economist—still less for having been a statistician. I remember him saying to me one day: "What's your boy's subject?" (He was devoted to children.) I said "Pure Mathematics." "Yes," he said, "Just like his father: all facts, no bloody vision."

Harris: Has becoming leader of the party changed you at all?

Wilson: It hasn't changed me, but it's changed the way I behave. For instance, I'm making decisions much more quickly. And making more decisions.

Harris: Why is that?

Wilson: Because they're there. I'm much more relaxed as leader than I ever was before, because I am free to follow my instinct. You need knowledge, advice and a grasp of the background, of course, when it comes to adopting a policy about something, working out a legislative programme and so on, but on the day-to-day handling of affairs in the House, the quick, tactical side of things, there simply isn't time to call a committee, or go home and read up your notes, or send out for a book about it.

The problems come up so quickly. I feel I am free now to decide by intuition. And this gives me a sense of relief because I know that is how political decisions—I mean the tactical ones—*should* be made and this in turn makes me feel less at odds with myself and consequently more self-confident and more efficient. Of course, I shall make mistakes, many mistakes, but they will be my own mistakes and I shall stand by them.

Harris: I once heard a Labour Party front bencher say: "You've got to hate the Tories." Do you hate the Tories as a class?

Wilson: I regard Freddie Trueman as the greatest living Yorkshireman. As a fast bowler he hates batsmen. When he turns to start his run he sees a batsman up there 40 yards or so away and all he wants to do is to get him out. And he sees red and starts his run. But when they draw stumps for the day he has a drink with him in the pavilion and some of his victims are among his friends.

When I'm at the Dispatch Box I pray to send 'em down as fast and straight as Freddie Trueman because I want to get them out.

The Tories and the Profumo Affair

If for the Labour Party 1963 was a disturbing year, for the Macmillan Government it was tempest-tossed.

First came the mud-slinging aftermath of the Vassall spy case. Late in March the Radcliffe Tribunal dismissed as groundless Press implications of impropriety or neglect of duty directed against members of the Government who had been Vassall's superiors at the Admiralty.

Then came the Profumo Affair.

Back in July, 1961, Mr. John Profumo, Secretary of State for War, had formed a liaison with Miss Christine Keeler, who was already involved with Commander Eugene Ivanov, assistant naval attaché at the Soviet Embassy.

Mr. Profumo's affair with Miss Keeler went on for six months and ended without having attracted any public attention. The two of them usually met at the flat of Dr. Stephen Ward, an osteopath and artist.

In March, 1963, a West Indian, John Edgecombe, was imprisoned for 7 years for trying to shoot his way into Miss Keeler's presence. She had been his mistress. At the trial she was called as a witness but had disappeared. She later re-emerged in Spain.

On March 21 three Labour M.P.s spoke in the Commons about rumours connecting "a Minister" with the missing witness. The next day, in a personal statement to the House, Mr. Profumo denied being in any way responsible for Miss Keeler's disappearance and added that there had been "no impropriety whatsoever" in his association with her.

In the weeks that followed Dr. Ward made contact with the Government and alleged that Mr. Profumo had misled the House.

On June 4 Mr. Profumo admitted that he had lied and sent a letter of resignation to Mr. Macmillan.

On June 8 Dr. Ward was charged with living on the immoral earnings of Miss Keeler. On August 3, a few hours before the court found him guilty, Dr. Ward killed himself.

A Leader on Lying

*The Profumo Affair stirred up intense public feeling.
People took it as dismaying evidence of a general decadence
in the country. We argued against this and suggested that
in public life some kinds of lying can be worse than others.*

Many people, including the Editor of *The Times*, have made up
their minds that the Profumo Affair is a moral issue and that it proves
not only the corruption of the Government but the spiritual and
moral delinquency of the nation.

But isn't such language exaggerated? The evidence produced so
far proves that Mr. Profumo was an immoral man who was not fit to
hold office in the Government; but it does not prove that other
Ministers were immoral and it certainly does not prove that the
nation is immoral. To lump Miss Keeler, as *The Times* seemed to do,
with the decline of religion, the faults of the affluent society and
the failure of the economy is ludicrous.

A case could be made, of course, that Britain *is* morally decadent.
(It always can be.) But it would have to be made with extreme care,
first defining what is meant by morals and discarding any illusions
that there ever was a Golden Age, in the nineteenth century or at
any other time, when all Ministers were pure and virtuous and all
ordinary men honest and hard-working. Even then it would not be
convincing, for it seems much more likely that we are seeing widespread changes in manners and morals (both sexual and other) some
of which are good and some bad. How much this—or any other—
Government can or should influence these changes is yet another
question.

On the whole it seems safer to stick to the morals of the Government. And here, while not denying the importance of private
morality in public men, public morality still seems more important.
To support dishonest policies which affect the lives of millions while
expressing outrage at a Minister's private morals shows a lack of
proportion. It will seem curious to many that Lord Hailsham and
Mr. Selwyn Lloyd should now wax so excessively indignant over
Mr. Profumo's lies when, as senior Ministers at the time of Suez, both
of them were able to stomach the far more serious lies that were then
told about our Government's collusion with the French and Israeli
Governments in preparing an attack on Egypt.

A Freudian View

One of our readers turned to Freud to explain the nation's behaviour in this minor crisis. He set out his findings in this Letter to the Editor.

Sir,—It is strange that no one seems yet to have applied a little Freudian insight to the national reactions to the Profumo affair. The way in which the clergy and others have taken this single incident as evidence of a general decline in morality; the way in which we are being exhorted by them to examine our own moral standards; the way in which a scapegoat is being sought so earnestly; the way in which certain people (and notably *The Times* leader-writer) are demanding an end to the affluent society and a return to blood, toil, sweat and tears—some of these things may be justified in themselves, but none appears to be a rational reaction to the transgression of Mr. Profumo.

However much concerned some people purport to be with the fact that he told a lie to the House of Commons (a place, after all, in which deceit is not unknown) or with the security aspect of the matter (which has not in fact, at the time of writing, been shown to exist), one must suspect that the real source of outrage lies in the fact that Mr. Profumo gave way to a sexual impulse—an impulse which exists in a state of precarious repression within most of us.

In *Totem and Taboo*, Freud wrote: "If one person succeeds in gratifying the repressed desire, the same desire is bound to be kindled in all other members of the community. In order to keep the temptation down, the envied transgressor must be deprived of the fruits of his enterprise; and the punishment will not infrequently give those who carry it out an opportunity of committing the same outrage under colour of an act of expiation."

In the light of this is it not hard to understand the widespread and uneasy, if largely unconscious, suspicion that we are all in some way guilty of Mr. Profumo's transgression. Nor is it difficult to see that this feeling of guilt is being dealt with in two distinct ways. Whilst some would seek to expiate it by self-punishment (*vide The Times* leader), others attempt to project it on to a scapegoat which is then driven into the wilderness—and since Mr. Profumo himself has resigned, no less a figure than the Prime Minister seems adequate to play this role.

But at the same time we are, of course, attempting vicariously to indulge the desires which we so strenuously condemn. To this end the Press provides its eager readers with pictures of, and information about, Miss Keeler so that they may in fantasy give vent to the

very wishes by the indulgence of which Mr. Profumo ended his
career.

Dorset.   R. T. OERTON

The Enigma of Stephen Ward

by Anthony Sampson

*The Profumo tempest petered out. An inquiry conducted
by Lord Denning, the Master of the Rolls, showed the
Government to have been "gullible but not guilty", as our
Political Correspondent put it. But the upheaval had claimed
at least one sad victim.*

What was the real motivation behind the extraordinary career of
Stephen Ward?

In spite of the examinations and cross-examinations, and all that
has been said and written about him, there are still many questions
left unanswered. From the evidence, and from the accounts of people
who knew him, some clues can be pieced together about this odd and
muddled man.

He was, from his youth, impelled by a restless, defiant daring. He
was brought up in Torquay, where his father—who took a first at
Balliol—was the vicar of a fashionable parish. Ward's father was a
gentle, scholarly man who was very popular with his staid parish-
ioners, and his mother was a formidable and sociable person, known
as "Ma Ward" and treated by neighbours with deference and caution.

Young Ward was clearly, from the first, driven to revolt against his
paragon parents. He did not believe in God—a fact that then worried
him a good deal—and he was inherently unstable. At the same time,
he had extraordinary charm and social dexterity. When he was about
18, for instance, he went with a friend on holiday to France, and
picked up a young French girl, whom he then took back to Torquay
and hid in the basement of Ma Ward's house for three weeks, until
she was discovered. This kind of prank gave him great excitement
and continued to do so, with diminishing returns, for the following
30 years.

His frenetic interest in girls continued unabated: but his pursuit
of them was so restless, so open and showing-off, that some of his
friends suspected that his Casanova activities concealed latent homo-
sexuality or impotence. He had occasional apparently serious affairs,
but they always petered out; and when, at the age of 36, he got
married, the marriage collapsed after a few weeks.

There seemed to be very little privacy about his life: he was a compulsive exhibitionist who depended on audiences to provide him with stimulus and confidence. As an osteopath, he had talents. As an artist, he was a slick illustrator. He was massively indiscreet and loved showing off right up till the end.

He liked to exercise his power over girls, and it may have been this, as much as sexual desire, that impelled him. He had strong, seductive eyes and a soft, cultured voice. He was amusing and good company. He was capable of great kindnesses. He knew how to reassure insecure girls, and how to give them confidence in public. With these skills he could, as he did with Christine Keeler, build up Pygmalion girls, whom he would enjoy showing off to his friends.

Part of his motive, no doubt, was the sheer enjoyment of the social game; part of it may have been not much more than the desire of an overbearing father to dominate a daughter. But part of it may have come from an obsessive sense of inadequacy, both sexual and otherwise.

In spite of the evident squalors and miseries of his life, he seemed to his friends to be fairly confident about his general usefulness and importance. He fancied himself as an amateur psychiatrist who understood the failings of others and helped to put them on their feet. He saw himself also as bringing the classes together, easing the wheels of society, introducing poor girls to rich men. It seems never to have occurred to him that other people might see him differently, as the jury at his trial came to do.

He was not an avaricious man, and he clearly wanted social acceptance, sociability, glamour, and the great world much more than money. It was this which made much of the prosecution's case seem inherently implausible. To depict him as a straightforward ponce, using his flat as a commercial brothel, seemed out of keeping with Ward's basic ambitions and the peculiar nature of his self-respect.

His political attitudes remain very puzzling. He was certainly "pinkish", much admired Russia, and loved talking about the evils of capitalism. But he appeared to have a very romantic self-dramatising approach, as he showed in the extraordinary attempts to act as an intermediary in the Cuba crisis. His friendship with Ivanov was certainly close: they spent weekends together at his cottage, and Ivanov used to dig for hours in a rockery known as "the Russian steppes".

But on the evidence so far the friendship does not seem to have had very serious political implications: it seems to have revolved around bridge and girls as much as Communism.

Ward, in his fashion, seems to have taken himself, both in his social and his political roles, quite seriously. At the trial he seemed quite composed and cheerful, sketching, joking and attending his

66

exhibition of drawings. The impression was created that he was shameless. But he must have been aware that the evidence, whether believed or not, was undermining his self-justification. Even if he had won the case he could never again have enjoyed the social position which sustained him: that back door had been slammed.

It may well have been that realisation which led him to suicide: he saw what the unbalanced poet John Clare called "the vast shipwreck of my life's esteems".

The Struggle for Tory Power

The Goverment moved into calmer waters and on October 7 Mr. Macmillan felt able to let it be known that he would, after all, lead the Conservatives into the coming election. But within 48 hours a sudden illness obliged him to announce his resignation—on the eve of the Party conference at Blackpool. Our Political Staff recorded what occurred there.

The news of the Prime Minister's decision was brought to Blackpool by Lord Home, who flew up on Thursday afternoon. He entered the conference hall at 5 o'clock and was introduced as the President of the National Union, the pompous and normally powerless body which comes into its own only at the annual Conservative Party conference. He read the message in which the Prime Minister told the party of his decision to retire and invited them to choose a successor.

The news confronted the party with a unique situation. Never before had the complex and subtle process by which it chooses its leader, by which the leader is said to "emerge", become involved with the hubble-bubble of the annual conference.

Traditionally the choice of a Conservative leader had been a matter for the few: soundings discreetly taken in Cabinet and Commons, elder statesmen giving their advice to the Queen, and the new Prime Minister called to the Palace. The mystery of the monarch had always been an important part of the "customary process". But now the whole party, including hundreds of constituency chairmen and members, was closely involved.

Not even the Labour Party, with its violent leadership contest and formally democratic system of selection, had ever faced such a situation. It was a far cry from 1957, when Macmillan had been chosen Prime Minister in preference to Butler. Then the soundings had been so discreet that all the morning newspapers had predicted Butler's appointment and all of them had been wrong.

From now onwards Blackpool was alight with rumour. But Blackpool opinion did not truly represent the balance of power in the party. The whole of the Cabinet, except Sandys and Noble, had booked in at the Imperial Hotel. But scarcely more than half the Conservative M.P.s were in Blackpool and they were swallowed up in the swarm of constituency rank-and-filers, many of them women and young Conservatives rooting for Lord Hailsham.

From Thursday onwards the Lord Chancellor and the Chief Whip were in play, taking soundings, waiting for the leader to emerge; and the man most obviously anxious about the soundings was Rab Butler, since Tuesday the acting Prime Minister.

It was Rab's second chance for the Premiership: and the ordeal must have been agonising. The abruptness of the news, together with his reticence about the succession, suggested that Macmillan did not want Rab to be leader. They had never been close; they had been wary of each other for a long time. Macmillan had made Rab his deputy, but Rab had heard the news of Macmillan's resignation only at the same time as other Ministers, an hour before the public announcement on Thursday.

Rab's first difficulty, when he arrived at Blackpool on Wednesday, was over the question of the Saturday speech which is by tradition the triumphant sole appearance of the Party leader. Macmillan had conspicuously failed to nominate a deputy for the occasion. It was a delicate question, for whoever was chosen would have a good chance to rally the party behind him.

As Butler entered the crowded lobby of the Imperial Hotel, the officers of the National Union were in session discussing the matter. There were Mrs. Shepherd, the bell-voiced chairman of the conference, Lord Chelmer, a successful London solicitor, a trio of Tory knights— Sir Max Bemrose, Sir Robert Davies, and Sir Dan Mason—and the new secretary, Mr. Cooke.

This portentous body, after half an hour, decided to invite Butler to take Macmillan's place on the Saturday. But the decision still had to be agreed by his Cabinet colleagues. Butler at once summoned all available Cabinet Ministers to Room 127. There were 10 of them, counting the Chief Whip, Martin Redmayne.

Butler, who presided, was quite firm. He proposed to accept. What had they to say? As it turned out, plenty. They suggested other possible speakers, including Lord Home and Lord Hailsham (who were not present). There was even an idea that the Chief Whip should read out the speech the Prime Minister had started to write. Maudling blandly suggested cancelling the rally and giving the delegates a half-holiday.

But after 80 minutes the meeting agreed, by a narrow margin, that

Butler should make the speech. Butler looked pleased as he descended the stairs, though he must have realised that this was only the opening of the battle.

By five o'clock on Thursday, Rab's prospects looked excellent. He had the most backing among his Cabinet colleagues. In particular, he had the firm support of Sir Edward Boyle, Sir Keith Joseph and Enoch Powell—the trio of highly professional and technically proficient Ministers with acute social consciences, who typified the new face of Toryism.

And then suddenly Lord Hailsham burst on the scene.

At the moment when Lord Home was reading out Macmillan's resignation to the conference, Hailsham was at Preston, meeting his wife and one-year-old daughter. When he returned, he had three hours before he was due to address the Conservative Political Centre. In those three hours he finally decided to renounce his peerage—the equivalent of a formal challenge. He made a strong speech to the C.P.C., speaking of the need to sharpen controversy sometimes, even if it meant making enemies as well as friends—an obvious dig at Rab. Then, in reply to the vote of thanks, he announced that he would renounce his peerage.

On television afterwards he insinuated a comparison of himself with Sir Winston Churchill. The next day he found himself fêted wherever he went, ostentatiously sitting among the delegates in the conference hall, walking through the lounges, silencing the spontaneous applause.

It now became clear that—with Macmillan out—Hailsham enjoyed strong support from some members of the Churchill and Macmillan families, who formed a small but important network of their own. Julian Amery, Macmillan's son-in-law, was the most ardent Hailshamite, and his applause when Hailsham made his announcement was ecstatic. Amery was even busily putting it about that Macmillan had indicated Hailsham as his rightful heir.

Maurice Macmillan too, was actively pressing for Hailsham, and so was his friend Christopher Soames, Churchill's son-in-law. Randolph Churchill turned up from America on Friday gaily announcing that the decision had already been taken to call on Hailsham; and began distributing badges with "Q" for Quintin on them.

Rab's old enemies from appeasement days were mustering their strength, and the right-wing of the party (always better organised than the left) were buzzing with Hailshamisms. But there were other more sober spirits said to be on Hailsham's side: Thorneycroft, for one, and Hare.

But as Hailsham's popular triumph grew, so his Cabinet colleagues became visibly more irritated by his flamboyance and jauntiness. The more the constituencies loved him, the more the Cabinet disliked him. He was less than tactful in his method of announcing his renunciation: he did not warn his Cabinet colleagues beforehand, and he did not try to assuage them. His critics said that he had finally wrecked his chances by moving in the wrong way, at the wrong time. But he could not have moved earlier without appearing to undermine Macmillan; and he could not have moved later without leaving himself dangerously little time to muster support. The fact was that whatever he did, he was bound to be criticised; for in this curious Tory game, as in a game of grandmother's footsteps, you could only safely move if you were not seen to move.

On Thursday and Friday, Hailsham was at his most boisterous and cocky. He revelled in television, jostled among the constituency people, and tramped up and down the corridors with a retinue of henchmen like Ian Gilmour and John Eden in his train. He posed before the cameras with his baby and the baby food. In fact, some people say it was the baby food, that dished him. By Friday morning a large section of the Tories had come to feel they had had enough. Whereas Butler might be unable to inspire the party to victory, Hailsham would inspire the wrong people with the wrong ideas. And so attention focused on the search for a third candidate.

The old names were recited once again. Heath—too inexperienced. Macleod—too left-wing, too tired. Maudling—yes, perhaps; Maudling still had much support from Tory M.P.s particularly the young and modern-minded.

But then on Friday morning came Maudling's speech. He was in a good position; the hero of the Budget, the master economist, the man with faith in Britain. Yet he made a speech so utterly flat that the Maudling campaign instantly ran out of steam.

And so the name of Lord Home came back into circulation. The Fourteenth Earl had made a speech just before Maudling. He managed to be both patriotic and international; he was jingoistic yet attacked the jingoes. Above all, he inspired confidence. He brought the house down.

As the compromise candidate, Home had many advantages. He was unquestionably Tory. He was aloof and disinterested. As one ex-Minister put it, "He'll be the first utterly *honest* Prime Minister the Tories have had for a long time" (meaning, of course, not a Talleyrand).

He was also, without being as wildly romantic as Hailsham, undoubtedly the patrician type, and in the powerful pre-election atmosphere it seemed increasingly important to have a leader (unlike Butler) who was obviously anti-socialist. However much the choice of leadership depended on personalities, there remained in the background the old rift between the Left and the Right of the Tory Party. Rab remained suspect as a liberal; and just as the right wing had defeated him in 1957, so it looked like doing so again in 1963.

There were cogent objections to Home. "A fourteenth earl doesn't

70

quite fit in with the idea of the new Tory party," one Cabinet Minister remarked. The idea of matching a Scottish laird against Harold Wilson did not appeal to everyone. But the temptation was strong to go for a leader who gave the impression of being above the battle and who could attract both wings.

And so, on Friday evening, as Lord Dilhorne sounded the Cabinet, Redmayne sounded M.P.s, and Lord St. Aldwyn talked to fellow-peers, the outline of Lord Home began to appear on the Tory radar-screen.

Late on Friday night it became known that Lord Dilhorne had persuaded Hailsham to wait and see before renouncing his title: word went round that Hailsham, and even Macmillan, were prepared to serve under Home. The Earl himself began to display unusual signs of excitement.

And then the Butlerites counter-attacked. If they could only hold the situation until everyone returned to the relative calm of London, they believed that their man's chances would be greatly strengthened. Butler's supporters in the Cabinet made it plain that they would accept Home only with the utmost reluctance, if at all: any such appointment, they argued, would be seen by the great majority of the country as a step back into Britain's feudal past.

The party managers began to think again.

The 'The Observer' (London) 1963

"Quintin, you're drowning the music!"

71

A Question of Evolution

by Michael Frayn

The leader-selection system used by the Conservatives was found fascinating by many outsiders, among them our Resident Satirist.

Evolved, that's what he was. Not elected, but *evolved*. It's the new idea. I'm all in favour of it, believe me, since the result has released me from the solemn oath I swore to join the Labour Party if Serjeant Quintin Tread-this-godless-generation-down-in-ammunition-boots was evolved, elected, or otherwise extruded into the form of a Prime Minister.

Yes, I'm a great believer in evolution. I'm not the only one. Every time I've turned the television set on in the past fortnight I've come face to face with some very reliable-looking man who believed in it too.

"It's a question of evolution," each one of them said.

"Through the normal processes of consultation," I would add shrewdly.

"Through the normal processes of consultation," he would go on. "Because, of course, the best way of choosing a leader isn't necessarily just by counting heads."

"Of course not," I'd say. "We have to recognise that some people carry more weight than others."

"I say!" he'd reply. "How jolly nice to find someone who understands!"

"Oh, I heard your friend talking about it last night. We agreed entirely."

"Did you? Yes, well the point is, of course, that if we just counted heads, the vote of someone who carries a lot of weight, like Alec, or Quintin, or myself, could be completely cancelled out by some ghastly little man no one's ever heard of, who might turn out to wear crêpe-soled shoes and say 'bottoms up'."

"How frightful for you!"

"I mean, if it was someone one had been at school with, one could go and talk it over with him sensibly. But a lot of ghastly chaps in R.A.F. blazers well, I mean to say, one doesn't know them."

"But you take soundings, of course."

"Oh, good heavens, yes! We take *soundings* all right. All the way down to R.A.F.-blazer level—and below. Oh, we sound them out all right. Get them on the phone, you know. 'Are you the ghastly little

72

tick who turned up at the conference in a made-up bow-tie? ' we say. 'Well, we're just sounding you out, old chap'."

"And you take note of these soundings, do you?"

"Of course we do. We note down: 'Sounds a decent enough little tick in his way,' or whatever."

"You get right down to grass roots?"

"Exactly."

"But do they carry any weight?"

"The grass roots? Good heavens, yes—they carry the most tremendous amount of weight. Alec, Quintin, and the rest of us walk over them all the time."

"In the Labour Party, of course, they still elect . . ."

"My dear chap, in the Labour Party they simply haven't *heard* of Darwin or evolution. Of course, it's just like the refrigerator or the motor-car—once one's got these things one can't think how one ever did without them. My word, if we'd had to rely on the *election* of species, mankind might never have got where it is today. If every little hog, tick, or sparrow had had his say, instead of soundings being taken among the fellows who really carried some weight, like rhinoceroses and brontosauruses, they might have picked some ghastly little insect as the Lord of Creation."

"I suppose they might. So all this 'election' business is just a lot of antiquated Socialist theorising, is it?"

"Well, what do you think, old chap? You know the slogan—'One man, one vote.' It's the old story of shortages and controls all over again. I mean, I can tell you for a fact that if the Labour Party wins the next election we're all going to find ourselves issued with ration books allowing us one vote each per election."

"Really? There'll be a black market immediately."

"Of course. Now, our approach is completely different. We say, let any man who has the initiative and the guts to get ahead and make a way for himself in the world increase his voting power as much as he can, and jolly good luck to him."

"That sounds fair enough, I must say."

"Meanwhile, let me assure you, we are sparing no efforts to ease the lot of the old-age pensioners, and increase their voting power to a full ·001 votes per person."

"God bless you for that."

"Naturally, now that the advantages of the evolutionary system have been fully demonstrated, we shall extend them from the Party itself to the country at large."

"At the General Election?"

"At the General Evolution."

"Will you be standing yourself?"

"Well, it's not really a question of standing or not standing."

"But you're in the running?"

73

"I can't really tell you whether I'm in the running or not. It's really simply a question of one's standing in certain quarters."

"One's standing? I thought you said you weren't standing?"

"I'm not. But one has a certain standing, you see, notwithstanding whether one's standing or not standing. I mean, where one's lying in the running is simply a matter of certain people's leanings."

"People of standing's leanings?"

"Of course. I need scarcely add, soundings will be taken of the leanings."

"They will? That's all right, then."

"Oh yes—running soundings."

"Running soundings of the people of standing's leanings?"

"Exactly. It's all a matter of evolution."

A Scottish Lord is Premier

In the end Lord Home got the job. Within a month he had renounced his ancient title and won himself a seat in the Commons as Member for Kinross.

An Observer Profile

Alexander Frederick Douglas-Home, the fourteenth Earl of Home, has a striking and unusual face—a triangle standing on its point. It is fine-boned and markedly without surplus flesh. His mouth is wide and thin-lipped, often tilting upwards to the left in an eloquent, faintly ironic smile. His hair is thin on top (it was auburn when he was young), but thick enough back and sides to allow him a minor version of the Westminster cut. When reading a speech he wears light and curiously antique spectacles and tips his head from side to side in a schoolmasterly way. His figure is slight and he has a deceptive air of frailty.

Home indeed has little pretension. Even in London he dresses without much obvious interest in the result. As Foreign Secretary he went about without retinue and sometimes walked to the Foreign Office by way of the Embankment, with no hat and with his hands in his pockets.

In his office, he commands great loyalty. He is punctiliously polite, remembers people's names and jobs, chats with liftmen and never stands on dignity. He can be astonishingly vague—he can lose his car, his documents, even a despatch box. He is not, in fact, very good at looking after himself, and in this his wife is crucial.

He is good and ingenious at drafting diplomatic Notes—he has just that touch of ambiguity which is so useful. He has a somewhat under-graduate sense of humour: he giggles easily, and enjoys verbal, quasi-literary jokes. He even keeps a joke book—divided into different categories—Scottish kirk jokes for speeches, broader jokes for men's clubs, etc.

The Homes (pronounced, as all the world has learned with proper reverence, Humes) were once great lords of the Border—virtually petty kings in their district. The society into which Alexander was born in July, 1903—he was given the name most often allotted to the head of his house—was still an affluent and buoyant one. Even today, earls are relatively common along the Border.

But Alec was allowed to grow up in surroundings less grand than some of those available to his family. The Home estates are broad, though not outsize. They are divided into the segments indicated by the hyphenated family name—the Douglas part and the Home part. The two were formally joined in 1857 when the eleventh earl married Lady Douglas of Douglas.

The Douglas part is by far the larger—53,000 acres of hill farms and 35,000 acres of grouse moor in Lanarkshire, below Glasgow. Here there are over 50 farms looked after by Mr. Robert Marshall Hamilton, Lord Home's factor. They raise black-faced ewes, Highland cattle and a small pedigree herd of Galloways. There are also 3,000 acres of forest, cared for by 30 foresters, and nine gamekeepers.

On this western estate stands Castlemains, not to mention Castle Douglas, the old Douglas seat (they were earls before the Homes), now a ruin. Castlemains is a 50-room shooting lodge—a plain grey house overlooking the main road from Glasgow to Carlisle.

On the Home side of this double inheritance, covering the extreme eastern end of the Border along the Tweed, there are 5,000 acres of farmland and a one-and-a-half-mile stretch of the river. Here, in Ber-wickshire, is the family seat, called The Hirsel (telephone: Coldstream 1) and full of treasures. It is an elegant eighteenth-century pile with several hundred rooms and is up a long drive.

But as a boy Alexander lived in the dower house, Springhill, be-cause his father had not at that time succeeded to the earldom. No estate agent would call Springhill modest. It is a big place, covered in red creeper, looking out over the Tweed, the battlefield of Flodden and the beginnings of England.

Alec's father—the thirteenth earl, and so inevitably known as the Unlucky Earl—appeared as a very simple man: amiable, kindly, really loved by most of his tenants. In the depressed twenties he used to take venison and sheep down to the soup kitchens in Douglas, then a mining village, and called many of the local miners by their Christian names.

Anyone he met and liked he would invite to stay: there were huge meals, lots of guests, immense shooting parties, and the wine always ran out at dinner. If the hock ran out you were given whatever was at hand, which might be port—so that half would be drinking hock and half port. You had to play round games after dinner.

He took some mild interest in politics—stood for Parliament in 1910 and later worked for the League of Nations. But basically he was a country gentleman, president of the Boys' Brigade for years. He was portrayed as the eccentric earl by William Douglas-Home, Lord Home's playwright brother, in *The Chiltern Hundreds*.

The play presents his father as an endearing, slightly bumbling, but also forthright character, at a loss about modern life and inclined to discuss it facetiously. Nobody could suppose this to be a portrait in the round, but it has, within its limits, what members of the family reckon is the truth. Indeed, some of the recorded attributes are noticeably reproduced in his sons—strongly in the playwright and to some extent in the fourteenth earl—the amused detachment particularly.

Alec's mother was a Lambton from across the Border—one of the family of the Earl of Durham. Home takes pride in his Lambton blood, naming it as the source of his political sense. He likes to recall that he is descended from the Lord Durham who wrote the famous Report on Canadian independence in 1839. Besides, his paternal grandmother was a daughter of Grey of the Reform Bill.

Alec's mother was the lively and more outspoken half of the marriage. She is still alive—in her eighties. When her children were young she was more in touch with contemporary affairs than her husband cared to be, and showed some streaks of radicalism in her opinions.

She is remembered for having sometimes taken her children to task, but never for sitting on them. She was, in fact, a woman of independent mind who encouraged her sons to develop freely in their own ways. Since then she seems never to have tried to direct either the political or the social behaviour of her family. She is a Conservative. She is also a convinced church-woman and it is perhaps here that Home most openly reflects his mother's influence.

He had an enviable boyhood, learning to shoot and fish in splendid natural surroundings, among people who liked his family. From this he went away to a prep. school in Hertfordshire and then to Eton, and everyone knows how well he did there. The other night a schoolfellow, Mr. Cyril Connolly, who is not a hero-worshipper, spoke on television with real admiration of Home in his Eton phase.

Home was President of Pop, the club through which, as monitors, the senior boys do their share in the government of the school. He was "a patrician—but a very tolerant one".

The slice of ripe Connolly prose describing Home at Eton is already famous:

"He was a votary of the esoteric Eton religion, the kind of graceful, tolerant, sleepy boy who is showered with favours and crowned with all the laurels, who is liked by the masters and admired by the boys without any apparent exertion on his part, without experiencing the ill-effects of success himself or arousing the pangs of envy in others. In the eighteenth century he would have become Prime Minister before he was 30; as it was he appeared honourably ineligible for the struggle of life."

Not all Home's fellow-Etonians took so romantic a view. Another contemporary recalls him for his slightly rabbity appearance, and his contorted bowling action.

For a few years cricket was an important part of his life. He played a few matches for Middlesex in the 1920s, and toured South America for M.C.C. in 1926-7. He was a useful medium-pace bowler despite his ugly run up: a good slip field, and a determined and brave, if ungraceful, batsman. Of his 66 against Harrow in 1922, on a bad wicket, it was said he made 65 of them off his thumb. He was always in line, and didn't flinch even though he was hit.

At Oxford he didn't get a blue, and he did get a third. When he went down no one thought they would ever hear of him again. Nor did there seem any reason to change that opinion when Home decided to go into politics.

From 1931 to 1937 he was a loyal and comparatively uncommunicative backbencher, concerned about unemployment in his own Lanark constituency; but he did not follow his colleague Harold Macmillan in rebelling against his party for permitting it. He was concerned, too, about the rise of Hitler, but far from rebelling against Chamberlain's policies, like Anthony Eden and Salisbury, he served from 1937 to 1939 as Chamberlain's Parliamentary Private Secretary.

Once he went with Chamberlain to a conference with Mussolini, where his job was to stick with his master and never leave him alone with Musso. The story is told of how, when the two leaders got into a small lift in a hotel, there was no room for Home: he had to race up the stairs, meeting the lift at every level, and seeing Musso's bald pate, with a large boil on top, appearing at each floor. He met them, panting at the top.

He was close to Chamberlain, but suspected that he would make a fool of himself when he returned from Munich: he was horrified at the "peace with honour" statement.

But he still publicly defends his old chief's policies. He still argues that until it became clear that Hitler could *not* be appeased and was in fact bent on war, Chamberlain did right to try to reach agreement with him.

While still active as Chamberlain's aide, Home's health gave way, and he spent from 1939 to 1941 on his back with T.B. (His brother

William thinks the contorted bowling action was the origin of the trouble.) He read prodigiously, his main purpose being to educate himself in Soviet affairs. He developed the view that the Russians were ultimately the real threat, and he was concerned lest the war with Hitler should divert Britain's attention from this fundamental truth.

In 1944, at the time of the Yalta conference, when good-will towards our ally and trust in her post-war intentions was at its zenith, he made a speech in the House of Commons warning Churchill and Eden that the Russians could not be trusted. His analysis of Russian motives and his forecast of Russia's post-war behaviour—borne out by events—amounted to a major attack on Government policy. For this he became unpopular with some of his fellow back-benchers, who, he says, started regarding him as "a bit touched".

He was among those who lost their seats in the general election of the following year. He came back into the House of Commons in 1950 but the next year his father died when he was actually in the House, so that he was at once stopped from going into the Chamber. By this time his views about the Russians had become more fashionable. The fall of Czechoslovakia, the Berlin blockade and the outbreak of the Korean war had changed the atmosphere. But for the next four years he devoted himself largely to domestic affairs.

When the former Chief Whip, James Stuart, became Secretary of State for Scotland in 1951, he asked Churchill to let him have Home as his Minister of State. Churchill, who, Home said, had scarcely heard of him, agreed. Stuart—now Lord Stuart of Findhorn—who always moved at a steady pace, relied greatly on Home's energy, loyalty and readiness to serve. These qualities became known, and in 1955 Eden had Home transferred to the Commonwealth Relations Office. Home was still very little known in the party, and—it now seems astonishing—practically unknown to the public, outside Scotland.

When he went to the Commonwealth Relations Office, he had for the first time to deal with a world beyond Europe. Although he tried hard to understand Africans, Asians and Arabs he has never succeeded in making the imaginative jump needed to understand their slightly aggrieved approach to life. He can appreciate their rational attitudes, such as their desire for non-alignment, their antipathy to racial discrimination and their ambition to fight their poverty; but he has never disguised his dislike of their emotionalism and the methods that it produces.

After he had left the C.R.O., his feelings were made clear in a speech at Berwick-on-Tweed in which he warned that the United Nations should not become the vehicle by which the Afro-Asians practised "a double standard of morality". Some considered the speech candid, others tactless. The Afro-Asians thought it offensive.

His political instincts on the Afro-Asian world have always been close to those of the right-wing of the Tory Party. So long as he was at the C.R.O., Lord Salisbury and his followers were content. Salisbury's resignation, significantly, came soon after Home left the C.R.O. in 1960.

There is only one cause he made his own while Commonwealth Minister: support of Sir Roy Welensky's Central African Federation. His devotion caused a former Governor of Northern Rhodesia to dub him "Sir Roy's postboy". Welensky seldom appealed in vain to him for help against the Colonial Secretary of the day—first Iain Macleod and later Reginald Maudling—two of Lord Home's present doubters.

It was largely due to his interventions in the Cabinet that British policy lagged in Northern Rhodesia and Nyasaland. In the end, Lord Home lost faith in Welensky: but by then he was already at the Foreign Office, and the Central African Federation was visibly crumbling. Welensky praised him again last week as Sir Winston's true heir.

Both at the C.R.O. and later at the Foreign Office, Home has identified himself with his party's right-wing on three crucial questions concerning Britain's relations with the Afro-Asians. He has firmly resisted applying public pressure on Dr. Verwoerd's Government, and was against South Africa's exclusion from the Commonwealth. Although he does not endorse Portuguese policy in Angola, he has opposed all suggestions to apply pressure on the Salazar regime. On the Katanga issue, his policies took Britain into open conflict with the U.N. Assembly and led to a sharp division with the United States.

In the Middle East he has continued to act upon ideas which were being officially questioned before Eden became Premier, notably the idea that a British military presence is essential to ensure British access to Persian Gulf oil; and to insist on our need of military bases in the Mediterranean and in Aden and "reliable" air routes through Africa to be used in the event of Middle East troubles.

In 1956-57 Home acted as Deputy Leader of his party in the Lords, and then, until 1960, as Leader. This was a very important, perhaps the crucial, step in his career. As spokesman for the Government in the Lords he revealed his capacities. As Lord President of the Council he was able simultaneously to make his mark in the Cabinet.

Home became Foreign Secretary in July, 1960. The appointment was greeted with a storm of indignation in the Press (including *The Observer*) and in the House of Commons. But in the Lords the Labour peers were well aware of his abilities in debating and diplomacy.

As Foreign Secretary for the last three years, Home has shown no Gaullist-type jealousy of the Americans and has got on well with them, even when there have been conflicts between British and American interest. He has not adopted an extreme attitude towards

79

the Communists over reaching a Berlin settlement or an activist attitude over Cuba, and it is possible that his candour and tough-mindedness have been positive assets in achieving better Soviet-American relations.

On Macmillan's decision to apply for Britain's entry to the Common Market, Home was loyal rather than enthusiastic. By prior agreement, he scrupulously left the negotiations and public speaking to Heath and never demonstrated the proselytising zeal of, for instance, Sandys or Soames. But he firmly supported the idea that Britain should not be squeezed out of a prospective partnership between a united Europe and the United States. It was the same anxiety to keep Britain in the main stream of the partnership which led him to insist almost alone inside the Cabinet las tmonth [September] that Britain must participate in the official talks on the possibility of a mixed-crew nuclear force.

In public, he has always taken the Gaullist-type view on the independent British nuclear deterrent as an essential part of sovereign power, arguing recently that but for Britain's bomb we could not have played any part in the test-ban negotiations. In private, however, his dedication to the independent British deterrent may be less than absolute.

In his general political philosophy, Home describes himself as a "liberal radical", a true descendant of the Lambtons, who saw change as a fact of life, not merely to be recognised but to be welcomed.

He claims that he supports the principles which his ancestor, Lord Durham, enunciated for the Empire 130 years ago—"dependence giving way to independence, independence changing to inter-dependence", but this to be done in accordance with another principle of "orderly withdrawal".

Firm in his attitude that Communists will expand whenever opportunity presents itself, he believes that the change for the better in Russian temper and attitudes is due to the rise of the new, scientifically-minded non-doctrinaire classes, and that it makes permanent co-existence possible, indeed predictable.

He shows a similar open-mindedness in domestic affairs. On capital punishment, for instance; he supports it only because he thinks the balance of evidence does not yet justify its abolition. He accepts the concept of a mixed economy and has said that the State should, if necessary, take central powers to deal with unemployment, economic expansion and population drifts.

Wherever he can be interested, he can be argued with; and where he can be argued with, he can be converted. If converted he will not hesitate to change his policies. But, because his ideas become ingrained deep in his mind, converting Home can take a considerable amount of time.

At such a moment it is inevitable that the Left should condemn the choice of Home because of his ancient lineage. The *Daily Worker*, mincing no words, says it has "put feudalism at the helm".

A determined Herald is said lately to have traced the Home line back to Macbeth. When the great power of the Douglas family in the Scottish Borders was at last shattered by James II of Scotland, three families scrambled for the pickings: the Scotts, the Kerrs and the Homes. The head of the Scotts is now the Duke of Buccleuch; the Kerrs provide both Lord Lothian and the Duke of Roxburghe.

In the following three centuries the Homes established themselves as a conservative, courageous and slightly eccentric family. Home has often shown the assured authority—and sometimes the apparently carefree independence of behaviour—which some might attribute to his background. He speaks his mind, even on important occasions, with a marked indifference to the effect he is liable to produce.

At the collapse of Britain's Common Market hopes, when he appeared on television to explain what had happened, an incredulous interviewer asked him: "Are you *really* saying that General de Gaulle deliberately *deceived* us?" Home replied: "Well, yes, in a way I am." He went shooting with his relation, Lord Lambton, not obviously caring what anyone might think, just when Lambton was publicly attacking Macmillan.

Home's domestic background is contented. Lady Home, the daughter of Home's headmaster at Eton, Dr. Alington, has no aspirations for smart society, wears homely clothes, and likes books and crosswords. Her mother, a Lyttelton, voted Socialist, and Lady Home has inherited her mother's social conscience.

The Homes tend to spend shooting holidays at Castlemains, which is shabby and comfortable and has a peeling brown front door. Inside are family oil-paintings, cosy sitting-rooms, a baronial-type kitchen, and a big gong. There are 14 bedrooms, plus eight for the staff. Life in the Home family runs to long walks and parties of mixed ages, while Home himself wanders about arranging the flowers, working with his feet up on a sofa, and endlessly looking for his spectacles.

At Castlemains he and his wife entertain a good deal. This year they had the Japanese Ambassador, and Mr. Macmillan and Lady Dorothy for the second year running—the Homes give up their own brass bed to the Macmillans.

The Homes only recently began to use The Hirsel, the official seat of the earldom. Lady Home is renovating it, has introduced a lot of open plan, has knocked down 22 rooms and the chapel and has just installed a lift. But most of the time Lady Caroline, the Homes' eldest daughter, has the place to herself. She divides her time between being assistant factor for the estate and serving the Queen Mother as a part-time lady-in-waiting.

It is still the custom on the Border not to send daughters to school. Lord Home's three had governesses and finishing schools. His second daughter, Lady Meriel, is a gay blonde who studied art and works in Bumpus, the London bookshop. The other, Lady Diana, recently married a businessman. Lord Dunglass, the only son, a good shot, is 20, and has just been sent down from Oxford for failing his exams. (Home's father was sent down, too.)

The Douglas-Home family are gay and witty, always visiting or on the telephone. As fortunes swayed in London last week, the Home clan were busily ringing each other up and laying bets. Home is himself of a quieter nature, but he has the same abundant energy.

On Sundays at Douglas, the Homes attend the Scottish Episcopal chapel. Home is not quite so religious as his father was, but he is a genuine churchman.

Lord Home's second brother Major Henry Douglas-Home holds that Alec has always been the most serious-minded member of the family. "We all had a wild streak in us," he says, "but Alec didn't."

There are evident streaks of originality, if not of wildness, in the brothers. William, the playwright, had marked pacifist tendencies. Even so, he enlisted during the war and was serving with a flame-throwing regiment when it found itself before Le Havre.

William was reluctant to see the town attacked, because he believed there were many civilians inside it and that the German commander was likely to surrender, anyway. When it seemed improbable that this point of view was going to prevail, he took matters into his own hands. He tied a pair of white Army-issue drawers to the aerial of his jeep and set out to persuade the Germans to capitulate. But he was stopped on the way, in due course court-martialled and sent to Wormwood Scrubs.

An officer who was with William at the time is satisfied that his motives were entirely honourable, even if his actions were excessively independent. When Alec visited him in the Scrubs, as soon as he set eyes on William in those woeful surroundings he burst out laughing.

Brother Henry is an ornithologist, living in a ramshackle house nine miles from The Hirsel. He farms, has a small herd of donkeys and 80 birds, mostly tropical, which he keeps in an aviary outside the front door and in rows of cages in the sitting-room. He is an eminent Bird Man on radio and TV (also appearing on Border TV as part of the McEwen folk-singing act).

Henry started bird-watching as a boy at The Hirsel, which is a natural bird-sanctuary. He is a particular expert on swifts and has invented nesting-boxes to which the same birds return from South Africa year after year. Last year Prince Philip became interested in the boxes when he and the Queen stopped off for a drink at The Hirsel, and Prince Philip has now had similar boxes rigged up under the windows at Windsor.

Remembering the day war broke out, when Lord Home was Chamberlain's P.P.S., Henry says that Alec rang him up and said: "Let's drive out to the Downs and look for some Chalk Blues. It's no good sitting here and brooding."

Nowadays, at shooting weekends, Home sets the pace—up at six, rallying the beaters with an almost military zeal. His long trips abroad seem occasionally to have exhausted his aides a great deal more than him.

Up on the Border these last few days the local people have perhaps naturally been inclined to speak of their Earl in glowing terms. But the fact is the locals do not know him as well as they knew his father. His old constituency has turned to Labour, and some of the voters in Douglas are disinclined, even now, to speak of him too highly. They say he is "hard on poachers".

But in the true Home country, at least, people see it as a grave thing that Lord Home might be parted from his ancient Scottish title. "It's no matter for Lord Hailsham," they say, "he's only second generation. But Lord Home is really *it*."

And people everywhere in Britain, most of whom owe the Homes no vestige of feudal loyalty, will no doubt admire a man who is willing to abandon so ancient a title in order to serve his country.

The Queen and the Tories

by Nora Beloff

Conflicting versions of how the lot fell upon Home were still being "revealed" some months after he had been chosen. At the end of January this year our Political Correspondent dealt with one of the more significant aspects of the event.

The last major political prerogative retained by the Crown—and now under debate—is a minimal last-resort influence on the choice of a Conservative Prime Minister. As long as there is no cut-and-dried electoral procedure by which the Conservatives choose their leader, the Queen may, if there is no agreed successor, find herself involved in the complex processes of selection.

The Queen's role has already been eliminated when Labour is in power, as the leader of that Party is chosen by secret ballot of Labour M.P.s, leaving the Queen with no alternative but to ratify their choice. But on the Conservative side, where the processes of consultation have not been institutionalised, the Queen may find herself having to make her own decisions on whom to consult.

Hard political facts narrow her choice and it is easy to over-emphasise how far she could deviate from certain obvious moves. None the less, there is here a relic of royal authority and the present Prime Minister has firmly set his face against any transformation of the system which would produce an automatic selection and relieve the Queen of her status of ultimate arbiter.

Earlier this month, Mr. Humphry Berkeley, Conservative M.P. for Lancaster, wrote to the Prime Minister suggesting that after their recent experience the Party should now examine new methods for democratising the processes by which they select their leader. The Prime Minister replied politely that nothing could be done just now but that he was not averse after the election to setting up a small private committee to consider the selection procedures.

Mr. Berkeley took this as a positive answer. But Government sources indicate that there is a prevalent feeling within the hierarchy, that an automatic poll would be a highly inflexible method for producing the best Prime Minister from the vast, straggling and essentially pragmatic body of men and women forming the Conservative Party. This feeling is shared by the Prime Minister and most of the recent contenders for leadership.

The question of the Royal prerogative itself, though on everybody's mind, is hardly likely to be publicly debated. On the Conservative side there is unanimity at least on the view that the Queen's role in the recent crisis was irreproachable. The Labour leaders are hoping that their redder back-benchers will not make remarks which might be considered offensive to the Royal Family and consequently cost the Party votes.

But reluctance to involve the Queen is not only a matter of tactics. As the evidence about the sequence of events in the last few hours before the new Prime Minister "emerged" accumulates it becomes increasingly difficult to substantiate the romantic thesis developed by Mr. Paul Johnson in the current issue of the *New Statesman* that the Queen herself intervened to favour a Scottish lord against an English commoner.

It is undoubtedly true that the Queen had been following with apprehensive attention the problems of the Conservative succession since they first arose early last year, knowing that when the crunch came she would inevitably be involved. It is also true that she is known in Ministerial circles to have a considerable grasp of constitutional law and, contrary to some reports, takes advice but not instruction from her three secretaries.

In the recent crisis she made her first official incursion at 9.15 on Friday morning, October 18, when Mr. (now Sir) Timothy Bligh, the Prime Minister's Principal Private Secretary, arrived at the Palace, bringing Mr. Macmillan's resignation. In Johnson's view she should have known by this time that the principal contenders in the Cabinet had rallied around Mr. Butler and should therefore not have accepted without demur Mr. Macmillan's subsequent recommendation of Sir Alec Douglas-Home as the man likeliest to command support.

But could the Queen really have acted otherwise? It would have been inconceivable for her to ignore the advice of the man who had been serving her as Prime Minister for seven years and who, though ill, was certainly not mentally incapacitated.

Macmillan himself since the previous Monday had set in train the "sounding" of the four elements of the Party: the Cabinet, the two Houses of Parliament and the constituency associations. Once she made the decision to seek his advice he left no room for further consultation. Short of telling him he was a liar or frivolously disregarding what he had said, she had to assume the Party was in broad (Macmillan himself never said unanimous) agreement that Home was the Party's first choice. The Queen could hardly conduct a rival poll of her own.

It seems reasonable to ask whether, in any case, the Palace was fully aware on Friday morning that there was a consensus among the chief contenders in favour of Butler. The newspapers knew and reported the all-night meeting at Mr. Enoch Powell's house attended by Messrs Macleod, Maudling, Errol and Lord Aldington. Those who attended subsequently revealed they had been in communication with Lord Hailsham by phone and that by midnight they were clear there could be an agreement to support Butler. But although the Press knew of the meeting it was some time before they discovered the nature of the agreement.

Furthermore, Mr. Martin Redmayne, the Chief Whip, who was invited to the meeting, is reliably reported to have taken away the impression that there was a movement on to stop Home rather than to start Butler. He certainly never transmitted any message either to the Prime Minister or to the Palace that Mr. Butler was emerging as an alternative choice as he did not himself think he was.

The Queen's secretary, Sir Michael Adeane, is reported by Randolph Churchill and others to have received more than one call from what Churchill calls the *"caballeros"* meeting *chez* Powell, but these might have produced an impression of turmoil and anxiety over Home rather than an indication of a categorical agreement on a different candidate.

In fact, a formal commitment of the principal contenders organised by Macleod, by which Hailsham and Maudling agreed that Butler was their first choice and indicated they would not join a Home Government unless he did, took place in Mr. Butler's offices at the Treasury only after breakfast on Friday morning. By this time the Queen was already receiving Macmillan's advice on the Home appointment.

It has also been said that the Queen acted with inexplicable speed: here again, once Macmillan handed over his omnibus report covering all sections of Party opinion, it is difficult to see what reasons could be advanced for further delay. It was the Queen's job to give Britain a Prime Minister able to command a parliamentary majority as quickly as possible. Once she had received Macmillan's resignation and after a brief private appointment with her own doctor, she lost no time in going to seek her ex-Prime Minister's advice. Her interview in the hospital lasted less than half an hour (the recommendations were in writing and there was not much left to say). Knowing that she had no option but to send for Home, the Queen could hardly have seen much sense in postponing the encounter.

Originally, expecting a later and longer meeting with Macmillan, the officials had expected Home would be received after lunch. As the Queen was back in the Palace by midday, as there was nobody else she could sensibly turn to, and as the whole country was waiting for the vacuum to be filled, it would have been, as one observer put it, "a mere charade" to delay action.

Former precedents have been cited, and it is true that the Queen herself had allowed a day to elapse on the two previous occasions between the resignation and the choice of a successor. But although the details of whom she met during these times are still State secrets, it can safely be assumed that she was engaged in further consultations.

Such consultations were this time ruled out by the comprehensive nature of Macmillan's memorandum.

The most important fallacy in the Johnson argument is the suggestion that the Queen joined Macmillan in imposing Home on the country. In fact, she might very well have pressed Home to accept an immediate appointment and by the ritual kissing of hands declared him Prime Minister. Mr. Macmillan, who, in the account he gave to Randolph Churchill, said that he predicted to Home there would be a "ghastly confusion" if there was any delay, would probably have preferred it if she had.

But in fact she took into account the existence of the "caballeros" and went right back to a precedent from the reign of her great-great-grandmother, Queen Victoria, calling on the candidate first to see if he could form a Cabinet before she declared he was officially appointed.

It is true that by calling on Home she gave him a flying start over his rivals but it is certainly not true, as Paul Johnson seems to think, that, from then on, the choice was automatic. On the contrary, Mr. Butler held out for 24 hours before deciding he would serve under Home and, had he refused, Maudling has now revealed that he would certainly have done likewise. And, without the former Deputy Prime Minister and Chancellor of the Exchequer, Home would have had to advise the Queen to send for Mr. Butler. At that point, with Mr. Wilson lurking in the background, the Conservatives would never have risked a second fiasco and the remaining last-ditch opposition to Mr. Butler's appointment would certainly have withered away.

It is perfectly possible to argue, as the "caballeros" still do, that if Macmillan had not precipitated the decision, the Party would have had time to re-examine the electoral risk at having an apparently anachronistic peer as their leader. This might have led them to rally either to Mr. Butler or to another of the candidates from the House of Commons.

It is possible—and must necessarily remain hypothetical—that had the Queen been fully informed of a rally of senior Cabinet members behind Butler, she might have preferred to stop and take further advice before calling on Home. Though even here it is difficult to see to whom she could turn for advice: all the prominent members of the Conservative establishment, except the contenders themselves, would probably have supported Home.

In any case, given the sequence of events, there is no case whatever for suggesting that the Queen's personal preferences were a factor in the final choice. But was it fair, some young Conservatives are now asking, to place such heavy responsibility on the Queen?

The answer seems to be that there is no indication that the Queen herself, or her advisers, feel she is carrying an unfair or unwise load of responsibility.

Life on the Island

Social Aspect

The Roots of Beatlemania

by Cyril and Peter Dunn

From quiet—or at least obscure—beginnings, a pop music group from Liverpool became the adored idols of our young ones and then a minor world phenomenon. Their names: George Harrison, Paul McCartney, Ringo Starr and John Lennon.

It doesn't do to knock the Beatles. Our own jazz critic, Benny Green, did so, almost by accident, on Granada TV the other night. Without any deep feeling one way or the other, Green said he thought there wasn't much musical value in what the Beatles do. Now he gets letters with menacing beetles drawn on the envelope and enclosures which say, for instance:

"Listen Mate, I jus won to say dat your gob on telly 2 night was last. The Beatles, mate, make a better and original sound than any other group. If you think you can make an original sound from your trumpitt and sacks then record it and see if people will buy it and mob you and Q up for you for days. If there were more groups as good as the Beatles this land we call Eng would be gear. So go buy yourself a surgical boot and go criticise yourself sum jazz."

Actually, dissenting voices are few and nervous. People may be found along London's Tin Pan Alley who say "Don't quote me, but . . ."

What they go on to say is never very harsh, They simply deny that the Beatles are creating an entirely new sound. "Speaking off the record and as a musician," one of them said, "so far as I'm concerned the Mersey Sound is no different from what the Shadows were doing two or three years ago. It's LOUDER—a terrific beat—but it's still rock 'n' roll music."

88

You won't find the Beatles themselves eager to deny this. There's an accumulating archive of Beatles *obiter dicta* at the Beatles Press Office and Fans Club H.Q., over a bookshop near Soho featuring in its window *The Psychology of Sexual Emotion*. Here one of the group is shown as saying: "This Liverpool Sound . . . well, we tend to think it's a lot of rubbish, really."

But Mr. George Martin thinks differently. He is chief record producer at E.M.I., now making the booming Beatle discs. Elegant and relaxed, with Prince Philip good looks, Mr. Martin is everything not usually associated with pop records.

"I didn't make the Beatles," he says. "They would have been great anyway." And he is quite sure they have made a new sound, that the sound-before-the-Beatles was an amalgam of Cliff Richard and the Shadows, and that the Beatles sound will be the pattern until the next pop-mutation happens.

But people are evidently drawn to the Beatles by factors other than the extraordinary noise they make. The main body of truly obsessed fans—the compulsive screamers—seem to be extremely young, taking in the 10—12 age-group as well as the teenagers. But even the grown-ups who reacted with sharp distaste to the Elvis Presley cult a few years back now speak about the Beatles with real affection.

Even the Queen Mother seems to have been impressed. She talked to the Beatles after the Royal Command Performance the other night. She asked them where they would be appearing next, and they said Slough. "Ah," said the Queen Mother, with obvious approval, "that's quite near us."

Musicians may find nothing unique in the Mersey Sound, but the Beatles are broadcasting the true and unique voice of Liverpool's working class and this is what most people admire. The Beatles were all born during the blitz on Merseyside. They have grown up in a tough, violent city and have developed an immense self-confidence.

The *Daily Worker* has cashed in on their Mersey Sound, calling it the voice of 80,000 crumbling houses and 30,000 people on the dole. The Beatle songs are certainly defiant—like numbers from a pop-opera about a council flats rent-strike.

The working-class accent is exaggerated, not refined away but made to sound as crude as it can be. But the tone is triumphant, not resentful. For the Beatles the battle seems over and won and now they're friends with everybody. Their fans are classless; a lot of the mail reaching Monmouth Street comes from public schools.

Mr. Tony Barrow, the Beatles' Press officer and record critic for the *Liverpool Echo*, thinks they're a success with the adult world in particular because they epitomise Northern Man—his naturalness, directness, the "truthfulness" behind those hard and nobby faces.

We found a fourteen-year-old high school girl taking the same line. "Well," she said, "you usually think of film stars, pop singers, etc.,

89

as living in glamorous places, Hollywood and so on. But the Beatles aren't like that. It's *Liverpool* . . . where *Z-Cars* comes from."

Others, mainly in the mid-20s age-group, are for the Beatles because they represent "a break with America" that started with a revolt against the Elvis cult and has run through Tommy Steele, Lonnie Donegan, Cliff Richard—a local, national pop, with strong working-class, do-it-yourself undertones. The fans now have people they can identify with directly, instead of "a remote American hero on a record".

The same group also find the Beatles typical of "a trend towards decency"—crude but direct about sex instead of sly and sentimental; high professionals with nothing bogus about their act. The Ancient British hair-dos and the group's clothes may strike the older generations as bizarre, but the young ones observe only that they are impeccably neat.

The Beatles are intelligent, too. "They've got quite a few O-levels between them," is how Mr. Martin puts it. They talk in a Goonish witty way and it all comes straight from under their own mops. They have no gag-writers yet. And there's also something beat and Kerouac-like in what they say.

Someone asked them to say what it was about Liverpool that excited people so much. "It's exciting trying to keep alive," one of them said.

There may be no special Mersey Sound, but the Beatles were born out of a staggering local upsurge of pop music groups. It's been throbbing under the sombre Liverpool surface for more than three years now, without attracting much outside attention until the Beatles hit the top.

We have been investigating Merseyside this week. It is a wild place. Our car was broken into outside a club called The Sink and a portable radio stolen. We also discovered a kind of frenzy to get on in the Mersey Beat scene.

One group called The Undertakers wear top-hats and black crêpe and have loudspeakers shaped like coffins. They once turned up at the Locarno carrying a dead cat and have been photographed in graveyards. Another amplified group call themselves the Ghost Squad. They wear white hoods and skull masks and look like white citizens on a night out in the Deep South.

Also on offer are The Four Just Men, The Riot Squad, Rory Storm and the Hurricanes, Jeannie and the Big Guys. Or you can have The Beathovens.

In the Cavern Club—the cellar-tunnel under a warehouse where the Beatles began—the huge invigorating Sound booms against the brick walls. Five hundred young people stand in the thick gloom and do "The Whack"—a kind of continuous twitch.

Only the bouncers at the door seem unaffected by it. Some of these have a ferocious reputation. A club member said that one of them once jumped down seven steps into the club and hit a drunk so hard that he fell on the cash table and broke its legs.

It's impossible to count the groups on Merseyside today. Failure and bursts of temperament make them chop and change continually, disbanding old groups, forming new ones. They spend between £1,000 and £2,000 "on the knocker" (hire purchase) for their guitars, drum kits and amplifiers.

A lot of them have the mop-headed Beatle look, but it takes more than this to get on if the Sound is wrong. Like the Beatles Ltd., the more successful groups are turning themselves into limited companies to help with their tax problems and make provision for the future, which seems close.

In the Mind-Benders Ltd., the four players are all directors and their average age is 17. They wear pink shirts, high-heel boots, tight blue leather and horse-brasses.

Most of the Beat clubs are in halls and old cinemas beyond the city centre. They're all doing excellent business. Some of the smaller clubs in the middle of Liverpool don't have groups, but just play records under purple lights and sell coffee. One of these is The Sink, a cellar-room under a snack bar called the Rumblin Tum. Members are issued with a black sink-plug on a chain instead of cards.

There are plenty of experts in Liverpool willing to explain the Sound. A young man in a black leather jacket said the city is a "crude" place and the Sound is crude, with an emphatic beat. One of the successful local promoters said: "There's realism in this city. It's a city of mixtures, but it's also grubby and very crude. Fundamentally, the music is like that. With the trad Sound the musician's saying, 'I'm doing you a favour. Sit still and listen.' It's not like that with the Beat. It tells everyone to join in—makes them join in."

But Liverpool's also a seaport, edged up against a wide estuary, a kind of dead end with a tremendous sense of community. And it's also in touch with America. New "sounds" reach Liverpool before anywhere else in the island because young seamen bring home with them American pop records not yet released in Britain.

Liverpool seems to breed self-assured, vital young people who are "jumping" in early boyhood and nowadays learning the guitar—by ear, from pop records—as soon as they are big enough to hold one. They have a ganging-up tradition—street gangs at one extreme, boys' clubs at the other.

The gangs, clubs and groups rate loyalty very high. And the unforgivable sin is big-headedness. The Beatles are still enormously popular in their home town because they have avoided this breach of ethics. In fact, the Beatles are strong on ethics altogether; at early record-making sessions they regarded over-dubbing with suspicion until Mr. Martin convinced them it was no more unethical than an electric guitar. If anyone shows off in a Liverpool group-performance, he's liable to have someone pull out the plug of his electric guitar in mid-phrase.

The Sound has its own newspaper—*The Mersey Beat*. It costs sixpence and sells 30,000 copies a fortnight. Bill Harry, the editor, works in an office above a wine shop. He says the current Sound movement developed from the "skiffle phase", which for some reason stayed on in Liverpool when it died in the rest of the country. The first group to play in the present style was Rory Storm and the Hurricanes, who started up in Liverpool seven years ago and are now working in Germany.

The Beatles' promoter is Mr. Brian Epstein, now on a business trip to New York, where our correspondent talked to him. He is a handsome, poised, urbane young man, rather amused by the "highbrow" interest now being taken in the group he helped to make famous.

He is a director of a family firm owning three record shops in Liverpool. His interest in the Beatles dawned when youngsters started crowding into one of these shops and demanding with a special intensity records of a pop group he didn't know about.

Mr. Epstein says he used no special forms of promotion to put over the Beatles. They just caught on like wildfire—a case of spontaneous combustion in the pop cult. He says his problem is to keep up with them. He thinks the fact that they write their own songs and music is an essential part of their authentic quality.

Our correspondent does not get from Mr. Epstein the impression of a brilliant manipulator, but of a shrewd young man who has caught the lightning. And the overwhelming emotional reaction of the fans to the Beatles is, Mr. Epstein says, as much a mystery to him as to anyone else.

Psychologists, however, seem less inclined to reckon this phenomenon mysterious. Beatlemania, they say, has a long pedigree. Apart from compulsive dancing to drum-beats among Africans, they mention the young girls known to have swooned when "the blades" swaggered through medieval Florence and squealed in eighteenth-century England as the redcoats marched by.

Some of these experts find the subconscious significance of guitars intriguing. They fancy that their female symbolism is evident and point out that pre-Hellenic stone statuettes of women might well be mistaken for toy guitars.

The pop cult is generally considered a rich field for psychoanalysis, but in fact it has been little investigated. As one psychoanalyst said sadly: "There are no funds for studying adolescents unless they are delinquent."

At all events, the fact that the Beatles and hordes of other groups like them have been rousing the young to frenzies in Liverpool and other provincial cities for years without attracting widespread adult attention suggests that this can be a fairly private world. Within it the teenagers create their own idols—and then lose them when the promoters raise these pop singers to national eminence.

Experts in the business believe this helps to explain the riots in the streets when the elevated pop-singers make their national appearances. The youngsters feel shut out and are reaching out to hold the receding idol. As these authorities see things, it also explains why new idols keep appearing.

"It's the younger kids who get something new going," said a Tin Pan Alley man. "They want someone new to excite them—and they want him to be their own."

What seems to have emerged is an age-group solidarity of a new intensity. The old play-group of the city streets used to be deliberately exclusive; shutting someone out—usually someone diffident and unglamorous—was part of the fun. But when the Beatles start hammering the Mersey Beat into the floorboards and swaying behind those guitars, anyone can join in and scream with her fellows.

We got this final piece of wisdom from a teenager who felt old enough to throw a tender light on the Beatle fans whom she saw as being younger than herself. Asked why she thought these young ones so readily joined the Beatle frenzy, she said: "Because they're lonely, of course."

Two Strange Happenings

by John Gale

(a) Black magic in Bedfordshire?

Dead pigeons litter mournful cabbage fields below the ruined tenth-century church of St. Mary's, Clophill, Beds., near the A6 road, where a Black Mass is supposed to have been held recently. Not far off a black cat lies flattened by a car. It is easy to see signs.

The bones and skull (found impaled on a metal stake) thought by police to have been used in the Black Mass are now locked in a cupboard in the vestry of the new church: they are those of Jenny Humberstone, wife of Lawrence Humberstone (a surgeon), "who departed this life January 30, 1770, aged 22 years."

"I've made up my mind just to quietly rebury them," said the Rector of Clophill, the Rev. Lewis Barker. "I shan't wait now. I don't think I ought to keep them locked up in the vestry.

"I don't know anything about Black Magic; all I do know I've learnt this week. It could be. I don't really feel convinced.

"It was the police who gave me the idea of this Black Magic. It'll take a team of men to put the tombstones back."

Up on the hill by the lonely ruined church, far away from any house, an elderly man was attacking a wild rose hedge with a bill-hook. His hands were bleeding. "It seems queer to me," he said. "I can't make nothing of it. Dammit: I should think those gravestones weigh over five hundredweight. I shouldn't think anyone would do that for a hobby. Though there are queer people about, aren't there?"

Just over a mile away, below slanting rays of light coming from a black cloud, was something like the skeletal framework of a huge gasometer: in the centre was a tangle of what looked like radar. Apparently you can sometimes hear "The Stars and Stripes" coming up out of this place on the wind at night.

"I don't think the general public know what it is," said the hedger. "And they say that the contractors putting it up don't know. They've got guards up there, police dogs, and all manner. It must be something secret."

Round the outside were shapes like silver-topped rockets. It might have been a giant's magic circle.

In The Rising Sun down in Clophill, the landlord, Mr. William Dickins, was puzzling things out. He said there had been a bit of excitement in the village the night before when a lot of young men calling themselves students had gone up to the ruined church in cars. People had wondered.

An elderly woman with wide-apart eyes and a dark young man with glasses and box camera entered the pub. "I'm a theological student," said the young man. "My friend, Mrs. Thorne, is very psychic. We've had tremendous do's at the college about things like this.

"Say you found your crucifixes upside down, you'd know there was something there. Or if the red vestments had gone. If you get that, you generally fear they've got them for a Black Mass. A Black Mass is generally by an unfrocked priest. They've got no other outlet."

"I can't think of anyone locally who's been unfrocked," said Mr. Dickins. "I came armed with crucifix, holy water, rosary, and everything else," said the theological student.

Mrs. Thorne described supernatural experiences she had had in Malta. "Just a minute," said Mr. Dickins. "One of those students we had here last night said he was from Malta." He shook his head. "I hope we get to the bottom of this."

At Ampthill police station they would give no official comment, but mentioned the Burials Act of 1857 (section 25) and the Malicious Damage Act (section 39): "Disorderly conduct in a burial yard," said a police officer.

In London, Mr. Francis Clive-Ross, editor of Tomorrow, a journal

94

of parapsychology, and an authority on goings-on, said: "I don't think it was a Black Mass or anything resembling it.

"If there are people seriously interested in this sort of thing they don't court publicity. And they don't leave evidence around for the police or anyone else. There's only one genuine account of a Black Mass in existence and that took place in the reign of Louis XIV."

Mr. Clive-Ross mentioned a man who kept coming in and telling him about terrific sales of black candles and a baby having been sacrificed in the south-east. "Tripe," said Mr. Clive-Ross.

"Someone claimed to be a witch. When I first met him he was no witch. He was longing to get in touch with someone who was." He didn't succeed, it seems, but met some enthusiasts. "They would strip naked and dance around. There was a spot of flagellation to help things on."

He produced a book with a picture of two men and two women in the buff drinking something at a magical session. What were they drinking? "Lord knows," said Mr. Clive-Ross. "Tea, I should think."

(b)   A cheetah on Shooter's Hill?

The cheetah of Shooter's Hill, London, S.E.18, was still puzzling people yesterday.*

Scotland Yard said three people in a car reported seeing it early yesterday morning. "It was 200 or 300 yards from Shooter's Hill police station. When they got out of the car it shot off. We're none the wiser. One of the chaps went up to it and reckoned he recognised it as a cheetah. But it bounded off."

In Shooter's Hill police station, Woolwich, a sergeant said these statements had to be checked. He could not give the names and addresses of the people who thought they saw the cheetah. "I wouldn't like to commit myself," he added.

Almost at the exact spot where the people thought they saw the cheetah was a middle-aged policeman with a labrador. He was just passing the time of day. "All the reports we've had are pretty authentic," he said.

In a large brick pub down the road they were preparing for a wedding. Nobody there had seen the cheetah, though the woman behind the bar thought it could have been a young one that had jumped from a car coming from Scotland or France.

"Now it's grown up," she said. "You never know, do you? It brings a bit of colour into people's dull lives."

* The Shooter's Hill mystery is officially unsolved, but seven months after this affair another animal was sighted near Cromer in Norfolk. Some people thought it was a cheetah.

She added that the *Daily Sketch* had had a very good story about plaster casts of pawmarks being sent to the London Zoo, which had confirmed that the animal was a kind of leopard. The *Sketch* quoted a Shooter's Hill police spokesman as saying: "This now rules out the theory of it being a large dog . . . it looks as though we are hunting a leopard."

Just at that moment a waitress with spectacles said: "It's just come over the news—you know, the news you get on transistor radios—that it's turned out to be a dog."

Back in the police station the sergeant didn't know anything about the story of the plaster cast: "It didn't originate here to my knowledge." As to the radio report about the animal being a dog, "that's rubbish too."

In a paper-shop a woman said, "The wireless says it's on the move again, doesn't it?" There seemed nothing for it but to go into the woods, which covered 750 acres.

There were some birds, a few squirrels, and some fungus that looked as though it had been coughed up by an animal. A Welshman in a back garden said he had spoken to a police control car: "They reckoned that the cheetah jumped over the front of their car."

Deeper in the wood a girl and three small boys with a black dog that didn't belong to them said they'd heard about the cheetah.

"Bertram Mills' Circus was passing Woolwich Common, and it must have fell off. Fell off a whatsisname. We can show you some big footprints at a drinking place." We went on.

Two park-keepers in brown hats said they had both been on leave. "You get these bits and pieces. You don't know what to think. It could be a dog fox. There's six or seven feet of undergrowth in Oxleas Woods. A chap done himself in and lay there three months."

We went on. Two more boys joined us: "Quite a lot have seen it or heard it," they said. What sort of noise? "A growling noise. A lady saw it. There was a dead fox, and the police tried to keep us back. We kept imagining we saw the cheetah. We were nervous."

At last, after struggling through deep bracken, the children showed us the drinking place, which might have been an old bomb crater. There were footprints, possibly those of a large dog.

"One, two, three, four pad marks, and two in the middle," said a small boy. "I think that's a cheetah. It can run seventy miles an hour. Do you think they'll catch it?"

Landscape with Horses

by Patrick O'Donovan

The racing at Goodwood, by immutable tradition, marks the end of the London season. After it is over, society puts away its grey top-hats and quits the capital. Some will prolong it a little at Cowes and the Irish horse show. But in theory they retire exhausted to the source of their income, which is land.

So Goodwood is geared to a sense of relaxation. It is essentially a country meeting on the estate of a duke. The men dress informally. Suede shoes and lightweight suits appear. The women do not dress to stun, as at Ascot. There are garden flowers in buttonholes, and the Queen slips in by a side door.

Of course all this applies to a minute part of the Goodwood crowd only. The rest is England, stripped to the essentials of decency by the sun, continually conscious of how much money is left, determined to enjoy and if possible to profit. And yet the curious society tradition somehow prevails. It is above all a holiday meeting, closer in feeling to the seaside than the stable. And it takes place on what is accepted to be the most beautiful racecourse in the world.

It occurs in a huge classical landscape of rounded hills and opulently curved woods. The course, a ribbon of purer green, runs along hilltops. The grandstands face the landscape like opera boxes. No building defiles the enormous view, and the cattle pose themselves pleasantly in the shade of trees.

Well before lunch-time the roads to Goodwood become snakes of cars edging their way towards the course. There are hundreds of buses, many of which have stopped once or twice on the way. There are determined men in sports shirts striding through the woods lost in their plans. There are lordly cars filled with the cheerful rich. There are overheated families loaded down for a day in the country. There are acres of parks for cars and buses which are packed like chocolates in a box. And in the end, the crowd, some 50,000 every day, is penned into the railed enclosures; it surveys the empty landscape; it looks as concentrated and pretty as a Victorian posy.

Racing is a curiously formal pleasure, and of course the more you know of it, the more pleasure there is in it. It has evolved its own elaborate pattern for a ritual of delight, and its complication is part of its attraction.

At Goodwood the architecture is mostly that of a nineteenth-century country railway station, though there is a splendid ducal box that looks like a remnant from a durbar. There is the members' stand, from which the profane are excluded by fierce and devoted exguardsmen. There is the grandstand, open to any with thirty-five shillings for a badge, and in descending order the Silver Ring and a high bald hill known as Trundle.

There is a row of beach huts, as hard to acquire as Rembrandts, each bearing the name of its hirer, where small parties lunch on gold-painted chairs off cold salmon and fruit salad and champagne. There are bars in every possible corner, places to lunch, and all nicely graduated to fit the varieties of the English purse and social hierarchy. If you go detached and are open to surprise, it is all very odd indeed. It is open only on these four days in the year.

Up on the Trundle Hill, it costs only five shillings to see the whole course and a great slice of Sussex looking like a travel poster. Here the atmosphere is almost self-consciously proletarian. The grass is trampled grey and littered thickly with cartons and torn betting-slips.

Young men have their shirts off: older men show braces. There are knotted handkerchiefs and babies in carry-cots. Determined men crouch on the grass with pencil, race-card and the folded page of some trusted newspaper. Beer tents survey the scene like temples on an acropolis. Hundreds just sleep in the sun and the noise. Food is dispensed like rations for the troops. And there is a sort of basic seriousness in the pleasure here that marks it off as a race crowd. It is much more than a beery day in the sun.

For those in the grandstand and upwards, a more elaborate ritual is ordained. The visit to the bookmaker or the Tote. The crowding into place for the race, the drift back to the paddock to see the winner led in and the new lot of horses saddled and then back to the book-makers da capo. It is a restless and busy form of pleasure.

Some people indulge in it because of a passionate enthusiasm for horses that can become almost a way of life. Some come for the pleasures of betting, which are far more than a lust for something for nothing. Some come because it is the done thing, some for a day in the country. Some come for all these reasons, and most come because all the various delights of a well-run course and a great occasion come together to make a satisfying and indefinable whole.

From two o'clock to five o'clock the central ritual is repeated. Each half-hour a troop of horses comes thundering into view. There is a glimpse of small, bent bodies in brilliant silk, a sense of supreme and marvellous effort, a second or two of beauty that surprises each time it happens and, for those who have involved themselves with money or personal loyalty, a climax of excitement that cannot be communi-cated. It is the supreme ritual pleasure and, like all rituals, a crashing bore to non-believers.

What a Year for Profit!

by Robert Heller

On Christmas Eve our Business Editor took a look at the year's champion shares.

Nothing makes for a happier Christmas than a charming tax-free capital gain. This has been a vintage year for these useful presents, much better than last. About the best you could have managed by a judicious purchase of shares on January 1, 1962, was a 174 per cent profit.

The champion share of 1963 has appreciated over nine times. Last year's combined profit on £1,000 invested equally between the Top Ten shares—an improbable stroke of genius—would have been £1,367. But the ten money-spinners of 1963 listed below work out at a total Christmas box of £3,229.

Two companies led the market this year and last—Bernard Wardle and Burton Son and Sanders, a good old Ipswich food group that gets forty per cent of its trade by feeding East Anglians. It is unique in another respect: the chairman and managing director is an M.P., Mr. Keith Stainton, the Tory saviour of Sudbury and Woodbridge.

Stainton arrived at Ipswich in 1956, when the company was in "a deplorable state". It's a case of the preacher practising: Stainton is a converted management consultant. *Profit on £100 invested on January 1: £165.*

You might well have discovered Burton's by following classic rules of investment. The same is true of Sidney Flavel of Leamington Spa. Its gas appliances are riding the boom. In 1960-61 the company lost £105,000. Within two years profits had soared to £256,000. Whether having *three* joint managing directors has anything to do with this devastating speed of turn-round, I wouldn't know. *Profit on £100 invested on January 1: £317.*

Bernard Wardle is another company bounding along on a boom, this time in cars. It makes upholstery fabrics. Wardle's went into plastics immediately after the war—a priceless chairman's inspiration, executed by the present managing director, confident Lancastrian Mr. Kenneth Berry. Berry is 54, says he feels 24. He also makes textiles where "there are some marvellous opportunities". *Profit on £100 invested on January 1: £226.*

Another quasi-textile favourite is Klinger Manufacturing, which makes machinery at Edmonton and had its spell of "rough water", says chairman Mr. William Castell, seven years ago. Castell is a tough war-time Lt.-Cdr. who worked himself and Klinger up from the bottom. Castell turned the company from making stockings to making money; he believes his technical director is "near to genius". The directors and staff exercised options to buy shares this year, and who can blame them? *Profit on £100 invested on January 1: £331.*

Investors in one or two other textile companies very happily multiplied their money. When I.C.I. injected £13 million into Viyella International (which promptly paid £10 million for British Van Heusen), the chain reaction made Viyella shares still more fashionable. Its chairman is 42-year-old dark and ambitious Mr. Joe Hyman.

For a man with no college education, Hyman has a remarkable reputation as an intellectual's businessman, or businessman's intellectual. Two years ago Viyella bought up Hyman's own textile business and installed the take-over victim as boss. Watch out for reverse take-overs of this type: they can work wonders. *Profit on £100 invested on January 1: £147.*

Another 1963 reverse take-over example is Easterns, the long-ailing furniture store group. It bought the "furniture supermarket" business controlled by the canny Mr. John James and the breezy Mr. Norman Williams. Williams knows how to sell furniture, while James is the free-lance Bristol financier with the near-Midas touch.

All of James's other multi-millionaire interests are privately owned; Eastern's is the only way in which investors can back a James horse. But he and Williams own about two-thirds of the shares, which must be a comforting thought. *Profit on £100 invested on January 1: £200.*

Ellsworth Estates is a special situation. Once a rubber company, it was put into property. In September two new men acquired control and joined the board. People who spotted this took a speculative flutter; the company is eventually to be merged with McManus and Co., a building company, and the speculators have fluttered to fine effect. *Profit on £100 invested on January 1: £200.*

Brayhead is even more special. In June Surtees Investments, itself only fifteen months old, bought the company and started pumping assets into it. Mr. Anthony James Richards, the chairman, is a very large (seventeen stone) and very able chartered accountant of 36.

Under the Surtees hat, Richards has been buying up garages wholesale. On Friday he signed contracts for the takeover of Boon and Porter of Hammersmith. The garages are also destined for Brayhead, which, like all such situations, would not have been turned up by anything more sophisticated than a pin. *Pin-money on £100 invested on January 1: £398.*

The B.M. Group is a similar case in point. Currently a stockbroker's pet, B.M. Group took off not after but just before Mr. Leon Selzer and friends joined the Board. Selzer, who used to be head statistician to Britain's farmers, doesn't know how the rumours escaped his security precautions. He says he can now sympathise with Mr. Macmillan.

The speculators hope that Selzer's other interests will be merged into B.M. Group's engineering business. Selzer first made his money by importing Alfa sewing-machines from Spain (hence his nickname, "Alfa" Selzer). He is also the man behind Imperial Washing Machines, Italian imports that compete with Mr. John Bloom on the door-to-door front. *Profit on £100 invested on January 1 : £492.*

The mention of John Bloom brings me to his English and Overseas Investments, just pipped by a small textile company, H. W. Phillips, for the share championship. Although the company has profits and is getting Bloom's Rolls Razor shares, its big fascination is the unknown. If, as expected, Sir Isaac Wolfson takes a stake, the future may fascinate still more. It may still be unknown. However, Bloom gets the palm as the man who made most Press revelations in 1963. *Profit on £100 invested on January 1: £753.*

Finally, on last year's evidence, it would not pay well to invest now in the leaders of 1963. If on January 1 you had invested £100 in the Top Ten of the previous year, your Christmas profit would be a paltry £196. It's no use having a backward-looking crystal ball.

Sex and the Unmarried

A Readers' Dialogue

The year was remarkable for a widespread questioning of the restraints imposed, by religion and by social codes, on sexual intercourse. The issue was first raised in February, when a group of Quakers issued a report—which we welcomed as "far and away the best study yet produced by any religious group"—calling for "a new morality". The debate which followed was started by Father Maurice O'Leary, chairman of the Catholic Marriage Advisory Council, who said in an interview that, according to Catholic teaching, the sexual appetite and instinct were good, but had to be controlled in a loving and permanent relationship, since in no other way could the overall procreative purpose of sex be achieved. Readers took up the argument, in a series of Letters to the Editor, re-invigorated from time to time by other items on the same theme appearing in the paper.

Kenneth Hassall, Reading: "Father O'Leary's view must be challenged, not as an attack on this excellent man, but because it has been the major cause of controversy over sexual morality and has led to misery and persecution.

"It is just not true within marriage, let alone outside it, that the only objective of sex is reproduction. Human beings are capable of fellow-feeling of a type unknown in the animal world, and I suggest the machinery of reproduction is becoming adapted for expression of this new inter-relationship.

"I hope Father O'Leary would not assert that my relationship with my wife has been any less pure since we decided to limit our family. Moreover, if we follow his contention, we shall find ourselves condemning pre-marital intercourse less vigorously if it leads to unwanted children than if it aims at avoiding this socially most undesirable situation. Similarly, some of the finest friendships of history were homosexual.

"The paradox of sex is that it can be one of the most ennobling or the most degrading of human activities and the determining factor is neither the marital status nor the sex of one's partner, but whether the physical relationship is accompanied by love and respect."

Among others who spoke later on this theme was an official at the Ministry of Education, who was then attacked for having advocated fornication. We pointed out in a Comment that in fact he had condemned promiscuity while giving it as his purely personal view that it was not immoral for engaged couples to have sexual relations, though it might be unwise.

Stephen Foot, London, S.W.15: "Certain subjects are not controversial; they are fundamental. Anyone who, whether in his private capacity or in his public utterance, advocated murder, theft, blackmail, or assault, would be regarded as a lunatic. Chastity is so clearly part of the strength of a nation that a man who queries the need for it is unfit to hold any public office."

Thomas Tempest, London, S.W.19: "Mr. Foot mentions several grave breaches of the criminal law, including murder, with the inference that these are comparable to unchastity. On what premise? All the offences he lists are unilateral acts of aggression upon passive victims—that is why they *are* crimes—not remotely analogous to the case of two adults who agree to have sex relations. . . . We have not got to such a pitch of reactionary moral fervour, surely, that extra-marital relations between sane consenting adults should invoke penal sanctions."

Matthew Robinson (19), *Saffron Walden:* "When will intelligent people cease attributing personal or national weakness to sexuality? The concept, for example, that Greece and Rome fell because of their inhabitants' free sexual behaviour is a preconceived idea which was taught to young people in the Victorian era. The Greeks' love of intercourse didn't prevent them building up a magnificent empire. Would anyone describe Napoleon Bonaparte, the finest general in the world, as chaste? Or the Duke of Wellington? And did promiscuity prevent Mozart from writing masterpieces? Indeed, far from causing their downfall, it seems to me that a little illicit love has helped a number of people on their way."

Stephen Foot: "Mr. Robinson's partly humorous letter demands a serious reply. Free sexual behaviour has its most harmful effect on family life. For an illustration of this truth it is not necessary to go back to the history of Greece or Rome. In the early days of the Soviet Union the so-called "postcard divorces" led to a rapid weakening of family ties. The result on a generation of children was so disastrous that the policy was reversed. Easy divorce was labelled "bourgeois" and abolished.

> *At this time we published an article by Dilys Rowe showing that at the last count in England and Wales about one baby in sixteen was illegitimate and that about one quarter of the unmarried mothers were between thirteen and nineteen years old, some of them still at school. Miss Rowe commented on the growing social problem of how to care for these pregnant girls and, thereafter, for their babies.*

Valerie King, Wembley: "The answer to Mr. Tempest was to be found in the article by Dilys Rowe. These illegitimate children were conceived by two people whose only thought was their own selfish pleasure. Surely this is an offence—an offence against the children?"

Francis M. Roads, Oxford: "The birth of illegitimate children is caused, not by pre-marital sex, but by pre-marital sex without adequate precaution against an unwanted pregnancy. The latter case is evidently 'an offence against the children', but it is a large step from the particular to the general. For surely the sane majority who have sex before marriage but take the necessary precaution never find their way into the statistics. We hear only of the unhappy cases. It is equally fallacious to assume that all pre-marital sex is pure selfish pleasure for the people concerned. Many young lovers regard sex as an expression of their love for each other—as something that is given to, not taken from, the other. In any case, sex is rather more than a pleasant sensation; for most people, once past puberty, some kind of sexual experience is just as necessary for mental health as are rest and recreation. Presumably married couples who continue their sexual relationship after they have finished having children are not indulging in pure selfish pleasure, yet the need of young un-married people for sex is if anything greater than for these."

I.F., *Birmingham*: "At twenty-one, I can lay no claim to high standards of morality—if morality in the unmarried young is to be judged in terms of virginity and chastity. However, from my own experience, I know that a *genuine* set of values and a balanced view of sex can come from a period of promiscuity. One cannot be taught that sex is for orgasm and procreation, not for ego; that making love is something two people do *because they know each other*, not *because they want to get to know each other*. These are things that must be learned by experience and often by hollow experience at that."

Jean Frazer, London, S.W.13: "The infuriating aspect of the prob-lem of the unmarried mother is the beastliness of the men involved. They destroy a girl's resistance by arguing with irrefutable logic that there is nothing immoral in sensual pleasure, by salami tactics and emotional blackmail. They make a girl feel abnormal or sub-normal, tell her she is cold, old-fashioned, and the like, and that she is driving a man into the arms of another girl. Even when men do not demand actual intercourse, they demand other forms of love-making, which leave a girl a virgin, but not virginal.

"I know three girls who have literally had to fight their way out of situations. One of my girl friends spent a weekend with her boy friend because he was pestering her so much. He assured her he would make sure there were no consequences. He didn't bother to do so; there are consequences. He has offered her an abortion. Another girl friend of mine who gave in was told, after her weekend with her boy friend, 'Thank you—goodbye'.

"I have been told, in so many words, that I must expect to pay for the cost of taking me out—and one of my girl friends once had the cost of her meal demanded of her because she had refused her date a session on the sofa.

"In all the cases I have quoted the men come from what the welfare worker would describe as good homes. Today a girl finds she just has to give a man sex—not merely to keep him, but to get him in the first place. Part of the trouble stems from the fact that fathers, although they would have a fit if a man made a pass at their daughters, think it desirable for their sons to gain sexual experience. They ignore the fact that this means that other men's daughters will suffer as a result."

J. Douglas Dant, Southsea: "If it were possible for teenage girls to attend family planning clinics because they have been encouraged to have a sense of social responsibility, the story would be very different. Other countries have moved in this direction, but it seems that in this country we are more concerned about punishing 'immorality' with unwanted pregnancies than using our knowledge to promote human happiness. The dilemma of the Christians is easy to understand. If fornication ceases to involve a risk of tragedy and becomes a matter of taste, it may be harder than ever to persuade people that it is sinful."

Schoolmaster, Wakefield: "What astonishes me is not so much that my pupils have the nerve to indulge in sexual intercourse, but that having done so (i) they consider speaking about the subject filthy, embarrassing and indecent, and (ii) they shun any girl in their group who is 'caught'! Where does this Machiavellian double-thinking spring from?"

A Postscript by Feiffer

Showing that the married have their problems, too.

© Copyright 1963 Jules Feiffer New York

Peace in Our Time?

by John Davy

Our Science Correspondent looked at ways of reducing the noise that afflicts us and had an idea for making airports quiet.

"Much more could be done," said the Wilson Committee report last week, "to quieten machines and processes in general."

This flat phrase hides a stirring prospect: there seems no doubt that, given sufficient incentive, the resources of modern technology could substantially hush the roar of most machinery in ten to fifteen years.

The present hubbub is largely due to insufficient incentive, too little research, and the lack of noise-consciousness among engineers.

Motor manufacturers are most noise-conscious. Nevertheless, the technical development of European cars is on a tack that aggravates silencing problems. High petrol costs encourage small, high-revving high-compression engines, to produce maximum performance from the smallest size. Bodies must be lightly built to match, and the result is a loudly buzzing beetle.

In America, where size and quietness are more significant selling points than petrol consumption, evolution has gone the other way, producing large, relatively slow-running engines and cars that seldom need to use anything near full-throttle.

A direct route to quieter traffic in Britain would thus be substantial cuts in petrol tax, and purchase tax concessions on cars meeting much stricter noise standards than those at present proposed by Mr. Marples.

This would not solve the problem of sports cars and motor-cycles, whose attraction appears to lie partly in the aggressive snarl of their exhausts. But this is not a *technical* problem: one of the quietest motor-cycles on the market has a water-cooled engine—the most direct way to quieten these machines.

Big diesel engines are a much more formidable problem. The exploding fuel makes the cylinders ring like a bell, and this is the source of much of the noise. The trend is towards lighter cylinders, which will make more noise.

Possible answers include rubber mountings and heavy shrouds round the engines; modifying the engines to produce slower burning —which means lower efficiency and the risk of more smoke. More far-reaching would be the possibility of composite cylinders that don't "ring" in the same way—perhaps incorporating plastics that will stand up to very high temperatures.

Then there is the prospect of new types of engine. The German Wankel engine, with its single rotating triangular piston, may be developed for heavy vehicles—and may lend itself to simpler, more effective silencing.

The "hydrostatic transmission" being developed at the National Engineering Laboratory near Glasgow may help. The engine will run at a steady governed speed, and could be placed anywhere in the vehicle.

The quietest practical propulsion for road vehicles is certainly electric. For specialised purposes—milk and bread deliveries, refuse collection at night—battery-driven vehicles are highly successful; their numbers on British roads are increasing by over 1,000 a year.

Their snag is limited range—around 40 miles—and some eight hours attached to an electric plug to refuel. Military research is producing great improvements in lightweight high-capacity rechargeable batteries, and a fibre-glass electric town runabout, with a 75-mile range and recharging time of a few hours, may appear on the market before long.

But the most hopeful prospect is a practical fuel cell. These devices —pioneered in Britain—convert fuel directly into electricity. The National Research Development Corporation is backing considerable research here, and intensive work is in progress in America to develop fuel cells for spacecraft.

One futuristic version being studied by Allis Chalmers involves a cell containing metal "fuels" that could be recharged by heating in a nuclear reactor.

Of more immediate importance is the fuel cell recently announced by the American General Electric Company, which is the first to work on cheap petrol-like fuels, at a reasonable temperature. It is still an expensive device—but five years' development could transform the situation.

A fuel-celled car would be propelled by electric motors powered direct by fuel cells; the "exhaust" would be innocuous water and carbon-dioxide; refuelling would be at a normal pump, and virtually silent vehicles would result.

One major problem remains: jet aircraft. Here the outlook is depressing. Very little can be done to quieten jet engines without making them hopelessly inefficient. As it is, B.O.A.C. estimates that using noise suppressors of Boeing 707s costs £16,500 per aircraft per year.

Heathrow, according to the Wilson Committee, is in the wrong place, surrounded by built-up areas, and faces the worst noise problem of any major airport in the world. The only final answer would be to move it, so that landings and take-offs pass over the sea.

A partial, but still remote solution, would be the reintroduction of airships. With modern technology they could possibly make a limited but significant come-back. They could rise silently from city centres to several thousand feet before starting their engines. They can never hope to compete in speed with aircraft, but for short hauls, or luxury longer trips, they might have possibilities.

Foreign Relations at Windsor

by Pendennis

This account of who was who at the great ball given by the Queen at Windsor Castle for Princess Alexandra's wedding guests is taken from the Table Talk column.

In the years immediately after the war, and even in the early years of our Queen's reign, courtiers seemed anxious to play down the Royal Family's foreign—and especially German—connections. Little was heard of the European cousins who came here, by the back-door as it were, to visit their royal relations.

Even with all the talk about getting us into Europe, little has been made of the fact that in the Royal Family we have one institution which has never been anything else but part of Europe. But there it is.

This weekend all is changed. With archdukes and margraves and German princes pouring in by every train and aircraft, London is once again the acknowledged heart and centre of royal activity. The latest scorecard suggests that about fifty European "royals" are coming over for the wedding of their cousin Princess Alexandra and for the great ball which the Queen is giving at Windsor Castle tomorrow night.

Prominent among them will be chips off the distinguished Hesse block, which also produced our own Mountbatten family. (Battenberg was the name given to Countess Julie Hauke when she married above her station into the Hesse dynasty: the origins of Countess Julie are not given very generous treatment in studies of the dynasty—a disappointment for Britons accustomed to the discovery, when commoners marry well, that they really spring—like the Ogilvys and Armstrong-Joneses—from Scottish and Welsh kings.)

The present Grand Duke of Hesse and the Rhine, Prince Ludwig, is coming to the ball with Princess Margaret of Hesse, daughter of the first Lord Geddes (of the Axe). It was they who entertained Princess Anne on her first visit to Germany last week, so she had no need to speak German. English, in fact, is the *lingua franca* of all these royal persons. Their nannies see to that. When, for instance, the Queen of the Hellenes, who is German (and known to some of her cousins as Frederick the Great of Prussia) wants to tick off her Lord Chamberlain, who is Greek, she does so in English.

Two of Prince Philip's four elder sisters married into the Hesse family; but tragedy overtook them both. Princess Cecilie was killed with her Grand Duke, her children and her mother-in-law in a terrible air crash in Belgium in 1937. The youngest sister Princess Sophie's first husband, Prince Christian, was killed on active service with the Luftwaffe. A daughter of this marriage, Princess Christina, the "Dolphin Square Princess", married a Yugoslav prince (Oundle and Clare College, Cambridge) but was soon divorced.

After Prince Christian's death, Princess Sophie married Prince Georg of Hanover, who will be partnering her at the Ball. Princess Anne was staying with them yesterday at the sprawling white Schloss Salem, where Prince Georg is the headmaster of Kurt Hahn's and the Duke of Edinburgh's old school, Salem.

The whole Salem property is owned, as it happens, by another of the Duke of Edinburgh's brothers-in-law, the amiable and easy-going Margrave of Baden. Both the Margrave and his Margravine (Princess Theodora, the Duke's second sister) will be staying at Windsor Castle this week. Their daughter, Princess Margarita, used to be a nurse at St. Thomas' Hospital, and lived in the nurses' home opposite. She liked her work there, but whenever she felt ill preferred to return to Germany. She was sometimes known as "Swabs" Baden and married another Yugoslav prince (also Oundle and Clare); and they, too, lived happily in England.

The Georg's of Hanover have three children, the eldest of whom, Prince Guelf, goes to school at Gordonstoun with our own Prince Charles and went ski-ing with him last hols.

Even this doesn't exhaust the Duke of Edinburgh's visiting blood-relations. His eldest sister, Margarita, married Prince Gottfried of Hohenlohe-Langenburg. She'll be over for the celebrations and so will her daughter Beatrix, former London art student and another of the Pimlico Princesses.

Another of the Duke's nieces, Dorothea, sister to the Dolphin Square Princess and "Puppa" to her friends, will be one for the tele-guests to look for on Wednesday: she'll certainly be among the prettiest girls in the Abbey.

Two young men who'll be on the floor at Windsor tomorrow with the Princesses of the blood are the sons of the Landgrave of Hesse—the Princes Maurice and Henry of Hesse, who prefer to be known by their Italian names Maurizio and Enrico. Their mother was an Italian princess who died a prisoner in Buchenwald concentration camp. Their father had been a friend of Goering's; but he failed to obtain her release. Prince Enrico is a painter who lives a bachelor life in Rome and Ischia and is liked for his sardonic humour. He and his brother have long been favourites of Princess Alexandra and her foreign cousins.

A great centre for all these people is Florence, where the Queen Mother of Rumania lives. She is the sister of the King of Greece, and, with her son King Michael (who lives near Hitchin, Herts), has had the extraordinary experience of living and reigning under the Russians. A handsome and courageous woman, one of the first beauties to have contact lenses fitted by Sir William Rycroft, she impressed even the Russians before they forced her out. (Once she had asked Vyshinsky why she and her son had been left. He pointed to a map and remarked: "When we find an obstacle, we go round it and come back for it later.")

Most of these families have known hard times, and there is a natural warmth and fellow-feeling between them. This is not always shared to quite the same degree by our own royals. Princess Margaret knows few of her foreign relations and to some extent takes after her grandfather, George V, who would not have been a keen Common Marketeer. Nor are Princess Margaret's languages any better than those of most girls of her age: she has no German and her French is fairly basic.

Nor is the Queen herself a linguist. But she enjoys welcoming her foreign cousins and likes to hear the family news. The foreign royals refer to her as "Lillibet", instead of saying "The Queen", as Princess Marina or Princess Alexandra, brought up in the English manner, would.

Of other British royals, Princess Marina speaks modern Greek, but doesn't claim to do so very well. She once told Paddy Leigh Fermor, the writer, that he spoke it better. Her accent in all languages has a trace of Russian: her mother was a Russian Grand Duchess and her surviving sister, Princess Olga of Yugoslavia, still speaks Russian well.

Prince Philip is, naturally, the most abroad-minded of the Royal Family. He likes visiting his sisters and gets on well with his German nephews and nieces. But he seems less keen on Greece. Most royals reckon to be able to speak the language of the countries whose royal families they belong to—Bernadottes learn Swedish and Schleswig-Holstein-Sonderburg-Glucksburgs learn modern Greek—but Prince Philip doesn't seem to worry about his inability to do so.

However, it is Princess Alexandra's day that all the royals have come to celebrate, and her choice of husband has pleased everyone, foreign relations included. One witty cousin wrote to say that he was so pleased the Royal Family had dropped its tiresome habit of marrying into double-barrelled families, like Mecklenburg-Strelitz, Hohenlohe-Langenburg, Armstrong-Jones, etc.

It isn't the first time, though. Princess Alexandra's first cousin,

111

Princess Elizabeth of Yugoslavia, married Mr. Howard Oxenberg of New York, who makes wholesale maternity wear. He is very handsome and was taken for a prince, at the last royal wedding, by Richard Dimbleby.

These two first cousins make a trio with a third—the Duchess Elizabeth of Austria. They have often holidayed together, and carry on with an affectionate intimacy which reminds one of a cross between Louisa M. Alcott and Tolstoy. The Duchess and her Archduke Ferdinand live very modestly near Paris, where they prefer to be known as the Count and Countess Klyburg. They have a six-year-old Archduchess daughter who is one of Princess Alexandra's bridesmaids and seems likely to steal the show.

Princess Alexandra (never known as Alix: her only nickname in the family has been "Puddy", short for Pudding) likes abroad too. She has adored Greece ever since she visited her grandmother in Athens as a child and saw the scores of stray cats that formidable lady allowed to haunt her garden. She also likes Florence, where her uncle Prince Paul has a beautiful villa. (It used to be called the Villa Demidoff: Potage Demidoff is a much tastier Brown Windsor: give a dish a name and be assured of immortality). In fact, Princess Alexandra likes everywhere, including Thailand. And everywhere likes her.

Sweated Labour in the Unions

by Peter Dunn

"Anyway," said the big shop-steward, arguing with the Regional Officer's assistant, "we pay your wages and don't you forget it."

The Regional Officer's assistant, who had been talking to a meeting of his members, went back to the trade union office and told the Regional Officer.

"Next day," the R.O. recalls, "I went to the meeting myself and sent 1s. 1d. down to this Willie Pep—that's what we call these whip-crackers. I let him stare at it while I talked to the men. Then I said to him: "I've come to the conclusion that 6½d. a year covers your contribution to the union officers' wages. Perhaps now you'll keep your bloody mouth shut for two years."

"This is much more of a full-time job than some of our members seem to have. One bloke rang up and complained because he didn't find me in the office. I told him that if he let me know when he was going to ring again I'd sit on a shelf and wait for him to pick me up and dust me."

Small wonder if, from time to time, trade union officers lose their patience with the Willie Peps. Most of them accept working conditions which their members would find intolerable.

The R.O., for example, gets £1,000 a year plus a Cortina ("You need it for increased productivity"). And he and his assistant look after 21,000 members in 800 depots spread across an eighth of the country. They work on average a 65-hour week and usually have meetings on 45 Sundays a year. They can attend meetings 50 miles apart in the same day and one of these is bound to be an evening job.

The members, for their part, pay 1s. 6d. a week in subscription (for which they get lawyers' services and accident, sickness, funeral and strike benefits) and expect their officers to be in ten places at once.

No one can really blame a shop-steward for losing his patience when he has a strike on his hands and cannot get a full-time officer down to the job from headquarters at once. But the big shop-steward's truculence about paying the R.O.'s wages, and the R.O.'s sarcasm in reply, are merely symptoms of a deeper problem. If trade union members want better service from their officers, they are going to have to pay more than 1s. 6d. a week to get it.

Meanwhile, leading officers inflate their meagre salaries with perks —houses, cars, committee-attendance fees. Others accept what is offered and do three men's work.

The T.U.C. made a vague pass at the problem in 1960 with a document about trade union finances, but it has yet to be tackled on the floor of an annual Congress. It is apparently considered a domestic issue for individual unions, not a matter for national concern.

There are, according to estimates, about 3,000 salaried trade union officers in Britain (compared with about 200,000 shop-stewards who work for little or nothing). They look after 8 million workers.

Past experience shows that the principle of equal distribution of wealth has its thinnest hours when the members are asked to vote for more money for their leaders. A couple of years ago the Foundry Workers refused in a ballot to give their officials a £2 a week increase.

This left the executives with £15 a week—less than the earnings of some of the people they represented. The decision was reversed last year, but it did show that when a worker becomes an employer he can be mighty mean.

Getting new men in to work for the unions is going to be difficult in these circumstances. No one today can claim the sort of background which gave the Regional Officer in the North his initial impetus to make it a better world.

"I worked as an apprentice in a tool room," the R.O. said, "with a group of old-style revolutionary Socialists. They all read Jack London's *The Iron Heel* and *all* the Upton Sinclair books. I don't push it down young people's throats, but you won't have met the type.

When the Strike came in 1926 they let the apprentices in to work but we all joined the union."

Working-class boys who go to grammar school or the universities would rather invent new soap flakes in industry today than go into a movement where the pay is low, the hours monstrous and promotion, to say the least, steady. The R.O., in any case, does not really want them.

"As I believe that no full stomach can feel hungry," he said, "neither do I believe that a man who has no practical experience can ever really give his best to industry. The unions spend a hell of a lot on education. But the university types being brought in by management today, while they're quite a good thing in an academic sense, seem to fall a little short when it comes to the actual clash of very opposite opinions. I find that they're very easy meat to deal with. I just overwhelm them."

It needs, in any event, a special kind of panache to face a mass meeting from the back of a lorry at 8 a.m.

"We'd called this meeting," the R.O. said, "and some wag at the back shouts, 'You've only come here to get us back'—as if that was something detrimental. I jumped off the lorry and went into a café for some bacon and egg. A bit later they sent in a deputation and asked me if I'd go back to the meeting.

"I'm absolutely fanatically engaged in this job. I'm very contented. I believe it's a way of life, a religion.

"I'm seeing one of the employers this afternoon. We'll sit down and if you came in 25 minutes later and heard us you'd wonder whose side who was on. But in a couple of hours we'll have sorted out the problems in this firm for the next couple of years. You won't hear of any strikes."

Our Old-Fashioned Ways with the Old

by Dilys Rowe

The pensionable-age section of the population has increased steadily from 6 per cent in 1911 to about 15 per cent this year, but old age has still taken the Welfare State by surprise.

Old workhouses have been pressed into service to house the old. Local authority homes, it is true, are getting better and better, but when the Ministry of Health published its latest report almost half the places provided by local authorities, mainly needed by old people, were in workhouses which the Minister of Health himself thinks should long ago have been pulled down.

The report points out hopefully that by 1972 the proportion will have dropped by 11 per cent. In cold figures this means that 14,000 old people will still be living in converted workhouses 10 years from now.

The arrangements made by local authorities for the comfort and well-being of old people are enlivened by the occasional flash of individual initiative, of the kind that gives the waiting world such a lift to read about after a natural disaster. But there is still no consistent nationwide recognition that when certain things are made easier morale in old age is higher.

The Ministry of Health admits that the variation in the number of home helps provided in the different parts of the country is not excused by variation in need.

All local authorities have power under the Public Health Act to provide laundry services for incontinent people living at home. Only 48 do so.

A few local authorities have followed suit since the Ilford Old People's Welfare Council pioneered volunteer night-sitters to sit with the sick, but most of the schemes are voluntary, and there are not many. For many old people a national scheme of this kind would mean the difference between home and hospital.

The old-age pension, like any emergency grant, covers bare existence, and has to be supplemented by national assistance, now called the supplementary pension, to overcome the inhibitions of those who do not like asking for what they consider charity, however much they need it.

It is useless to change the name of National Assistance. By any other name it is distasteful, and one of the worst effects of not giving old people an adequate pension, which can be regarded as a citizen's right, is the reinforcement of a class system stratifying old people in a particularly cruel and rigid form.

At one end of the scale there are, for example, the old people in the slums of North Kensington. Many of these spent most of last winter in bed trying to keep warm. They will probably end up in the condemned workhouses. And at the other end of the scale there is, for instance, the elderly widow of a professional man.

She was discovered, in an attic in Hertford, living mainly on bread and milk, by an official of the Royal United Kingdom Beneficent Association. This body helps gentlefolk. Luckily she qualified for aid. One hundred years old this year, the Association is spending about £1,000 a day on helping people of "the right class" whose need is established. Help is mainly through small annuities or with places in the association's residential homes. The recipients for annuities are chosen by a method with which Mrs. Proudie would have felt completely at home; subscribers are issued with lists of applicants twice a year and can have as many votes as they want for 5s. a vote.

The general secretary of the association hates the word gentlefolk and wishes someone would invent another. He dislikes having to make the invidious distinction. But looking at the passport of an elderly woman, he said: "Now looking at that photograph I'd have my doubts, but let's see. Widow for many years of a member of the Irish Constabulary, education stopped at 14, occupation fancy work, the referee says the society must judge for itself." She was out. We moved on to a more cheerful case. "I'd have no doubt about that face, oh yes, splendid old lady, teacher of English abroad, yes, she's all right."

The Distressed Gentlefolks' Aid Association runs some of the finest residential homes in the country, and spends over £70,000 a year on helping 2,000 people with money to enable them to live independently at home.

These organisations are as necessary as they have ever been since their foundation as patronage charities, for one of the curious effects of the Welfare State's disregard of the old is to have revived the category of gentlefolk, and to have re-created the need for the kind of charity that flourished in Barchester.

The Spectre at the Christmas Feast

by Patrick O'Donovan

There is an ancient Scottish poem whose refrain consists of the absolutely honest words: *"Timor mortis conturbat me"*—the fear of death oppresses me. This fear is a sign of life. It is laid upon humans with their flesh. Most of the time we manage to put it aside, to rationalise it almost away, to postpone its consideration, to forget it for days at a time.

Perhaps it is because it is so little considered that the arrangements for dying are so inadequate. Not everyone dies of a set disease in a hospital. And happy and rare is the man who can linger among his children and grandchildren to die, loved and cared for, in his own bed. The lot of the rest is not a pretty one.

Everyone dies alone. But in many the loneliness becomes so terrible that it becomes a reproach to our whole society. All over England there are wards and hospitals where old men and women wait for the inevitable. There is one L.C.C. place that I have had to visit.

It is enormous. It is lined with beds. It is as busy as a railway station. It is never quite quiet. It has the smell of old age about it, of incontinence and sorrow. Each bed contains a man who may for a few hours sit in the sun, spend a shilling or two in the pub across the road, but few of whom will ever again sleep anywhere else.

Those who can sit dressed beside their beds in a private world consisting of their chair, their locker box and their wallet under the pillow, are fortunate. They are cared for by nurses, some of whom are coloured, some foreign, some Irish. These are, of course, underpaid and overworked. The nurses give an overwhelming impression of devotion and exhaustion. Theirs is a genuine work of supererogation. They could not be praised too highly.

The patients are not easy. They are all apparently profoundly unhappy. It is marvellous to watch a pert little West Indian girl flirt a smile out of an old man or to watch an Irish girl teasing another into saying his rosary. There is a necessary, underlying toughness in them. They carry a burden that society has long since weakly surrendered. And an Anglican priest, plump in his belted soutane, twinkling and cheerful, represents almost alone the outside world, kindness, the personal touch and love.

Of course it is terrible to be old and unwanted. We have found no solution to the problem of how to cope with such ordinary people—even though the people who fail to solve the problem will, as likely as not, experience it themselves in the end.

The modern flat is no place for slow death. The modern housewife can hardly double as a nurse. Only a few can afford the odd £40 a week demanded by a nursing home for easeful death. There remain places like this, ill-designed, under-staffed, at the tail end of the queue for welfare in the Welfare State. And only a few of them are able to give these ordinary people any work that hints at the idea that they are not useless.

Of course there are other places. The Sisters of Charity run hospices for the aged and the dying. They are remarkable places. Death here is accepted as a normal and natural thing. The easy religion of the Irish sisters is not insisted upon. Old nuns will sit up all night to hold the hand of a frightened man. In surroundings that shout of mortality and dissolution, they are as cheerful as kindergarten teachers. But because they accept neither bribes nor influence, because they are open first to the lonely and the hopeless, it is as hard to get into their houses as into the most exclusive London club. They have waiting-lists—for dying.

But the people in this predicament have no voice in the State. There is no pressure group of people plucked protesting out of bed-sitting-rooms or unconscious off the street. They do not write to the papers. No one pleads their cause. And yet we will be them some day.

This is Christmas—a feast that brings a sort of horror to such people. It is the cruel reminder, the brutal suggestion that now they are genuinely alone. The nurses can do their best. But the faded, beady eyes are still on the door looking for visitors. The smell is still there. The overcrowding is still a fact. The rejection by ordinary life still overwhelming. The unseen queue for admission still stretches from here to suffering. If anyone wanted a cause to be angry over, to shout about and to fight for, here is one ready-made and waiting with its arms outstretched. But where do you begin?

A Cold Hard Look at the Welfare State

by Michael Frayn

The fog of emotionalism which has always obscured the subject of the Welfare State is lifting at last. After all these years the cold light of reason is beginning to filter through.

The Institute of Economic Affairs has interviewed some 2,000 married men and found that more than half of them—of all classes and politics—thought that individuals should be allowed to contract out of State education, health, and pensions schemes, or that the benefits should be confined to people in need.

This, it seems to me, is plain common sense. Take my case, which I should imagine a great many readers will find typical. I pay £1 a week in national insurance and pension contributions, and a great deal more by way of tax. But during the last 12 months, since I have been neither ill nor out of work, I have seen not a penny in return.

People like us have got the dirty end of the welfare stick. We have to pay contributions like everyone else. But we are too young to draw pensions. We are too healthy to need much medical attention. We have chosen to live in the South of England, and to work in progressive industries like entertainment and property development, where we are unlikely to find ourselves unemployed. Since we work in well-ventilated offices and take care to handle no machine more dangerous than a typewriter or a slide-rule, we are highly unlikely to enjoy any benefits for industrial injury.

Where is our money going, then? Let us not mince words. It is going to support people with incurable diseases, who will be taking money out of the scheme and putting none in for the rest of their lives.

It is going to couldn't-care-less young men who got their hands caught in the conveyor belt, or fell off the scaffolding.

It is being used to finance the birth of illegitimate babies—indeed to encourage illegitimacy by enabling illegitimate babies to get as much orange-juice and cod-liver oil as legitimate ones.

It is buying drinks and cigarettes for unemployed Belfast shipbuilders, who couldn't be bothered to move to London, or to go to the university and train as television personalities. (And remember, men who are unemployed pay nothing at all themselves towards their own unemployment money!)

The truth of the matter is that people fall into two groups whose interests are diametrically opposed, and they are divided in a way that cuts right across their social class and political loyalties. There are the bright, successful, healthy, young people who pay the money in. And there are the slack, unsuccessful sick, old people who draw it out.

Now those of us who happen to be in the first group have nothing against the others. But if we set all woolly-minded sentiment aside and bring a little cold logic to bear, it is obviously in our interest to contract out of the system and look after ourselves. What we want to see is a system with benefits reserved exclusively for those in need, and therefore, to be fair, paid for exclusively by those in need.

This would have great advantages for all concerned. Our sturdy independence in contracting out would set a fine example to the old, the sick, and the unemployed. It would dissuade us from going off to America to avoid tax, and so depriving the country of our expert knowledge of television satire and property speculation. It would put money in the pockets of people who would know how to make good use of it—we shouldn't be tempted to waste it, as others might, on the degrading scramble for materialistic luxuries like cars and washing-machines, since we've got them already.

It would make the welfare services more democratic. The two-class welfare system, with a second-class service provided by the State, and a first-class one paid for by the individual, has worked well enough as far as it has gone. But a great many more people could afford the first-class service if they were not also burdened with the costs of the second-class one.

And after all, it's a sensible division of advantages. Since we healthy young people go to the doctor less often than old, sick people, we naturally expect to find on the few visits we do make, cleaner, better-decorated waiting-rooms in more desirable houses. For those who are chronically sick it's naturally more of a bread-and-butter occasion, and the sagging canvas chairs and peeling chocolate distemper strike a rather more suitable note.

Then again, the two-class system saves money for everybody. If newspaper editors and Cabinet Ministers had to join the queue for National Health beds, and send their children to understaffed State schools, they would certainly start insisting on the standards to which they are accustomed. The extra cost would fall on the unsuccessful as well as the successful. The more we can channel off the able and influential people into their own private systems, the more economically we can look after the nobly uncomplaining remainder.

If logic counts for anything, the range of two-class services will have to be extended until all unnecessary contact between the two halves of the nation has been severed. Then, in time, we could move all the Bright people into Southern England, and resettle all the Slack people in the North, where they would have generous reserves set aside for them in the historic Slack homelands, like Tyneside and South Lancashire.

They would, of course, enjoy a considerable measure of tribal self-government in Welfarestan. At any rate, they would be entirely responsible for their own welfare. Seeing that they would all be sick, aged, or out of work, it's a subject in which they should be quite well qualified.

The Delinquent Driver

by John Davy

After every public holiday the road-accident figures are greeted with cries of anguish. This year road deaths over Christmas are up 70 per cent on 1962, which gives good cause for even sharper anguish than usual.

We seem to think that if we lament road casualty figures loudly and long enough they will vanish into thin air. The exercise relieves guilt feelings—for every driver knows that he has on occasions driven in such a way that he might have killed somebody—and allows the matter to be decently dropped until the next festival of exorcism.

Our ambiguous attitude to the whole business becomes evident as soon as action is proposed. The idea of speed limits at weekends or on motorways is opposed; a vehement action is fought against breathalysers, although the drunken driver is the most universally condemned of road offenders; radar speed checks are resented, and in between peak accident periods the motorist is frequently represented as persecuted, heavily taxed and underprivileged.

Our split mind on the subject derives directly from the dual function of cars. They are part of the necessary machinery of modern life. But they also offer psychological satisfactions.

Some of these—notably the pleasure in exercising a skill—probably enhance road safety. But others certainly do not. A powerful vehicle offers unique opportunities for releasing aggressive and competitive emotions in padded comfort. Sociologists have often commented that the roads are a jungle in more senses than one.

Efforts to come to terms with the motor car in a technical sense—by building better roads, extending speed limits, etc.—will only nibble at the problem if we do not succeed, at the same time, in deglamorising driving.

At present, the publicity of motor manufacturers and the writings of many motoring correspondents enhance the image of the motor car as an outlet for what are, in essence, delinquent impulses. Reviews of new cars nearly always begin with an account of their powers of acceleration, rather than of their comfort, reliability, safety or quietness. Smaller and smaller cars are being equipped for higher and higher speeds, for the pleasure of the "keen motorist".

It is, of course, true, as motoring fans never tire of pointing out, that high performance is not in itself dangerous. Good acceleration and brakes, properly used, make for safety. It is also true that inadequate roads make a major contribution to accidents. The road-building programme is certainly not big or urgent enough, and there are administrative absurdities, such as county boundaries where the surface changes suddenly from well-gritted tarmac to an icy death-trap.

But the best roads and the safest cars are useless without responsible drivers. And the most urgent need is for a much more critical look at the whole social context in which motoring proceeds.

Last May, *The Observer* reported the striking findings of Lieutenant-Colonel Willett, who has shown that, in one county at least, a high proportion of serious motoring offenders had a previous record of criminal or motoring offences, or both.

Willett also underlined the general tolerance of motoring offences —the widespread feeling, shared by magistrates and juries, that "there but for the grace of God go I". This makes motoring law into a book of rules governing a sporting contest between motorists and the police, rather than a means of protecting society from delinquent behaviour.

To bring about a more sober psychological adjustment to the motor-car age is clearly a long job. But it could be hastened in several ways. A major need is for more study of the individuals involved in accidents, preferably through interviews with independent investigators as near the time of the accident as possible.

The courts should take previous criminal records into account when hearing motoring cases, and should be given the power to experiment with more imaginative sentences: in America and Germany offenders have been sent to work at the scene of accidents and in hospital casualty departments. And Mr. Marples's suggestion a year ago that wrecked cars should be exhibited in town centres could be taken up.

At the moment, one feels that the outcry at the accident statistics masks a deep unwillingness to face their real source. However much our ordered and unadventurous lives may need a jungle to escape to, we cannot continue—as at present—to leave civilised social standards behind as we depress the accelerator.

Round the Clock at Crockford's

by Maurice Richardson

Gaming clubs on the island had more than sixteen million members during a year of gambling boom. Most of them were bingo clubs, but in rather more exclusive surroundings, such as those described below, business was also brisk.

The *chemin de fer* room at Crockford's in London is L-shaped and dreamy, decorated in French casino style with satin-panelled walls and a suggestion of Empire. The light pours down on the five kidney-shaped tables, making them look like green pools. In between you seem to lose yourself in a diffuse, pink-beige, half-glow half-gloom.

This is the indescribable gambling-house atmosphere, asexual, quasi-religious; somewhere between a lunatic's bank and a eunuch's lupanar. Here you begin to understand the truth of Dostoevsky's dictum : that a real gambler must also enjoy the act of losing.

Britain's all-time record gambling boom gets bigger every day. London is becoming the capital of *chemin de fer*.

£   £   £

To find its heart, in so far as a gambling boom can have a heart, you must go to 16, Carlton House Terrace. Here, behind a cream stucco front of total respectability, flanked on either side by the Foreign Office and looking out over the Mall, is Crockford's Club. The original Crockford's was founded in 1827 by William Crockford, a picaresque adventurer and near-villain of the humblest origins, and closed in 1845. Crockford was supposed to have died of a broken heart after his horse, Raton, lost the Derby to a ringer. In fact he died before the off, but as dead owners' horses were automatically scratched his friends kept him propped up in a chair in a bow window until the race was run. In 1929 the club was restarted by Colonel Beasley, the bridge player, and in 1934 moved to Carlton House Terrace.

Since a *chemin de fer* room opened there in December, 1961, following the new Betting and Gaming Act of 1960, the Club's profits have been described by a police solicitor at Bow Street as "staggering". They amount to at least £10,000 gross a week. It is impossible to determine the exact figure of money wagered in one year across its tables, but it cannot be much less than £25 million.

£   £   £

Old night-life hands say that the present chemmy wave dates from the war, when there was an outcrop of private but professionally organised gambling parties, some run by bookmakers. Play was high, sometimes with £40,000 changing hands in a night. The promoters, after providing champagne, supper and transport, would clear anything from £1,000 to £5,000.

After the war, the wave seemed to have spent itself. In spite of currency restrictions, the English somehow found money to play with at Le Touquet and on the Riviera. Then, in the late fifties, Mr. John Aspinall started his careful private parties; one-night stands that moved round from house to house, making legitimate holes in the loosely framed gambling laws.

As soon as the new Act was mooted, the passion swelled up again. It had always been there. The English, with a few possible exceptions such as the Chinese, the Irish, the Greeks, the Negroes, the Arabs, the Jews, and the Australians, are the most addicted gamblers on earth.

There are other *chemin de fer* clubs in London today where play is higher than at Crockford's. It can be very high indeed at Mr. Aspinall's elaborately decorated club at 44, Berkeley Square. It has been on occasion astronomically high at Les Ambassadeurs in Hamilton Place, run by Mr. John Mills, night-club proprietor and former Polish soldier, where the record loss in one night was more than £100,000.

It has been exceedingly high at the 21 Room run by another night-club proprietor, Mr. Harry Meadows, and high at the River Club in Grosvenor Road, and at Quents, in Hill Street. But nowhere else has the atmosphere and drill of a French casino been so carefully reproduced and nowhere is there so consistently steady a volume of play as at Crockford's.

In France, casinos charge a commission, the *cagnotte*, of 5 per cent of the bank's winnings. In Britain, under the new Act, gambling clubs may charge only seat money. At Crockford's, if all five tables are full—there are seven on gala nights—£450 is taken in seat money per hour.

There are about 1,200 chemmy players at Crockford's out of a total membership of 2,200, including the sedate bridge players, for whom the club was founded, and the poker school. Of these 1,200, not more than 800 are regular gamblers.

They, and their guests, who can play for cash or on their host's credit, represent a wide variety of professions. There are rag-trade bosses, factory owners, property men, landowners, peers, bookmakers, trainers, jockeys, hairdressers, diplomats (including an ambassador), a few barristers, a solicitor or two, surgeons, actors, a very few brokers and jobbers, one or two jewellers.

There is the occasional professional gambler who claims to live by defying probability, and some optimists who hope to win at chemmy some money that will not be taxed by the Inland Revenue. One of these is a South Coast bingo proprietor. The ladies include rich widows and proprietresses of launderette chains.

£   £   £

The moving spirit of the chemmy operation is Timothy Langham Rokeby Holland. He is chairman of Crockford's Ltd., the company which in 1961, for £48,000, acquired Carlton House Terrace Ltd., owners of Crockford's Club since 1934. He comes of a bridge-playing family. His mother taught him to play bridge at the age of seven. Three of his aunts, members like himself of Crockford's, play bridge for England. One of them is married to Captain Alan Black, R.N., who is now managing director of Carlton House Terrace Ltd.

Holland, who is 35, is a middle-weight, square and solid, with light-brown mousy hair sticking out in tufts. His complexion has that special pink glow you see only on men with incomes of more than £10,000 a year and strong livers. His nose is a thin, bony, convex beak, slightly out of the straight.

Holland is quick and impulsive. One moment he seems boyish and eager and young for his age, as he splutters carefully about the iniquities of the present taxation system. The next he expresses public-spirited sentiments like a cautious chartered accountant.

He is friendly and unstuffy, and not in the least smooth. He happily admits to being rich and brought up rich. He is unmarried, has a house in Sunningdale and a flat in Hill Street. His parents were Yorkshire. His father was a wool merchant. His mother was a Miss Rokeby, from the family that owned the Rokeby Venus of Velasquez.

Holland was at Harrow and did his military service in the Coldstream Guards. Then he went into the family wool business, Holland and Sherry Ltd., of which he remains a director, but before long he began to feel an itch to become a financier and founded Ridge Securities, the private company which he used as a base for his Crockford's operation.

In this he was joined by Bill Meaden, an old night-club hand—he used to run the Empress—with valuable experience and connections. He is a dark, clean-shaven, inveterate bowler-hat wearer, a bit diffident and much more like the secretary of a provincial rugger club than a night-club boss. He has a naval background, R.N.V.R. and R.N., and a particularly soothing touch with the old ladies.

The other former naval person, Captain Black, suggests the actor Roland Culver playing the part of a balding but gingery, nobbly but good-looking and well-preserved senior naval officer. His favourite expression is "offside". This was Black's first job after retirement. He seems delighted with it and his naval training comes in useful for the odd gambling hours.

Black, who lives in Blackheath (during the last two years of his naval career he was at the Royal Navy College at Greenwich), shares a room at Crockford's with Edward Mayer, the present secretary. Mayer is a barrister who hasn't practised for some years now, a tall, white-haired, dedicated bridge player and bridge correspondent of *The Times*, who refers to the chemmy players as "those addicts" and is a man of sardonic wit.

There are two French managers at Crockford's—M. Sammy Denoun and M. Louis Wiel—and one or other of them is always on the spot. Both are from the casino at Le Touquet with which Crockford's has a tie-up. There is not much these two don't know about running casinos. They acquired some of their experience the hard way on the other side of the cloth, running the banks at baccarat. Denoun is a short, stocky, swarthy man, rather like a sawn-off Sam White—the *Evening Standard's* Paris correspondent—and almost as sociable. He is a great favourite with the regulars at Crockford's. He has been in casinos most of his working life. Wiel, commonly known as M. Louis, is the same size and colour, but plump and round. He started off as a law student.

Both tell you that their money is hard earned in terms of hours. Both avoid pep pills and drink very moderately. Denoun's favourite drink for a late or all-night session is milk and soda. Wiel is a chain smoker. He says he has his own private system of meditation to avoid the occupational boredom that can be one of the hazards of casino management. He always feels starved of fresh air and has a passion for mountains and scenic railways.

£   £   £

On Saturdays, Sundays and Wednesdays, play at Crockford's begins at five in the afternoon. The management call these early sessions "our cocktail parties". First to fill up, nearly always on the stroke of five, is the old ladies' table. Play here is not astronomical, but you could lose a few hundred if you had a bad run.

Four or five of the nine players at this table are evidently women of over 60. One wears a pink tulle bow on top of her mauve-rinsed hair. Two in black, with loads of modern jewellery and huge soft handbags like Titanesses' wombs, sit together and chat, occasionally croaking *avec* as they stake a modest £5 counter against the bank.

The oldest of all the gambling old ladies is 87. She once broke the bank at Cannes. She wears a green velvet cap, and her profile looks as strong as a Cornish cliff. She has a middle-aged companion with her because she can't always see well enough to count the pips of the French numberless cards. She bancos and wins five *coups* in succession.

The men wear dark suits and look lacquered and ageless, anywhere between 45 and 65. You get some surprises when you hear them speak. That small, dark bald person with a face like a lobster-claw must be either rag trade or bookmaker? But he talks like a colonel. The most duchessy lady of all has an acute Cockney accent.

The early evening is one of the chummiest periods, when the room feels quite like a club. But chemmy has them in its grip. At 8.30 there is some talk of dinner, but they decide to stay put and keep nourished on turtle soup, laced with sherry, and raw beef sandwiches. On they go into the night, trying to draw cards to make up nine.

£ £ £

Wednesday midnight and three tables going. The old ladies' table is empty now, though one or two of them have stayed on. Two £3 tables and the £5 table are still playing. At one of the £3 tables an exceptionally pretty dark girl, in a gym-dress tunic in green-and-red check that makes her look at a distance about 16, has a run of seven winning banks and wins about £400. (You don't see many pretty girls here as a rule.) She sits smiling at the pile of counters in front of her. A big bald man beside her pats her thin smooth little hand with his pudgy mottled paw. He seems very proud of her luck.

She looks like a French starlet. He looks like a film producer. As usual it's hopelessly difficult to guess right here. In fact he is her father-in-law, and a property tycoon. Her husband, his son, is the dark young man with a thick mass of curls in the chocolate suit and a beautiful dark-crimson tie with gold stars on it. His watch and gold bracelet couldn't be worth less than £500. Everything about him looks elegantly foreign, including his crocodile cigar-case as big as a Testament and his amber cigar-holder, like a great honey-coloured waste pipe.

But as soon as he speaks you don't need to be Professor Higgins to know he comes from east of Aldgate Pump. So do they all. It's a family party and mum is there too, in full mink against the cold, beaming at them from a corner armchair and tucking into a box of *marrons glacés*. This game must be chicken-feed for them. The bank passes to a pair of quiet, smooth, pale young men. They go banco for £30, win two banks, let the bank pass and punt very cautiously.

Somehow the £5 table always gives you the impression of being the most crowded. After midnight now, creeping into the small hours of the morning.

The youngest of the old ladies has moved on here. She's been at it now since five in the afternoon. A formidable ash-blonde warrior type in a gold lamé tunic, she is anywhere between 55 and 60; large head: long, wedge-shaped features.

She plays with an air of rapt concentration. Next to her is a woman, perhaps in her thirties, with untidy brown hair and a pink

126

open-air face. She is wearing a rather scruffy-looking pony coat. Diagnosis: English county. Accent, so far as you can judge from the way she says "banco", corresponds.

But what are we to make of this pair? The player looks like an intelligent professional man, keen and crisp and pink with thick tortoiseshell spectacles. His chum sits behind him, a little back from the table. He is a small person with a knobbly, knowing, wrinkled face. There seems to be some sort of social symbiosis between them.

The player bancos for £50 and loses to a natural 9. *"Neuf à la banque,"* croaks the croupier. The player turns to the little chum and the chum jerks his head slightly. They get up and leave the table. They are a barrister and his clerk. The clerk's job is to see that his master doesn't exceed his limit. "That, anyway, is the theory," says the barrister. "In practice when I lose he always likes to take my place and see if he can't lose some more trying to win it back."

£   £   £

Saturday night is always a late night. The big linkman with the forked beard who looks as if he is turning into a statue of Porthos will be helping people in and out of cars and flourishing his giant umbrella until breakfast time.

1.15 a.m. A Jewish bookmaker is grunting as one of the porters helps him off with his galoshes. A well-known character actor, one of the most indefatigable gamblers in London, glances at his watch. "Don't look so worried, dear boy. The Rabbi can't get you. It's long past midnight. You're not breaking the Sabbath."

All four tables in the main room are packed and there are about three times as many spectators, kibbitzers who may stake, non-playing friends and relations, as seated players. The high-play table in the ante-room has been full for hours.

At 4 a.m. the smallest table, the £2 seat, packs up. But the other three and the high table are still going strong. At 5.30 the £5 table finishes, but play at the high table holds out until 7.30. Not bad for the time of year and the weather. In summer the record late was getting on for midday.

The atmosphere has quite a hint of Saturday-night jollity and it lasts well into the small hours. This is a night when you get members bringing friends who have never played before. The "old ladies" would hardly know their table now.

A sharp, ferrety-faced grey man is teaching a big chap with that particular shiny red complexion, that must mean Smithfield meat market, how to run a bank. He nudges him as he turns up his cards: "No, you big git," he whispers, "this isn't pontoon."

There is a good deal of "card, please," "banco," "I'd like to come

127

in," and not quite so much casino French. But the croupier manages to keep up the tempo.

£   £   £

The croupiers are paid about £5,000 a year. All are croupiers of the first class. There are three classes of croupier in France, all licensed by the police. A croupier of the third class is not necessarily any less honest than his colleagues; he is likely to be slower, though.

Speed is essential. A doddering croupier could easily halve the table's profits. The Crockford's croupiers are marvellously quick and deft. Tact, and a special unobtrusiveness, is another useful quality. A croupier mustn't throw his personality about, but may exude a faint aura of sympathy. He must have enough character to assert his authority if necessary, but no suggestion of aggression; no first-class croupier ever looks tough.

Inside and outside 16, Carlton House Terrace, the Crockford's croupiers lead a life apart. Some have left wives and families in France and fly home whenever they can. Several are quartered in flatlets in Chelsea Cloisters. Their ages vary between 35 and 55. Some are dark, some sandy; all are small with rather tired, wistful faces.

In Crockford's they have their own quarters, deep in the vast basement; they have a snug rest-room and changing-room, with a rota of times when they clock in. One of them, a patriotic Corsican, has a large, bright picture of Napoleon pasted on his locker. They have their own little dining-room with their bottles of red and white wine.

£   £   £

The grandest hours of a gambling saloon are not the earliest, said Balzac. Even at 2 a.m. on Sunday morning the atmosphere at Crockford's can be relaxed. The high table is always a kibbitzer's paradise. The piles and piles of counters, including the rare £5,000-er, look impressive. After experiencing a round of the shoe here, play at the other tables never seems the same again.

Nine players. Two of them women, smart, middle-aged blondes in black, one of them French. Three or four preternaturally calm and solid-looking men in their sixties or late fifties, looking as if they could afford to lose for ever. One younger man, dark with a red face and a crinkly nose; something about him suggests the racecourse. He laughs a lot but he seems to be taking it seriously because he's undone his collar and loosened his tie.

Who's this fellow with the head of grey curls and the brown, lean face, playing all the time with a string of beads? Must be a Greek. Now at last we are beginning to see a bit of international cosmopolitan form. Wrong again. The shoe is emptied: conversation breaks out. He's not a Greek at all. He's some kind of Scottish-Yorkshire mixture. His young wife comes and stands behind him and tickles the back of his neck for luck. It's her crystal necklace he's been playing with.

But sitting next to him there really is a genuine Levantine with a string of amber beads. Might be Greek, but looks like Syrian or Lebanese. Arabs have a passion for chemmy. The biggest knocker Crockford's has on its books is an Oriental potentate not here tonight.

Two of the calm businessmen sound like Leeds. Quite a few of the big gamblers in London today come from the Midlands and the North. Crockford's has started up a chemmy club in Leeds with a £2 and a £3 table: not big enough for the really ambitious ones, though.

The game may be bigger at the high table, but it's no slower. The shoe flies round. If, as a spectator, you want to follow the play you have got to get used to the French numberless cards, otherwise they will be swept away before you can count the pips.

Back in the big room all four tables are still going. How often do you see that haggard, twitching look which is supposed to mean ruin? One pretty young woman in a dress like a Christmas tree seems haunted down at the end of the £3 tables. She has a small pile of counters worth about £30 in front of her; her hands have formed a harbour wall round them, but they've all slipped out to sea inside five minutes. You could have bet they would from the expression on her face, a born loser's.

£   £   £

Just how much is lost and won? At the lowest table, where it costs £2 for a seat for one round of the game, about half an hour, it is perfectly possible to lose or win a few hundred. At the high table, which is surrounded by a gilt rail rather like an altar, it costs you £10 a seat, the minimum stake is £5 and the maximum opening bank is £200: you can lose or win several thousand here without the slightest difficulty. As Captain Black says: "It may not be so much by Continental standards, but it's quite enough to drop in one night."

According to Holland, the most anyone has lost at Crockword's so far is "a bit over £20,000". He denies categorically as "out of the question, beyond the bounds of possibility", a rumour that one well-known golfing millionaire lost £40,000 between 7 a.m. and 9 a.m.

Holland and his colleagues are emphatic about not allowing play to become too high (there seems to be no limit under the Act). The last thing they want, they tell you, is for anyone to be ruined. It interrupts the steady flow of seat money.

Nothing, with the possible exception of an empty gaming room, distresses the management more than seeing people constantly lose money they can't afford. "It's bad ethics," says Holland, "and bad ethics mean bad debts."

The club claims to be extremely strict about banker's references. "We would refuse membership to anyone who is salaried only, or the owner of a small one-man business," Holland says.

"Members are responsible for guests. Cash is okay, but if we get to know that somebody is playing who can't afford it, we do our best to bar them. Trouble is you often don't get to know until they've started losing. We don't automatically allow bridge- or poker-playing members into the chemmy room. Not all of them can afford it."

£   £   £

Sunday morning, 5 a.m. The non-Greek Yorkshire Scot, conspicuous by his grey curls, strolls in from the high table, changes a few £100 counters and starts punting from the sidelines at the only £3 table still playing.

At the high table most of the faces have changed, now. The two solid-looking businessmen are still there, also the younger man with the undone collar. The rest are new; some have moved in from the £5 table. A girl of about 23 with a sharp greyhound face and slightly underhung jaw goes banco for £200 and wins five banks running, playing like an old hand. She has a pile worth about £1,500 in front of her. An elderly man rather like a pale Mr. Punch comes up and pats her on the shoulder. Surely not another household party. This place is like a family outing.

Two more graduates from the £5 table. One is the county lady in the pony coat. The other is an ageless dark man with an enormous face like a lunar landscape. His cigar is the biggest in Crockford's. Yet you feel he might be a case of chemmyitis.

He plays at the old ladies' table. He plays at the £5 table. Here he is now chasing his luck on the principle of win a few hundred at the low table and see if you can turn it into a few thousand at the high table. He plays with great deliberation. No one could possibly look more cosmopolitan : if he turns out to be a rag-trade king with a villa in Hendon it will be intolerable. Now he speaks in a thick foreign accent. He is, in fact, a diplomat, a representative of a tiny State whose affairs are seldom pressing.

7.5 a.m. Sunday. Last coup at the high table. There's been a good deal of levelling out but the pony-coat lady has had a rough time. The diplomat has pulled up with a run of five winning banks. The calm, solid Midlander is still a few thousand up. He bancos again. The diplomat deals him a three and a two, making five. He taps the table to show he stands. The diplomat turns up his cards. A Queen and a three. He's got to draw. He draws with a quick flick of his long yellow forefinger. Ace. All over except for a cup of soup.

Foreign Correspondence

Ghetto Pilgrimage of Grief

from Patrick O'Donovan

Warsaw, April 20, 1963.

Just 20 years ago the Jews in the Warsaw Ghetto decided to resist their exterminators. They decided to die fighting rather than go patient to their deaths.

To celebrate this gesture, Warsaw this week has been crowded with quiet and sad-eyed strangers. They came from all over the world. Their stories have a familiar ring. This one recognised her child's body from a mass grave because of a tartan ribbon round its head. That one lost wife, children and parents. This one looks 70 and is 40. That one is not quite normal. They have brought with them a load of grief, racial horror, that is a little too heavy for humans. It has been a holy and terrible occasion.

Warsaw is a martyr among cities. It rose four times against the Germans. Every citizen has a story to explain the mystery of his survival. Death was casual and chancy here. It was a matter of which tram you caught, which road you took home. It was even worse for Jews.

Before the war, there were 330,000 Jews in Warsaw. Despite the endemic anti-semitism of pre-war Poland, this was part of the heartland of Jewry.

In the early years of the war, before the nature of the Final Solution was quite clear, the Jews were tidily settled in a part of Warsaw that had always had a Jewish majority. Most of it was a solid, rather Germanic-looking district where housewives cooked Borsch and served dumplings and there were lace doilies on almost every horizontal surface.

The Jews were brought in from all over Poland, until there were 500,000 of them in this ghetto. The streets were sealed with wire. There were 15 entrances guarded by soldiers. Often there were 15 people crowded into a two-room apartment. There was little work and little food. By mid-1942, 100,000 were dead of hunger and unnecessary diseases. Then the deportations began, which, of course, ended also in death. The Germans attacked the place on the Monday in Holy Week (Holy Week is the traditional time for pogroms). The Jewish resistance lasted longer than that of the French Army. A few score survived. And the ghetto was destroyed. Today there is a ghetto monument in Warsaw. It has the usual heroic, wild-haired group of supermen at its front. It has a sad frieze of patient men at its back. On its black marble plinth it stands in appalling isolation.

The ghetto has vanished. Its street plan has been erased. Where the heavy balconies overhung the respectable streets, where the fires burned and the middle-class jumped from their windows, where the young took aim and perished and the old put on their prayer shawls and said aloud, as they died in their various ways—"Hear, O Israel, the Lord is our God, the Lord is one. Blessed be the name whose glorious kingdom is for ever and ever"—where the scent of death once ruled there is now a nice housing development. Blocks of people's housing, nothing fancy, nothing expensive. There is no grass yet in the squares.

There is a pock-marked military prison that has survived, and the ruins of a classical building with a few letters from the name of a king left on its front. It is all neat and decent and a credit to the new Warsaw, and the whole district cries aloud for vengeance.

To celebrate the occasion there was a meeting in the Palace of Culture, where unnecessary things were said about politics and the Jewish action was given an exclusive Socialist bloc validity. It did not matter.

Some went to pray in the single surviving synagogue. It was built in the last century by a merchant called Nosik, and it is broken and battered and poor. It survived because it was made into a stable. It is hidden among ruins and the bald patches left by war.

Some went to the cemetery where some of the Jews lie. They said that bold, proud prayer with which this gentle people remember their dead—"Magnified and sanctified be their name"—asking nothing.

And they attended a ceremony before the ghetto memorial. A company of Polish soldiers presented arms. A band played an anthem. A general spoke interminably. And then began the procession of delegates. It came of a queue that curled round the square. They came from all over the world. They carried inscribed and ribboned wreaths as if they were gifts for the needy. The men wore hats and some of the women wept proudly. Drums were beaten steadily all the time. The line crept in awe up to the monument. Soldiers heaped up the flowers.

A seven-branched candle-stick flamed on each side of the cumulus of flowers. Men wore their medals and women their black. A great crowd watched, but uncertainly. This was a private occasion. This was the awful privacy of the Jews. And, God forgive us all, it only happened 20 years ago.

The Displaced Germans

from Neal Ascherson

Bonn, June 8, 1963.

Timmendorfer Strand is a cheerful little resort, where couples lick ice-cream and make their dogs splash about in the Baltic for bits of wood.

But under the pine trees, there is a strange new monument. It has no words. Instead, it bears a bronze map of Germany, a map which gives the passing foreigner a sudden pulse of fear.

For these are not the frontiers of 1963, nor even the officially valid frontiers of 1937. This is the giant Germany of 1914, the eastern border surging forwards to the Vistula and north to East Prussia, flooding over the territory of what could only be a partitioned Poland.

That pulse of fear beats for the Czech farmer who reads in his paper about a Minister of the Federal Republic who tells a rally of 300,000 Sudeten expellees that Chamberlain's Munich pact with Hitler is still in force (he tells them each year, and he told them so last Sunday). It beats for the Polish schoolchild, shown a German newspaper headed "Achtung Breslau! tomorrow, the Germans are coming!" (It was on the news-stands in May.)

The whole world is frightened of the 10 million Germans who were expelled from their homes in East and Central Europe when the Third Reich collapsed. And yet, so far, only the Germans themselves have understood that these millions are a spent force in international politics, and hardly a danger even to German democracy.

This is difficult to believe when one reads about the gigantic rallies —300,000 Sudetens at Stuttgart last week, 250,000 Silesians tomorrow in Cologne—when the pictures come in showing ranks of marching youth in uniform, shadowed by banners and pounding their drums, when the Press reports the speeches of all Germany's party leaders promising the expellees "self-determination".

It is hard to believe when ex-Nazis enthuse for the refugee groups, or when attendance at the rallies rises 10 per cent in three years. Yet it is so.

Two recent symptoms tell much. One was the virtual extinction of the Refugee Party (B.H.E.), slaughtered in May at the Lower Saxony elections in a State with the second biggest proportion of refugees. Another is the current row over a television poll, which is asking the ex-inhabitants of Breslau where their children were born, and whether they now belong to a refugee organisation.

This the refugee leaders violently object to, and the implication is obvious. They have some 2,500,000 members, but between meeting

133

old friends at a rally and voting for a "revanche" party there is evidently a wise and widening difference.

A Pomeranian rally at Godesberg was pathetic rather than alarming. Middle-aged men, often painfully scarred, circled the hall with their wives to the rhythm of old-time waltzes. At tables, each marked with the name of a Pomeranian town, fellow citizens shook hands and drank beer quietly.

A hand-out suggested that refugees with cars should buy a Darmstadt number plate (DA) to commemorate Danzig, or Altena (AL) for lost Allenstein. But it was a poor land, often, that they left, and life is better by the Rhine. The refugees, still sentimental, are every year more securely integrated.

If the rallies get bigger, so do many festivals in the world, from the Hanover Fair to Highland gatherings in New Zealand. If refugee bodies are still active, one should remember first that they are brilliantly organised and second that they have long payrolls of permanent staff.

The younger German generation is tired of their claims; at a Press conference this week, a Silesian organiser could be heard begging the German (not the foreign) Press to stop their hostile reporting of his rallies. As for their elders, there are endless tales about what leading politicians have said about the refugees late at night, with glass in hand.

Yet tomorrow both Chancellor Adenauer and Willy Brandt will be speaking to the Silesians at Cologne, and no doubt telling them once again what they want to hear.

Even now, no party dares to be the first to break the great taboo and say what, for the most part, it really thinks: that the Oder-Neisse line will have to be accepted as Germany's eastern frontier, that Munich was an act of aggression, that to demand "self-determination" for the expellees at a future peace treaty would ensure that it never got signed, that refugee politics have made a sane German foreign policy almost impossible.

They are still afraid of the refugee vote, imprisoned in a democratic but vicious circle, while the paper tiger of irredentism roars on and frightens Europe.

In the Valley of Pebbles

from Patrick O'Donovan

Vaiont Dam, October 12, 1963.

It was once a charming valley, filled from side to side with small green fields, vineyards and orchards. It was dotted with brightly painted farmhouses, each commanding its tiny estate. It was hemmed by the steep slopes of the Alps.

The road through it runs north from Venice to Cortina, for the ski-ing, and to Innsbruck and Salzburg. So it had wine shops that advertised in careful German and restaurants and small hotels and a reasonable prosperity.

Today, the valley, at least half-a-mile wide, is a vast, glinting expanse of pebbled mud, with the River Piave picking its shallow way down the barren plain.

Almost facing the high church is a narrow valley between sheer mountain walls. It points, at right angles to the Piave Valley, almost straight at the place where the village of Longarone stood.

It is cut by a dam, taller than it is wide, graceful, castellated along its top usually in shadow. And when the water came over its top, literally sloshed over by a rock fall, it shot out as from a tap, directed, concentrated, accelerated, out of its valley.

It crashed down on to the green fields below; it rushed across towards the village; it roared up and over the rock—perhaps a hundred feet high. It destroyed the church and left its tower and a painting of the Holy Family. It tumbled across the cemetery and fouled the fallen angels and the shattered crosses with oil and wrack. It broke open tombs and tore off the wall of a columbarium to show the coffins.

It turned and, scouring and grinding everything in its path, went off down the Piave Valley for its deadly journey towards the sea.

The essential fact is that it left nothing behind it.

Longarone and half a dozen other villages, the farms and the wine shops do not exist—except for those small parts that stood above the water. Still on the map, the villages are not on the face of the earth —even as ruins. And all the fields and growing things, the top soil, the trees and the people went with them. The valley floor is featureless.

About 30 bruised and broken people are in hospital. There remains now the finding of the dead, the prevention of epidemics, the opening of roads. The valley here can never be restored.

There has therefore been no call for an international rescue operation. The Italians have coped swiftly and efficiently. The Americans sent helicopters and a fleet of ambulances. But it has been mortuary work.

Hundreds of Italian soldiers and dozens of lorries and bulldozers have been mobilised in the valley. Later there will be need of money and the means of helping the survivors and of rebuilding the farms down river that were not utterly wiped away. Now they are busy cleaning up.

Up in the churchyard, a company of soldiers rebury the long dead. Others pick their way over the valley of sand searching. There is nothing to salvage.

Dead cows are carried away in chains at the back of breakdown lorries. Bulldozers push back the rubble at the edge of the flood. There is the smell of chlorine disinfectant. Helicopters go over and over the waste in the endless ugly search.

Every now and again, a small procession can be seen picking its way from the far side of the valley, over the mud and stones. It consists usually of four men in grey smocks carrying a stretcher covered with a white cloth.

The body is put into a red ambulance and the ambulance speeds away out of the valley—even though there is no real hurry.

Some 1,700 have been recovered dead. Perhaps 3,000 died in the path of the flood that killed 12 miles away from the dam. No one knows what lies under the new smooth valley floor.

Opposite the church tower of Longarone, the dam still stands in the shadows of its own valley. A chip has been knocked off part of its top by the flood. And the rock-fall is now piled up, visible on the other side, behind the highest dam of its sort in the world. It almost fills the basin of the dam.

A New Island for Iceland

from Matthias Johannessen

Reykjavik, November 16, 1963.

Today I have seen a new land on fire rising from the sea—a new creation making its mark on the map of the world.

It has been fine and clear in the south of Iceland and this was an unforgettable sight as the steam clouds from the submarine volcano close to the Westman Islands rose to 25,000 feet.

The new island is now 1,500 feet long and 130 feet above sea level where the depth is 60 fathoms. It is rising still and today it has been observed from ships and aircraft.

The south of Iceland, where the capital, Reykjavik, is situated, is always liable to earthquakes and eruptions. Today, from the coast about 50 miles from Reykjavik, I watched the column of steam, black then white, ever changing and rising. It reminded me of the column from an atomic bomb, though certainly more beautiful and much more wild. At the top the rays of the setting sun may be seen like a crown to the new-born island.

Thousands of people in cars, eager to see this wonder of Nature, are leaving the city of Reykjavik for the coast. In the highlands is Old Hekla, now more peaceful than in 1947 when it erupted.

Many people said Iceland is getting much larger and they could not conceal their patriotic pride. Others said this would mean an increase in Iceland's territorial waters. The new island would now become the southerly part of Iceland.

In the Westman Islands everyone has been out watching it. Hardly any work is done. All are spellbound.

The Westman Islanders welcome their new neighbour. They hope the eruption will not touch their own town carrying ash and lava: but they are optimistic. The children have been given a holiday from school to see a sight that will remain in their memories until they are old.

Scientists are also busy. Some think the island will disappear again. A coastguard vessel has got to within 500 yards of the eruption. Observers aboard said the island is made of pumice and lava. As it rises and the craters get above sea level, the eruption gets more like a land-borne volcano.

Icelanders have already begun thinking about its name. Some want to name it after Olafur Thors, who handed in his resignation as Prime Minister on the day the eruption started.

Others want to name it after Saint Brandan, an Irish monk who was the first to see the ocean burning near Iceland in the fifth century, 300 years before the advent of the Vikings.*

This new land of fire recalls to Icelanders the 1,000-year-old-poem, "Edda". In the poem powerful wonders of nature are described as "Earth rising from the sea." The proximity to wonders of nature has from the first put its stamp on the thinking and poetry of the Icelanders.

Icelandic and foreign ships have been warned not to approach too near this latest eruption as unexpected flood waves might rise and rock formations might endanger the ships.

Many fishermen want to know if the eruptions will influence the fishing as this is the chief spawning place south of Iceland. Time will show if it will harm the fishing industries of the Westman Islands, where hundreds of fishing boats are stationed. Trawlers of many foreign nations fish these areas, among them the British.

* *In the end it was named* SURTSEY, *meaning the island of* SURTUR, *the Nordic giant who stoked the fires of Hell.*

The Disgrace of Big D

from Cyril Dunn

Dallas, Texas. November 30, 1963.

People who live in this city call it "Big D". They've always used the top of their corporate voice to boast about anything thought likely to spread their fame—the tallest office building west of the Mississippi, the biggest and richest Baptist Church, the only bank with a lobby ceiling of pure gold.

Now, suddenly, Dallas finds itself on everyone's lips everywhere in the world, but in a terrible context. The appalling prospect confronts it that in the end Dallas will be remembered only as a place where somebody important was assassinated, like Sarajevo.

Some confused citizens are still inclined to boast, perhaps from force of habit, perhaps from a longing to feel normal again. The cab driver who brings you in from Love Field, one of the city's airports, invites you to agree that "this has sure been an historical week for Dallas", makes a sight-seeing detour round by "where it happened" and brags about knowing Jack Ruby, the night club operator who shot Oswald, the supposed assassin.

Most people you talk to seem hurt and ashamed. They feel that Big D has been disgraced. But they also insist that fate has hit them unfairly; they vehemently reject the idea that they ought now to be tormented by feelings of guilt. "This could have happened anywhere else" is what they go round saying, repeatedly.

And they refuse to let anyone admit guilt on their behalf. The millionaire Mayor of Dallas, Earle Cabell, is in some trouble for having made a faintly apologetic speech. "It has occurred to me these past few days," he has said, "that perhaps we have spoken too proudly of ourselves." Only the strongest emotion could ever have induced a mayor of Dallas to say that.

We were with a group of Dallas people when news of this act of civic self-abasement reached them. A woman obviously dressed by Neiman-Marcus, the Dallas store that dictates fashion to the incredibly rich women of Texas, lifted a proud chin and said: "I don't want him to apologise for me. I don't see why I should. I haven't done anything."

Even so, Dallas is being blamed for what happened to Kennedy outside the Texas School Book Depository, as perhaps no other American city would have been. There are obvious grounds for this, though they don't strike an outsider as being particularly firm.

The dead President was not universally loved in this city, certainly not by those who set out to control local political opinion. They still hate his brother Bobby and are not ashamed to be heard saying so even now.

Dallas is also by reputation a favoured resort of the Extreme American Right, notably the virulent and muddled inmates of the John Birch Society. When Kennedy fired General Edwin Walker for recommending the Birchite doctrine to his troops, it was to a shabby frame house in Dallas that he withdrew, still shouting, and here he flies Old Glory upside down whenever he sees the nation sliding another few yards towards Communism.

Dallas is also uncommonly rich in the fundamental religions. Their "chapels" in downtown Dallas have the size and grandeur of cathedrals and a bigger cash turnover than our own Church Commissioners. Some of them foster political extremity. One notable swayer of men has preached against evolution, against racial integration and, with particular spirit, against John F. Kennedy for President.

These Dallas vanguards have encouraged acts of political violence, unwittingly no doubt. But they are acts which would seem laughably trivial to, for example, the French. In the 1960 campaign Lyndon Johnson was mobbed in the lobby of a Dallas hotel and someone stuck pins in Lady Bird, his wife. And only last month Adlai Stevenson got into a fracas when he came here, with some hardihood, to speak on United Nations Day. People spat in his face and someone whacked him over the head with a placard allegedly inscribed "IF YE SEEK PEACE, ASK JESUS".

The Big Businessmen who run Dallas were dismayed by what happened to Stevenson, not because they are at all attached to him, but because of the damage this incident seemed likely to inflict on the Dallas image. So they set out to make the Kennedy visit last week a flawless success.

In the first reeling moments after the shots were fired some radio reporters, knowing the Dallas background, leapt to the conclusion that this must be a Rightist act. Now, of course, it is believed that Oswald was "a hate-spitting Marxist", to use the local phrase. General Walker and some others are satisfied that this clears Dallas of all blame. As he sees it, the shooting was simply a part of the Communist plot, and one of its first aims was to get Texans disarmed and left helpless.

But the odd thing is that although most Americans prefer the quick and uncomplicated explanation of any bewildering event, people do not feel that the city is entirely absolved by this one and keep calling for changes in the nature of the Dallas community as an act of redemption.

Dallas has deficiencies that an outsider may sense. Its ordinary people are kinder in chance encounters with strangers than almost any others except Tynesiders. But the city itself lacks grace and seems soulless.

Nobody could think the entrance to the Triple Underpass a fit place for a great man to die. It has a kind of cheap grandeur—concrete colonnades round an amphitheatre of grass, now patched with wilting flowers. In the background stands the great square box of masonry from which Oswald fired and the nineteenth century county courthouse, like a Teutonic fort, quite terrifying in its ugliness. The whole of downtown Dallas bears a chilling resemblance to Johannesburg, but is, if anything, more desolating because the local black people are subdued and self-effacing.

Dallas is the great financial and commercial city through which the zooming wealth of Texas is processed. It stands on the plain like an ill-constructed computer, the towers of the money moguls rearing beside the old two-storey frontier-type premises such as the Lazy-hour Piano Bar. The place has no old-established working class and no productive roots in its own site. "The only crop Dallas grows," said someone, "is money".

For twenty-five years this city has been run by a group of rich and powerful businessmen known as the Citizens Council. Stevensonian liberals, offered a rare chance to speak out by the presence of foreign reporters in Dallas, have been trying to establish some kind of mystical link between this group government and the assassination, though, not, of course, a direct one. They have argued that this rule by Boss Men has nurtured "an atmosphere of hate" in which even a lunatic act of violence might happen. They fervently believe that Kennedy's death at the Triple Underpass will mean the end of Boss Rule in Dallas.

It might be thought logical for a community of this sort to have such leaders. What they work for is "a proper climate for business" and this could well appeal to young Americans who come here to make fortunes.

But the Boss Men have foreshortened the democratic process. For years the formally elected rulers have been their choice and their agents. The Boss Men have decided what's good for Dallas and as a result people at the shabby end of town have suffered. Above all they are accused of having used crushing weapons against intellectual and spiritual dissent. Perhaps their worst fault in this horrible context is that they have kept alive in Dallas the old image of America to which the dead Kennedy was opposed.

Diplomacy Down on the Range

from Godfrey Hodgson

In President Kennedy's day, correspondents had now and then to follow him to sophisticated sea-shores—to "the other White House" at Cape Cod in New England or at Palm Beach, Florida. But President Johnson is a Texan and owns a ranch.

Austin, Texas. December 28, 1963.

The Chancellor of West Germany, Dr. Ludwig Erhard, arrived here by air today. He was welcomed at the airport by President Lyndon B. Johnson and the two men went straight to the Johnson ranch—fifty miles or more from here—for a two-hour talk on Berlin and Germany's position in Europe. . . .

When we got there, the only man who was at home in every sense today was the rancher of the L.B.J., who is also President of the United States.

He welcomed his guest under the live-oaks in the front paddock that runs down to the Pedernales River.

It was a real old-fashioned Texas barbecue. And it was also a virtuoso performance on the instrument of modern mass persuasion. Nothing was entirely artificial; yet nothing was accidental either.

The result was as intended: Dr. Erhard and his party and a couple of hundred reporters who have been spending Christmas down here, will carry away an album of images that will not fade.

There was the dusty farm track, lined with German and American flags. Half a dozen big Army helicopters stood around the midden. Walter Jetton, "kingpin of the barbecue men," handed out 300 lb. of spare ribs in paper napkins to hands more used to diplomatic canapés. Three youths plunked guitars and yodelled until they were shushed for the Secretary of State to say a few words about East-West relations.

We reporters wedged our paper cups of beer into the roots of trees and struggled to get the grease of the meat off our fingers so that we could scribble notes.

The officials, with even less practice down on the range, were even more self-conscious.

But the Johnsons took the whole thing in their stride. Mrs. Johnson, in green, and Lynda, aged 19, in red, escorted busloads of reporters round the back pasture, and showed them the family graveyard and the old schoolhouse.

The President was game for anything. A globe-trotting woman

141

correspondent opened up at him in German. He explained that he
went to school in German and English until the third grade; most
of his neighbours are descended from 1848 German settlers.

"I have forgotten most of it, except the dirty words," he said. But
it struck me what was left sounded more like German than the woman
reporter's efforts.

He volleyed back tricky questions about screw-worm and what
permits he needed to build the dam that keeps the Pedernales full of
water on the Johnson place. Then he mounted his horse, demonstrated the "Tennessee Walk", a strange lopsided pace that cowboys
use to stay in the saddle all day. Students of horsemanship noted
that he has a firm seat and good hands.

But to me the day on the ranch gave some true insight into the
very complex man who is now the President of the United States. He
really does like people; but he also understands how to make them
like him. He has his roots in the stony valley of the Pedernales; yet
he understands Washington as few have done.

I left the barbecue amused, but impressed, and sure that was how
I was meant to leave. And I remembered something Lynda Johnson
said as she showed us the one-room schoolhouse where her father
started school. "It may not look very civilised, but really it is."

With the Kurdish Rebel Army

from Gavin Young

*By crossing the Congo border at night, Gavin Young made
his way secretly to the rebel H.Q. in Portuguese Angola.
To get the first full story of the Naga rebellion against
India, he walked for eighteen days through the Burmese
jungle. To reach the Kurdish National Army at war with
the Government of Iraq, he again travelled alone across a
wild mountain frontier.*

For an outsider the road to Kurdistan and Mullah Mustapha
Barzani's Kurdish national army is long and arduous. It begins with
Buchanesque telephone calls and discreet meetings with gruff Kurdish
emissaries in New York, London and Paris; cryptic letters must be
exchanged with shadowy men in West Germany or Switzerland.
There are rendezvous in the Middle East ending in furtive journeys
by night across lunar landscapes to remote mountain frontiers.

For this correspondent, the final introduction to Kurdistan was
heralded by a long, cold wait in a hushed border valley; a protracted

flashing of signal lights that seemed unromantically futile until the appearance of a dim figure in turban and baggy trousers announcing in cheerful Arabic: "I've come to take you to headquarters. My name is Abdul Wahab. Don't worry. I'm the best-known smuggler in Kurdistan."

Clearly marked though they may be on the map, Iraqi Kurdistan's frontiers on the ground are extremely hard to determine. The best authorities are the local smugglers, who cross them several times a week. The frontier region is a petrified sea of bare mountain ridges riven by deep, lush valleys and icy torrents.

The Kurds live simply and well off the long, wide strips of cultivation and gardens and orchards heavy with grapes and pears and pomegranates. The hills that shelter them slope gradually from east to west until the sudden drop to the Kurdish cities on the plains—Irbil, Kirkuk and Khanaqin (the oil centres) and Suleimanya—held by Iraqi Army garrisons that seldom venture out except in massive convoys protected by tanks.

Iraqi operations are severely hampered by the fact that motorroads are exceedingly few in the mountain areas. Stony hill tracks, usable only on foot or mule, wind through village after village where armed Kurds, in or out of uniform, offer unfailing hospitality to friends and a murderous reception to enemies. For the Arab Iraqi troops the majority of Kurdistan is simply impenetrable. "We haven't seen an Arab for four or five years," said some villagers in the west.

In the east, nearer the front line, where the valleys teem with marching columns of Kurdish *Pesh Mergas* (partisans), almost every village is cluttered with platoons of large, moustachioed men slung with bandoliers, revolvers, submachine-guns and rifles.

At Kurdish political headquarters, in a wide ravine deep in the hills, there is a solid, no-nonsense atmosphere. In a three-roomed office with large glass windows, typists hammer their Olivettis under wall-maps streaked with red pencil and paper arrows marking Iraqi positions and units. Uniformed men come and go with coded messages between the office and the wireless room that links headquarters with the five Kurdish military commands—and with the two hero-worshipped generals, Barzani in the north, young Jallal Talabani in the south.

Two officers in charge—both former Baghdad Civil Servants—produce the nationalist newspaper, *Khabat* ("Struggle"), for clandestine distribution throughout Kurdistan, and even to Baghdad.

Near by is a battle school where new recruits—and there seem to be plenty of them—are taught the arts of ambush with live ammunition and "shell bursts" of gelignite. Sometimes they have a curious audience of Iraqi prisoners, mostly bewildered-looking youths in tattered clothes from homes in the hot south.

Still more prisoners—soldiers and policemen, ignorant victims of

143

what to them is evidently a pointless war—are clustered in a former jail captured by the partisans. Here 228 of them are paraded at dawn and led out to build new houses for Kurdish war-refugees.

A notable inmate is the former Iraqi C.I.D. boss from the Kurdish city of Suleimanya, Major Hamid al-Qadhi. A glum figure with handsome features and a fearsome reputation as a policeman, he was "lifted" from his car by the Kurds while on his way to a party. As an officer he is excused work. He posed for photographs at the door of his cell in pyjamas and overcoat, smiling wanly at Kurdish officers who had been his subordinates before they absconded from the police force.

The hard, well-disciplined, unfailingly confident Kurdish soldiers are impressive. The quality of their officers can be attributed to two main factors: the first, that Kurds are a dynamic people with a long martial history, many of whom were able to achieve high office in the Ottoman Empire and later to play an important rôle in the intellectual-political life of post-1918 Iraq; the second, that while formerly some of the best units and officers in the Iraqi Army were undoubtedly Kurdish, many, if not most, of these have now deserted to Barzani's national movement.

In central Kurdistan today one frequently meets large parties of Kurdish soldiers whose officers and N.C.O.s are clearly educated professionals, often speaking English, eager perhaps to recall some happy experiences at, say, the Staff College, Camberley, or the British Army's Small Arms School at Hythe. A number of Kurdish N.C.O.s I met had had fifteen or twenty years' service and some had served in the Arab-Israel war of 1948. Such training and experience coupled with the Kurds' natural aptitude and enthusiasm for guerrilla warfare, make formidable opposition for the Iraqi Army, which even Brigadier Aref probably would hesitate to class among the world's top ten.

The Kurds have plenty of small arms. Most of them the Russian Kalashnikov semi-automatic rifles and Diktariov light machine-guns, the Brens and British .303s, were captured from the Iraqi Army. So were the two-inch mortars and bazookas that recently began to play havoc on occasion with the Iraqis' Soviet and British tanks.

What they *could* do with, Kurdish officers say, is a few dozen heavy mortars. Their ever-repeated grouse is that they have so far received no outside help of any kind. And they are only mildly amused by the story they tell of the reply of the Soviet military attaché in Baghdad to his American opposite number who asked him why Russia supplied Iraq arms to crush the Kurdish people: "But this is the best way for us to supply the Kurds. They capture our weapons—the Iraqis foot the bill." It has cost Kurdish lives to build up the arsenal.

Kurdish military tactics follow a predictable guerrilla pattern and the partisan army is certainly no rag-tag affair. Kurdish officers have read the by now standard textbooks by Mao Tse-tung, Giap and Che Guevara.

"We can't face the Iraqi Army's tanks and planes in an open, pitched battle," explained the young Kurdish General Jallal Talabani. "We haven't got heavy guns. So we allow the Iraqis to occupy certain villages, then isolate them: force them to call up reinforcements, then ambush the convoys. We're good at that."

Because of these tactics and consequent supply problems Iraqi garrisons outside major towns are few. Often they consist of 200 to 300 men hemmed in Beau Geste forts, unable to move outside. Inaccurate supply drops by parachute have greatly benefited the Kurds. If periodic large-scale Iraqi offensives have achieved temporary success, decisive victory is frustrated by the impossibility of holding large areas of hill-terrain indefinitely. Even what seems to be an Iraqi plan to isolate the Kurds from their city food supplies and starve them out has so far failed. The partisans I saw are far from starving—the Kurdish interior is a land of milk and honey.

They eat bread, eggs, yoghourt and chicken stew from huge communal trays; sometimes there is lamb or turkey. They drink innumerable glasses of tea at all hours of day and night. Sugar and tea are smuggled over the Turkish and Iranian frontiers or bought clandestinely from Kurdish or Arab merchants inside Iraq: so is the petrol for a number of Land-Rovers and Jeeps—a few of them "borrowed" from Unicef teams in Iraq.

The time may come, Kurds say, when the partisans will be strong enough to attack the larger Iraqi-held towns. But they point out that, even if they took them, occupation would be ruled out by the certainty of Iraqi counter-bombing and swirling street-battles in which Kurdish civilians would be the main victims.

Suleimanya, one of the largest Kurdish cities, is almost completely surrounded by partisans established on a horse-shoe of enveloping hills. I saw Kurds manning camouflaged slit-trenches with bazookas and machine-guns dominating a main road already blocked by tank traps and mines. Young partisans described how they occasionally enter the city in civilian clothes and visit their families or make contact with the urban "underground" groups which report on troop movements and the activities of Kurdish collaborators.

Significantly more and more Kurdish recruits are young, city-bred and middle-class. A high percentage are students, doctors, lawyers. While in the north Mullah Mustapha Barzani directs a largely tribal force, in the centre and south the Kurdish revolution seems anything but tribal. Here urban Kurds are fighting side by side with hill peasants. There is a rule that no boys under 18 and no women may join up; they "must keep the homes alive".

Typical of the "new" Kurdish leader is Jallal Talabani, a thirtyish, much-travelled intellectual who is also a dynamic military commander. He led the Kurdish delegation to the abortive "peace talks" in Baghdad after the fall of Kassim (some of his fellow delegates are still in jail there). Now he commands two important military sectors and is an influential member of the Kurdish Democratic Party's six-man *politbureau.*

He lives close to his troops in the field. A short, cheerful figure, he likes to sit cross-legged in a circle of partisans and villagers, explaining party policy, joking, almost invariably addressing them by name. He works far into the night dictating orders by the light of a pressure lamp, commenting crisply and often acidly on news broadcasts from Baghdad.

Talabani told me: "We don't hate Arabs. I have an Arab colonel on my staff. We just want to be treated as Kurds and equals in one Iraq nation. We're not demanding a separate State." One day we walked through the rubble of a burnt village. It was still warm and smoking; the streets rutted and churned by Iraqi tank tracks. "You see what we are suffering. This sort of thing doesn't subdue us. Can't they understand that in Baghdad?"

Talabani and a 49-year-old writer and poet, Ibrahim Ahmed, are the prominent Democratic Party theoreticians. Talabani described Ahmed, who was then outside Kurdistan, as "leftist, progressive—like Sekou Touré of Guinea". Both men believe that one-party "centralised democracy" is the essential initial political formula for an autonomous Kurdistan in a federal Iraq.

Talabani vehemently denies that the Democratic Party is Communist-inspired, despite Barzani's twelve-year exile in the Soviet Union. In fact, Kurdish party "political guides" scattered through the country are at pains to explain to partisans that Communists are to be regarded as a threat to the nationalist movement. In one Kurdish jail I talked to several Kurdish Communists arrested for trying to distribute Communist literature.

Like other Kurdish officers, Talabani talks bitterly of the "double standards" that preclude even diplomatic support from the Afro-Asian group at the United Nations or elsewhere. "Frankly, we would have been better off if the British administration had stayed. Then all Africa and Asia would rush to support our struggle—it would be against a European Power, you see, and respectable."

It seems clear that 59-year-old Mullah Mustapha Barzani, the prestigious Grand Old Man of Kurdish nationalism, is no longer his people's sole inspiration and leader—although this implies no conflict between himself and his younger colleagues: "Barzani is just one man in a national movement," explains Talabani.

In the quiet, watered valleys, the bullet-scarred houses or the massive mountain caves many partisans live in, the feeling of isolation is sometimes very strong for the hundreds of Kurds who have given

146

up careers, families and a whole way of life for a seemingly endless prospect of battle and hardship. Men such as Colonel Namek Abdullah, a middle-aged ex-regular officer with grey, cropped hair and a hard, lined face, who said goodbye to a wife and four children in Baghdad a year ago and gravely explains: "I talked the situation over with my wife. She insisted that the only honourable thing was to join the partisans. I've no regrets, even if my four-year-old son is grown up before I see him again."

Or men such as one gnarled old Kurd who has already lost two brothers and a son in the war. Clutching his Russian automatic rifle in a group of partisans forty years his junior, he said savagely: "Iraq has to get money from Kuwait and arms from Russia, Britain and America to fight us. They send tanks up here like flocks of goats. That shows how strong we are. I have given more than three of my family because every Kurd killed is my relative."

A Night as Nkrumah's Prisoner

from Anthony Sampson

Accra, January 18, 1964.

Ghana, perhaps not surprisingly, is in a jumpy state about its security since the last attack on President Nkrumah; and the visit of Chou En-lai, the Chinese Prime Minister, last week, increased tension. The combination has not made the job of a journalist an easy one, as three of us discovered last Thursday.

We had tried, the night before, to find out about a rumoured reception for Chou En-lai. The whole visit had been surrounded in mystery; no schedule had been announced; plans had been proclaimed, then cancelled; and it turned out afterwards that the Chinese had specifically asked that no correspondents from unfriendly nations— particularly Indian or American—should be allowed near.

In Tunis, where America is much more popular, Chou En-lai had been quite visible and security was apparently casual; but in Ghana, apart from a morning's visit to Tema, he was almost invisible.

So we tried, on the Wednesday, to seek out the reception. We set off—a man from *Time*, a man from N.B.C., the American Broadcasting Company, and myself—in an Austin Princess which was (it so happened) the only hired car available but which turned out to have a special magic.

We went first to the State House, the official guest residence at which Chou En-lai was staying, but there was no one there. Then later we set off for the castle, a big white fortress above the cliffs where Dr. Nkrumah has been staying since the last shooting.

We drove up to the big black gate, the sentries immediately jumped with their bayoneted rifles pointed straight at us; but the man from N.B.C. explained that we were following Chou En-lai, and we were allowed into the courtyard outside the main entrance to the castle.

A guard came up to us; we explained that we were looking for a reception and he said—as was now obvious—that there was none; and we drove off, leaving our names at the guard's request. We thought no more of it and went back to dinner with an American diplomat.

The next evening drinking on the terrace at the Ambassador Hotel, two of us—Jim Wilde of *Time* and myself—were approached by a courteous detective who asked if we could come to the police head-quarters to be questioned. We went off immediately, to the brand new building of the police and waited in that bare and timeless world of police stations everywhere. We were obviously caught up in the slow machinery of interrogation.

I was questioned for about half an hour by the polite detective. I was asked why I had been to the castle, what we had said to the guard and what our business was in Ghana. There was a mixture of grimness and laughter, very typical of Ghana, together with a rather alarming sense of limitless time. After the questions the detective was waiting to hear from the police commissioner and he brought two books down from the shelf for us to read.

He gave me a book by J. B. Priestley and the book he took for himself looked very familiar. I asked him what it was and he said: "It's called *Anatomy of Britain*. It was given to me by the Ghana High Commissioner in Tanganyika." I felt a sudden intense relief as if meeting a long-lost friend. I asked him if he knew who had written it. He looked down at the book and then at the sheet of paper in front of him. He said, "It's you!" and burst into laughter. From that point I felt much less seriously worried.

Soon afterwards the telephone rang and the detective said the Commissioner would see us in the morning. He took me, now separated from Wilde, down to the car, and I was told I would go back to the hotel. But the car passed by the hotel, and went into the police station at Jamestown, the old and rather seedy quarter of Accra. I was taken inside: it was a small police station of the early colonial period, with crumbling walls and a strong smell: and I realised rather abruptly that I was going to spend the night there.

I was asked, with rather tentative authority, for my watch, belt, shoes and tie. I asked to be allowed to ring up the High Commissioner, trying to put on a gunboat voice, but was not allowed to. There was a certain joviality about the place which made it hard to be cross. I was put into a cell—one of two in the police station—with a wooden board and a blanket, and locked in.

I lay awake listening to the extraordinary variety of Accra noises through the night—the patriotic songs, the drinkers leaving the Seaview Hotel, the early morning cock-crows. I felt rather relieved at not having to take any more decisions.

I was allowed out of the cell for a breakfast brought over specially from the Seaview Hotel, and was able to talk to my neighbour in the next-door cell. He was an engaging man from Timbuktu, clothed only in a towel, who presided over the cells with a dignity and grandeur of a prince receiving homage.

Then the special branch arrived and drove me back to the hotel to search my room. They found a not very friendly article I had been writing, and other papers. The searches were stern and humourless. I was driven back to police headquarters, with Wilde and the *New York Times* correspondent, Lloyd Garrison, who had also now been taken, presumably by mistake. We had all by this time been in touch with our embassies.

We waited endlessly at headquarters; we were taken back to the hotel for lunch; then back for more waiting. The atmosphere was still timeless and rather Kafkaesque, but humanity kept on breaking through.

Then at last we were taken in to make statements and for more questions. "Why do you write these unfriendly things? Why do you say these things about us?"

Soon after we were, all three of us, taken before the deputy commissioner, a very amiable man who had our statements before him. He said he accepted our accounts, explained that there had been a misunderstanding and that Ghana was very anxious about security, and apologised for keeping us. We were free. An American diplomat was waiting outside to drive us back to the hotel.

A Proud People Facing Death

from Anthony Sampson

From the former Belgian territory of Rwanda, early this year came shocking news of wholesale massacre. Our roving correspondent sent us this account after seeing some of the refugees in neighbouring Uganda.

Kampala, February 15, 1964:
Along the low slopes of the Oruchinga valley, in Southern Uganda, are scattered 20,000 refugees from the slaughters of next-door Rwanda.

They are all shapes, sizes and conditions; but the most striking are the tall, thin men and women, with long fingers, wide eyes and fastidious noses, whose shape proclaims that they are the Watutsi, the disinherited rulers of Rwanda.

You can see them standing and sitting by the bare camps, with all their history in their faces. Thousands arrived only last week in lorryloads, not from Rwanda, but from the Uganda frontier—where they had already been settled, but from where they had been up-rooted to prevent them organising raids.

They bring nothing with them but a few gourds, a grass mat, a shirt or two; and they are dumped on the open slopes, without any kind of shelter.

The boys set about cutting down papyrus stalks and elephant grass to make frail round huts; but the elder ones just stand, and watch, and talk, while the rain pours down. They look, as they are, unshake-ably proud.

For, in spite of all the horror of Rwanda in the last six weeks, the the Watutsi are still determined to go on fighting. They cannot face the facts of their exile and humiliation.

There are probably not more than 500,000 Watutsi left in Africa : like lions, they are a rare, proud breed, becoming still rarer.

Their history is dangerously romantic. For Europeans the Watutsi, with their air of the noble savage, have always had a special fascina-tion. Even Belgians fall under their spell, fall in love with their women—or their men—and cannot escape them. But this position as the white men's favourites has, in the end, helped to undo them.

Long before the white men arrived, the nomadic Watutsi had come down from the Sudan in the fifteenth century, with their cattle and their arrogance, and conquered Rwanda and its surrounding regions. They enslaved the Bahutu—the local Bantu tribe—and established their own monarchy, with a Mwame at their head.

They were immensely tall, they lived off milk for most of their childhood, and they had (and still have) a deep contempt for all other black men.

The Mwame kept his court which, like the Kabakas in Buganda, existed as a feudal enclave in the midst of simpler tribal societies.

Then, in the 1950s, the wind of change blew through Rwanda and Belgium. The new Belgian Government, becoming anxious, veered away from the Watutsi and began to encourage the Bahutu. The Bahutu, sniffing democracy, rebelled against the Watutsi in the first of a series of massacres, and when the Belgians instituted elections the Bahutu achieved a majority. Belgium, as lamentably as in the Congo, left behind an insoluble problem. By the time of independence, the power of the Watutsi was already broken, their king exiled, and thousands had fled to the neighbouring countries—Burundi, Uganda, the Congo and Tanganyika.

But they could not accept their fate. They disliked the strange people, they were lazy, and they kept their loyalty to the Mwame. The toughest of them organised "The Cockroach", a secret terrorist gang to recapture Rwanda. They got money and support from friendly tribes and more mysterious sources—including, according to some, the Chinese (though such a grotesque alliance seems scarcely credible.)

They raided Rwanda from time to time and then, last Christmas, launched their reckless two-pronged raid from the Congo and Burundi, which nearly captured the capital. But the cost of the raid in reprisals was appalling; and the chances of this small aristocratic minority ever regaining Rwanda must always be remote.

The massacre of the Watutsi seems for the time being to be finished, though there are still reports of murders in country areas. But the desperate conflict remains; the exiles still talk about guns and money, and are longing for a new chance to break into Rwanda; and 250,000 Watutsi are still inside the country, a helpless prey to reprisals.

Now the refugees remain on the beautiful but unwelcoming hillsides of Uganda. It is an extraordinary sight, these exotic and elegant people, still seeming very serene, speaking fastidious French, dropped in this empty valley.

Rousseau might well have admired it: but it is a desperate situation, desperately in need of help. The whole valley, unbelievably, is run by a nineteen-year-old Lancashire schoolboy (who came out for a year's voluntary service overseas) and a Red Cross nurse, and they are impossibly overworked and understaffed.

The Uganda Government has given what help it can, and has bravely accepted all refugees, but it has its own problems and needs, and this is an international responsibility.

What will become of the Watutsi? Like other defeated rulers, they have brought much of their misery on themselves and they remain terribly self-destructive. But they are a fascinating people, and they need protection—from themselves and from others. They have been caught up in the most ruthless of all Africa's upheavals, and they have paid for it horribly.

What Went Wrong in Africa?

by Colin Legum

Early in 1964 there were fresh outbursts of violent revolt in some of the new black States of Africa. In Zanzibar the Africans overthrew their new but mainly Arab Government. Then came a chain of mutinies in the black armies of East Africa.

The ominous turn of events in Zanzibar, Tanganyika, Uganda and Ghana is only a small part of the story of what is happening all over Africa. Three regimes were toppled in French-speaking Africa within the last twelve months. In Dahomey and Togo it was the result of Army mutinies; in Congo-Brazzaville the Army stepped in to end populist revolt. There have been two recent attempts to overthrow the Ivory Coast Government. And there have been serious plots against the Governments of Senegal, Chad, the Cameroun, Tunisia and Morocco.

The first war between two African States, Algeria and Morocco, is still hanging fire. An incipient war is brewing between the Somalis, Ethiopia and Kenya.

A massacre of the proud Watutsi is still going on in Rwanda. A revolt by the non-Arab tribes of southern Sudan is now being put down. There is mounting violence in South Africa. And there is a full-scale armed revolt in Angola. Already, all but five of the thirty-six independent African States have abandoned any pretence of practising parliamentary democracy.

It is hardly surprising that people are feeling that something has gone wrong. Can it be, they ask, that colonialism was ended too soon? That perhaps, after all, Africa is not yet ripe for independence? That, by "pulling out", the West opened the sluicegates to anarchy and Communism?

What is happening in Africa today was not only forseeable but foretold. The sudden ending of firm colonial rule over an entire continent could lead only to an era of turbulence—even if there were no ideological world struggle playing around Africa's shores.

It was never a part of the case for ending colonialism that this would automatically lead to the emergence of peaceful, stable, and parliamentary societies; the long history of Europe itself, not to mention Latin America, was there to discourage such facile optimism.

The case was twofold: that alien rule was morally indefensible; and that it had also become increasingly unpractical and unrewarding. Getting out of Africa was, therefore, as much for the good of Europe as for the Africans; to have tried to stay on would have produced a situation much worse for us than the one which confronts us, and which—awkward as it is—is by no means specially threatening to the West.

Unfortunately, too many people (including African leaders) seem to have made the mistake of equating freedom from alien rule with political freedom in Africa. But although these two freedoms are utterly different, the ending of alien rule is an essential first step in the process of democracy finding its own indigenous roots.

Colonialism did not leave behind it either the example of good democratic Government or the means for achieving it. The new States were left sadly lacking in three major requirements. First they were, with few exceptions, desperately poor; to add to their difficulties, the nationalist struggle greatly raised the peoples' expectations of a better life. Second, they lacked trained manpower in almost every department of State. Third, they lacked national cohesion. All were artificially created out of diverse tribes and are separated from one another by artificial frontiers.

In one form or another these three elements have played a major part in each of the crises that has followed independence. Nor were these early crises helped by the kind of Constitutions that were often given to the new States. In Zanzibar, for instance, the Constitution, which denied power to the majority of the electorate, created the conditions that invited an armed revolt to overthrow "the Arab-controlled Government".

One of our chief mistakes has been in the training of Africa's Armies, which have become a more crucial factor in the new States than was generally expected. Yet the Army is the only institution in all the former colonial territories (British, French and Belgian) where Europeans have been retained in the top command—albeit at the request of the new Governments.

The result was that, after independence, the Army alone was expected to take its orders from Europeans. While African politicians, Civil Servants and even policemen could get rapid promotion, the inexperienced African Army officer could not. Resentment of this situation caused the revolt of the Congo Army against Lumumba, and of the Togo Army against President Olympio. It also set off the mutiny in Tanganyika and threatened to start one in Kenya and Uganda.

The link between these two events and Zanzibar is that the disgruntled Armies of the mainland (who had made their discontent known to their Governments nine months ago) were galvanised by the success of the *coup* in Zanzibar: it showed that Governments were neither sacrosanct nor unmovable.

The mutinies in Tanganyika and Uganda had nothing to do with the Communists; they may have had more to do with Sandhurst, which trained the officers of Tanganyika and Uganda to regard themselves as an *élite*; and *élites* don't like being treated as subordinates.

Western observers of the African scene have reacted variously to the emergence of "strong Governments". On the one hand many criticise all measures taken by the new Governments to prevent the fissiparous tendencies from tearing their new States apart. But when things have gone seriously wrong (as in Zanzibar and Tanganyika) often the same people have criticised the African Governments' failure to act firmly enough in anticipating trouble.

Like it or not, it is clear from the experience not only of Africa but equally of Asia and the Middle East, that the democratic procedures known in North-Western Europe offer no substitute for "strong Government" during the transitional period after independence. Gaullist France—or, if things get even worse, the "Peoples' Democracies" of Eastern Europe—rather than Britain, seems to be the likely pattern of development.

But even if one understands why single-party rule is mostly inevitable under present circumstances, that is no reason for believing that democracy has no future in Africa. There was a time when democracy had no place in Europe.

Democracy, where it exists, has only emerged out of prolonged struggles for power. It is unreasonable to suppose either that Africa will be able to take a short cut to democracy or that Africans are inherently incapable of producing democratic societies of their own. If the swing today is towards the single party State, the swing tomorrow will be against it. Africa will, no doubt end up in much the same way as other continents, with a wide variety of Governments.

What can we learn from these first years of African independence? The essential lesson is that the mutinies, revolts and *coups* have their roots in real problems; and that, even if Communists and other neo-colonialists try to exploit them, the original causes remain real.

There are a number of realities about modern Africa which need to be understood if Western policies are to have any chance at all of successfully helping Africa's leaders to win the long-term battle for democracy—for their own sake as much as for ours.

First, Africa's poverty and backwardness are conditions which its energetic leaders refuse to accept; they are determined to advance rapidly into the technological age. They still prefer to do this in co-operation with the West if its policies are geared towards their objective. However, they have come increasingly to feel the Western policies are not being as helpful as they should be, especially over its trade and aid policies.

Second, it is quite impossible for Africa to grow strong, economically or politically, under the conditions of Balkanisation which characterise the post-colonial era. By the time the remaining colonies become free, there will be at least fifty African States; they will share among them only 225 million people—a little more than half of

India's population. If one remembers that more than half the total population is concentrated in only five countries, the enfeebling smallness of the other States can be imagined. The drive for Pan-African unity is bound to grow stronger, and the disputes over sovereignty sharper. The opportunities opened up by these rivalries have already been noticed by the Communists and some others.

Third, Africans will not accept "racial inferiority" in any form. This means that whatever their disputes with each other, they will certainly find common cause in fighting the white minority Governments of Southern Africa. It means, too, that they will assert themselves in international affairs to stake their claim to political parity with the more advanced continents.

These three realities are expressed in a revolutionary spirit which is more in tune with the ideas of the Communists than of the West. African socialists seldom look to social democrats for inspiration; they tend increasingly to look to the authoritarian Marxists.

Does this mean that the Communists are likely to gain ground rapidly in Africa? So far, they have gained very little. Their adherents had a finger in one of the attempted *coups* in the Ivory Coast as well as in the plot in Morocco. They have successfully infiltrated the group of young Ghanaians responsible for the policy of the ruling party's theoretical organ, *The Spark*. They have a number of supporters in the new Government of the Zanzibar People's Republic. On the debit side they have lost a lot of ground in Guinea and in Egypt, and they have failed to retain much of their influence with the African Freedom Fighters.

The reason for this is that they, too, are baulked by yet another African reality: the strong belief in non-alignment.

Even if some African leaders are beginning to feel that the Communists perhaps have more to teach them about their economic problems than has the West, they nevertheless strongly resist the entanglement of Communist alliances. This attachment to non-alignment does more than anything else to baulk the Communists.

The opportunities, therefore, for the West to establish a friendly relationship with Africa remain as great as always. But to take advantage of these opportunities the West must try to understand what the African revolution means to the Africans, instead of assessing it only in terms of Western interests. And having understood the true mood of the African revolution, the West should reformulate its policies to make them less equivocal in African eyes, and make Western policies more comprehensible, more meaningful and acceptable to the real needs of the African revolution.

Having withdrawn from Africa for sound political reasons, the West must now resist the temptation of still trying to "run the show", and should concentrate instead on protecting its proper interests, which are only economic and diplomatic.

People

Stalin Face to Face

by Hugh Lunghi

As interpreter with Winston Churchill at his great encounters with the Russian leader, Mr. Lunghi had a rare opportunity to study Stalin at close quarters.

Stalin has been dead ten years and buried twice—once mummified and on display in the mausoleum in Red Square, and then out of sight at the foot of the Kremlin wall.

In Russia eighteen months ago three people said to me, "Stalin has gone, but his shadow is still with us." But only one of them, an older man said it with a shudder, as though the ghost might yet materialise.

According to latter-day Communist Party leaders who knew him —led by Khrushchev—the man who created the long-lasting shadow was clearly a monster, guilty of unspeakable cruelties, bestialities, mockeries, outrages; a mass murderer. I observed Stalin closely over a period of six years, and he could give a totally different impression.

At the war-time conferences and banquets I saw and heard Western leaders praise and flatter Stalin in public and private, and in turn be flattered by him. I saw them shake him warmly by the hand which (so Mr. Khrushchev has since told us) was responsible for the deaths of "thousands of absolutely innocent people". I shook that hand myself on many occasions, was patted on the back by it, and received glasses of tea from it.

Had I been in a position to add my praise and flattery, no doubt I should have done so with the rest—at least to begin with. Only later, and perhaps because as an interpreter I could stand back and observe the man and some of his mental processes, did I wonder.

Part of the answer to the riddle lay in his contrived inaccessibility. The build-up of atmosphere before one even approached the gates of the Kremlin had its effect, if only subconsciously, on even the most hardened statesmen.

We, and all foreign visitors, were always instructed to report to the Borovitsky Gate of the Kremlin, at the farthest point diagonally from Stalin's quarters.

We drove to the Kremlin past clusters of three or more police permanently stationed at each road junction, who telephoned the next cross-roads, and thus passed us down the route.

A black saloon pilot-car led the way up the fifty-yard drive to the main portal. As soon as we passed the outer gate a bell, set off by a photo-electric cell, started ringing continuously. The arched portal contained guard rooms on either side, and a major of the MVD, the blue-capped, uniformed secret police, inspected our chauffeur's documents and peered inside the car, while three or four N.C.O.s on guard duty stood around. All wore revolvers.

Only when we emerged from the gateway inspection did the warning bell stop ringing.

In the entrance hall of the Kazakov Senate House we would be saluted by another pistol-carrying MVD guard of a colonel and two or three captains and lieutenants. A lift took us, in the charge of the colonel, slowly up two floors, and down long and high corridors, at each turn of which stood one of the armed praetorian guards to the remote place where Stalin waited.

Apart from the armed guards, the corridors were deserted. There was the same chilling silence inside the building as outside in the deserted grounds. An odour of Makhorka, the coarse black Russian tobacco, reminiscent of stale cabbage, seemed faintly to pervade the building.

Massive double doors were padded with greenish-brown quilted hide. Through one pair we entered the ante-chambers of Stalin's suite. A small posse of armed officers, the personal bodyguard, clustered at one side of the ante-chamber, at their head a squat man in the uniform of a general. Without announcing us, he quietly opened the double doors leading into a panelled study-conference room.

At the other end of it, a few paces in front of a desk, stood a humble-looking little old man. His withered left arm was somehow drawn up and bent at the elbow so that his upturned hand rested against his solar plexus. His right hand was cupped under the left one.

He wore a plain grey tunic buttoning right up at the neck, and decorated only by the small gold star of a Hero of the Soviet Union. His trousers, with sharp creases, were very wide, so that they only just revealed the tapering, square-ended shoes with built-up heels. He looked like an old-fashioned uncle.

As we entered he took a step or two towards us over the fine carpet, his interpreter just behind and at his side. Stooping, with his head slightly inclined, so that he looked nobody in the eye, Stalin shook hands with all our party. His grip was firm but not heavy; his hand not large, but square and rather soft. The hand-

157

shaking was repeated all round with the interpreter in grave and formal courtesy.

Stalin invited us to sit at the long green-baize conference table, extending along two-thirds of the side of the thirty-foot room, on the straight-backed dust-sheeted chairs, at the end nearest his own flat-topped desk. On his desk stood three round upright containers filled with dozens of sharpened pencils, a couple of pads, a heavy marble inkstand with cut-glass wells of red and blue, and a marble-based metal table-lamp.

Stalin sat, not at the head of the table, but opposite us with his back to the wall, on which hung portraits of Russia's great captains of the past, Suvorov, and Napoleon's opponent, Kutuzov. Our backs were to the windows, which at night were curtained with white-silk blinds.

On the table were ashtrays and several green-and-gold striped boxes of Dukat and Luxe, the top-quality Russian cigarettes with cardboard holders. Stalin would help himself to these frequently. Only once or twice in six years did I see him smoking his pipe.

During the talks Stalin would pick up a pencil and doodle, drawing sometimes geometric figures which developed into savage-looking animals, sometimes black, thick, curved arrows like those used on military charts.

After an hour or so, glasses of lemon tea, in silver filigree holders, would be brought in with petit-fours and chocolates. No alcohol on these occasions.

Stalin can hardly have been more than 5 ft. 5in. in height; strongly and squarely built, but not broad. At this time, during the war, he was 64, but his movements were smooth and cat-like. His hair was iron grey and still fairly thick, and his moustache bushy. But his sallow skin was wrinkled and his pock-marks showed, except when thickly covered with the talcum powder he was treated with after his evening shave.

His prominent nose with its elongated nostrils appeared more hooked from the habit of narrowing and wrinkling up his rather muddy eyes.

But hardly did one recover from the surprise of seeing the remote emperor cut down before one's eyes to almost less than human size than the sound of his voice produced a second shock. It, too, was curiously colourless, his delivery flat and monotonous, with a marked Georgian accent.

Up to this time I had heard the Georgian accent only as a joke. In the music-hall, or in telling an anecdote, any Caucasian accent is to the Russian language what Wigan Pier Lancashire is to English. For the first few seconds I found it difficult to take Stalin's words seriously. It made him seem for a moment faintly ridiculous.

Stalin, I soon noticed, was deliberate in making the best of his disadvantages, and often he liked to get his interlocutor off on the wrong foot. Though he habitually fostered the image of a modest man, telling visitors with a self-deprecatory air of humility that he owed all to "the people", he played the gambit hardest in my experience when he received Lord Mountbatten at the Potsdam Conference of 1945.

In his opening greetings and compliments, Lord Louis spoke of Stalin's achievements in peace and war. Stalin replied that he had done his best, but that really it was to the Russian people he owed everything. He returned to this theme several times during the conversation as if to play up the gulf that lay between him and his princely guest.

At the Bolshoi Theatre gala performance in honour of Churchill's visit in October, 1944, Stalin withdrew to the rear of the imperial box to allow Churchill to take the plaudits. It was only after I had seen this kind of performance on other occasions that I became convinced it was part of a calculated act to convey the picture of a modest leader in the image of Lenin; but in Stalin's case a kind of inverted vainglory, along with the apparent artless manner of his speech and the ultra simplicity of his dress.

I never saw Stalin behave in an overbearing or arrogant way to any foreigners, but he behaved thus to his own colleagues. Rarely in six years did I hear him laugh—a dry, repressed sound. The loudest laugh I heard from him was when Field-Marshal Montgomery was ragging Molotov at a Kremlin banquet. Montgomery had chaffed Molotov over the riotous and lazy life which he pretended the sombre Soviet Foreign Minister had led on visits to New York. Stalin elaborated on the joke, dragging it out until one got the uneasy feeling that there was some menace in it. Molotov would stolidly submit to being the butt of Stalin's ponderous jokes, but I never saw any sign of mutual irritation.

But I saw Maisky go pale when Stalin toasted him at a banquet, referring to him as the "poet-diplomat". There was an earlier poet-diplomat in the Russian foreign service, Alexander Griboyedov, Tsarist Ambassador to Persia. He was assassinated in his embassy in Teheran and the Tsar did not avenge his death.

One day Stalin's own interpreter, Pavlov, was scared stiff by his master. Someone had presented Pavlov with one or two volumes of Burns or some other Scots or English poet. Stalin had evidently heard about it and in his presence exclaimed in seeming jest, "Pavlov is getting too friendly with the foreigners." After that it suddenly became hard to have my usual friendly chat with Pavlov before and after meetings. I tried to invite him to meals, but he refused, even a semi-official party invitation.

At receptions a tomb-like silence descended on the company and a chill that seemed to cut off the Russians' very breath at the moment

Stalin appeared. As soon as he spoke the tension eased a bit, but did not disappear.

Never do I recall having felt physically sick at the relationship between two human beings except when I saw Vyshinsky, the diplomat and ruthless public prosecutor, in Stalin's presence, Vyshinsky behaved like a frightened dog, bending, nodding in assent, and backing away from his master, and Stalin quite clearly despised him. Before one of the conference sessions at Yalta I overheard Stalin say to a group of his lieutenants, including Vyshinksy, "With Vyshinsky all things are possible. He will jump over anything we tell him."

The gradations of fear of Stalin, which ran from the trembling aged waiters at the Kremlin banquets (with plain-clothed MVD men standing behind them—one to every two or three) up to the most beribboned military chiefs, were fascinating to observe.

He treated politicians—the Maliks, Zorins and Gromykos—and the top-rank soldiers—Bulganin, Vassilievsky, Koniev, Voronov—like messenger boys and batmen, and they behaved like that in his presence.

Among the diplomats, Litvinov seemed to me to lose least dignity and self-respect, but Litvinov always seemed withdrawn into himself. Only Molotov, more closely engaged, seemed to be free of the nagging anxiety that haunted the faces of the others. Stalin mocked him openly, and Molotov took it all impassively.

The relationship reminded me of that between a headmaster and a favourite sixth former. When technical points were under discussion, as with the currency problem during the Kremlin talks on Berlin in 1948, Molotov had done his homework and produced the answers for Stalin, sometimes leaning over to correct the master's figures. I never saw any other among Stalin's advisers dare to interrupt or correct him. At Stalin's funeral on March 9, 1953, Molotov, Malenkov and Beria delivered orations. Only Molotov is reported to have wept. I believe it.

At social functions Stalin asked admirals to get him glasses of tea, generals to fetch coffee. Bulganin, once dilating on the merits of Pertsovka, the peppery vodka served with cold sucking-pig in aspic, told me "all Soviet army generals" drank this fire-water. Perhaps it was to give them Dutch courage. Bulganin himself, sitting next to me at such a meal, kept his eyes and ears fixed on Stalin, straining to catch every word and gesture. Once, when Montgomery after dinner was asked by Stalin if he would like to see a film in the Kremlin's private cinema, and declined on the grounds that he was bent on an early start for England next day, a look of horrified disbelief seemed to pass over the faces of the assembled Soviet brass, and from the murmur I caught the word *Smelo*! ("That's bold!"). But when Stalin turned deliberately and eyed them they were silent immediately.

The nearest I ever saw to affection in Stalin was in his treatment of Voroshilov, but there was no warmth in it. Voroshilov stood in Stalin's military ménage as a glorified old retainer. Stalin treated him rather like a useless old dog kept on as a reminder of more adventurous days. In Soviet mythology, Voroshilov was one of the great cavalry captains of the civil war against the Whites. He turned up everywhere in his marshal's uniform and was still a member of the War Council, but Stalin would humiliate him at will.

At the first plenary session of the Tehran conference Stalin said he had not expected military discussions and therefore had brought no military experts. But, he added, Voroshilov might do and would try his best. Voroshilov, who sat looking at Stalin with his beady eyes, did not bat an eyelid.

Stalin's manner towards foreigners was quite different. He was seemingly deferential, never allowed himself to be seen disconcerted, but yet liked to disconcert others. In the Kremlin in 1948, three years after Potsdam, Stalin received three Western representatives who had come to try to get some solution to the Berlin blockade. He scarcely waited for the greetings and preliminaries to be finished before he shot out at the Western delegates: "Have you any delegated authority to negotiate?" Stalin knew that the talks were meant to be only exploratory at that stage; his gambit served to grab the advantage, put the Westerners on the defensive.

He repeated the tactic at the next meeting with: "Do you want to settle the whole thing now? I've got a plan for Berlin. It is all written out ready for us all to agree to."

He blew hot and cold as it served him. He would send Churchill, and occasionally Roosevelt, abusive telegrams about the alleged failure of Allied convoys to deliver war materials to Russia. But when Churchill's envoys, Eden or Ismay, visited Stalin shortly afterwards, he would be unexpectedly full of sweetness and light. I have heard him turn from menaces to bewildering reasonableness in less than a minute; switch from elaborate courtesy to vulgar vituperation just as fast, all without raising his voice.

He practised many forms of "one-upmanship". When Montgomery once visited him he took as gifts to Stalin a couple of his own books and a case of whisky, which I carried into Stalin's study. Stalin scarcely gave a glance at the case, and his first words to Montgomery as he indicated the gifts, but before Montgomery had got through his formal greeting, were: "Yes? And what do you want from me?"

He kept the "one-upmanship" going all through that interview. Towards the end, Montgomery produced an autograph book and politely asked Stalin if he would write in it. Stalin acted as though he did not understand (though I remembered that at Potsdam Stalin himself on one occasion walked round the banquet table collecting autographs on a menu). But now he continued to affect non-comprehension, until Montgomery had been forced into the situation of seeming to be begging. Then he rose slowly from the conference table, walked over to his desk, picked up a pen and without pause wrote in the book. Montgomery passed it to me to translate. Stalin had simply written his "regards to the British soldiers", and signed it "Stalin".

He had a flinty sneer for Churchill at Potsdam when the Briton spoke of the hardships that would face the British people in the coming winter if they were compelled by Stalin's proposals for the Ruhr to supply part of Europe with coal out of their own depleted resources. Stalin chipped in that Russia was in a far worse plight. This was true enough, but then Stalin added that he could tell the conference just how things were in Russia, but that if he did he was afraid Churchill would burst into tears. Churchill flushed slightly and looked glum.

One of the Stalin myths that still persist abroad is that he had a brilliantly rapid mind and always spoke to the point. It is true enough that he had a clear head and a good memory and kept his objective constantly in view. But if Stalin spoke briefly and to the point it was largely because he was incapable of oratory. The only times I ever heard him speak at length were in reminiscence (as when he was at pains to convince Allied leaders that he, and not Zhukov, was the victor of Berlin). On such occasions he might speak for up to three minutes.

Also, speaking through interpreters was an ideal method for Stalin. It gave him time to collect his thoughts.

Stalin on his feet had a monkish manner of clasping his hands either over his stomach or higher, keeping them clasped even when making gestures, by simply turning his palms slightly outward but without taking them from his chest, and this particular attitude symbolised for me his locked-in nature. But I saw innumerable manifestations of cruelty, harshness, craft and meanness, cold desire for vengeance, guile and suspicion, but all of them subservient to a seemingly infinite capacity to bide his time.

Stalin wore many masks. Two weaknesses impossible to hide permanently were vanity and fear. Both seemed to me compounded in an inferiority complex. Most Western leaders who met him have asserted that Stalin was a brave man. In so far as ruthlessness and fixity of purpose demand courage, Stalin possessed some portion of that quality. But if unnatural and intense preoccupation with personal safety and morbid fear of death indicate cowardice, then Stalin was also a coward at heart.

At Yalta on the day Stalin was due to come to dinner at the Vorontsov Villa, where the British delegation lived, the business of protecting Stalin's life began in the morning and was more extensive than his host, Churchill, realised. Red Army men and women constantly patrolled the gardens already, guarding the British, but that morning reinforcements moved on to the mountain sides behind, and others strengthened the patrols in the gardens seaward.

A magnificent wide stone staircase, leading down through the gardens, is flanked with sets of marble lions. The Russian guards inspected every one in case it held explosive. The whole roof of the villa was then searched. A few hours before time for dinner all the rooms giving on to the dining-room were locked, so that if one wished to go, say, from Churchill's map room in the Moorish section to the wing, one had to leave the villa and go round to another entrance.

A marked symptom of Stalin's fear was his preoccupation with ill-health. Allied leaders have reproached Stalin for compelling older men such as Cordell Hull, and sick men such as Roosevelt and Churchill after one of his illnesses, to travel thousands of miles to speak with him instead of meeting them at least half-way. Stalin gave the excuse that his doctors forbade him to travel long distances or by air. He often spoke about his poor health, but never joked about it.

Major instances of Stalin's fear of losing countenance have been recorded by others; it was minor instances of inferiority complex that I observed. Though he would rarely look you in the eye when speaking, I noticed that when photographs were being taken he would jockey for a position on a step higher than anyone else, or ease himself up any slight slope. At Potsdam he insisted childishly that it was his turn to be first to sign the final communiqué.

At Potsdam, Truman produced Army Sergeant Eugene List to play Chopin at a banquet given by the Americans for the British and Soviet delegations. Stalin, not to be outdone, produced a symphony orchestra.

If there was any man among the Russian leaders more colourless in appearance, manner and speech than Stalin, it was Molotov. It was hard to escape the feeling that this was one reason why Stalin found it agreeable to have Molotov around. Furthermore, Molotov stammered, and this meant that by comparison even Stalin's flat speaking voice showed up well.

He liked flattery (this was obvious to any close observer), but he hadn't the Khrushchevian self-confidence to welcome familiarity. I was at the dinner table in Yalta when Roosevelt told Stalin that he and Churchill between them called him "Uncle Joe", and I think Stalin was genuinely piqued.

In June, 1945, Stalin had acquired the supreme military title of generalissimo, and the first time after this I interpreted directly to Stalin was at Potsdam during the audience he gave to Lord Mountbatten. Pavlov indicated to me that he not only expected to be addressed by this title each time, but have it prefixed by *Gospodin* ("Sir"). Stalin had insisted on it. When one had to put *"Gospodin Generalissimus"* into, say, the instrumental case, it became even more of a tongue-twister, but Stalin obviously enjoyed its use. Stalin, who spoke no language but his native Georgian and Russian, could not bear it when others showed sufficient learning to speak a language other than their own.

He had a basic inferiority complex, He took an obvious pleasure in humiliating, denigrating, or simply scoring off others. I believe that it was this basic inferiority complex that led Stalin to the ultimate irony : that while he claimed (as he told Mountbatten) that he was a man of the people, in reality he isolated himself from the people in order to survive above them.

Only a tiny fraction of Russia's 200 million people ever saw Stalin in the flesh, and most of them only on a remote balcony at Red Square parades. Even fewer knew where he lived and worked. The closest most Soviet citizens got to Stalin was through an ordinary letter-box set in the Kremlin wall and labelled with his current Government or party title—not his name. Here, wretched petitioners hopefully dropped their pathetic pleas for mercy for some relative or loved one being persecuted to keep Stalin alive and in power.

Stalin made his people not only afraid of him, but afraid of one another. When the midnight knock of the secret police was almost as familiar as the postman's, the sick joke in Moscow was of the house concierge knocking at a door in the night and crying, "Don't be afraid, citizens ! It's only a fire in the house ! '

Sukarno: Creator of Indonesia

An Observer Profile

When a shrieking mob of several thousand Indonesian youths burned and wrecked the British Embassy in Jakarta [in September] and savagely stoned 20 members of its staff, one man alone could with certainty be held to blame, President Sukarno, who has used his mesmeric hold on his country's 100 million people to whip up mass hysteria against the new Federation of Malaysia.

Every so often history throws up a national leader so closely identified with his country that he becomes an accepted stage figure whose histrionic posturings are sanctioned by some tacit international convention. De Gaulle comes to mind, with his preoccupation with la gloire. So, however, does Mussolini. Sukarno is such a man. He personifies his country as Churchill typified war-time Britain—though he is no more like Churchill than Bali is like the Isle of Sheppey.

Scattered across 3,000 miles of tropical ocean, from the Indian Ocean to the northern threshold of Australia, the 3,000 palm-fringed islands of the Indonesian Republic lie like pieces of some exotic un-assembled jigsaw puzzle, each with its own magical name—Sumatra, Java, Kalimanthan, Sulawesi, Timor, Flores, Moluccas, Bali.

Sukarno, absolute leader of this nation, is a revolutionary with the instincts of a sultan. He wants to be loved, flattered, revered and never opposed. Flamboyant, indefatigable, he is full of theatrical gestures. His favourite costume is a gold-braided uniform with fawn trousers, capped by a black Indonesian fez which conceals his baldness. His large, luminous eyes dominate, even conceal, a flat, slightly puffy face. In repose his full, sensual lips, like R.A.F. wings, droop fastidiously.

His motives for unleashing the outburst against Malaysia are complex but underlying them is the rage of a man whose delusions of grandeur are impeded. Sukarno has dreamed of a Neutralist Indonesian Raja—the restoration of a half-imaginary Javanese empire which would embrace Malaya and the Philippines and dominate South-East Asia. In this context, the anti-Communist Commonwealth Federation of Malaysia, linked to the former colonial Power by a defence treaty, appears as a monstrous geo-political intrusion. But the campaign of "confrontation" will be cunningly calculated blows rather than a flurry of swipes that might invite bloody retaliation.

His methods were well illustrated during his skilful 12-year campaign of diplomatic and economic coercion to browbeat Holland into ceding neighbouring western New Guinea to Indonesia without a fight.

Jakarta approached the United Nations four times, rallied the Afro-Asian bloc and the Soviet camp to Indonesia's cause and tried to shame the Netherlands into submission. All debts to Holland were repudiated. Dutch nationals obliged to leave the republic. Dutch assets worth several hundred million pounds were taken over, and diplomatic relations were severed.

This entire operation bore the stamp of an inglorious tactician who favours anything from deception to blackmail which will break the enemy down and avert the need for frontal assault. Last year Dutch New Guinea duly ceased to exist and on May 1 this year the Indonesian flag rose over the republic's new province—"West Irian".

Throughout his political career, Sukarno has compounded savage bluster with devious compromise in order to win his victories painlessly. He began campaigning against the Dutch for Indonesian independence in 1927 and during the next 15 years was almost continuously in jail or exile. Yet he opposed the wishes of nationalist hotheads and consistently called for a policy of non-violence, of passive non-co-operation with the colonial authority.

During the war he ostensibly collaborated with the Japanese while continuing to work for the future sovereignty of Indonesia. Even after the Japanese surrendered, in August, 1945, Sukarno, conscious of the continued presence of their troops, declared Indonesia independent only after younger supporters forced him at pistol point to do so.

But although he may never have matched his aggressive and provocative words with bold deeds, his purpose holds. For he believes that he alone knows what is best for Indonesia, that he is the republic's God-given national leader and that its salvation depends solely on him.

He may not be far wrong. To the spices that drew Columbus across the Atlantic in search of the Indies have now been added Indonesia's new wealth in contemporary coin—in rubber, tin and oil, whose export earns her up to £250 million a year. But the fifth-largest nation in the world was still in 1945 a broken necklace of islands peopled by simple, sarong-clad kampong-dwellers who were always split into mutually distrustful ethnic groups and, after more than 300 years of Dutch rule, had lost any sense of unity beyond their common colonial experience. If these were to be fused into a modern nation, they above all needed a dynamic unifying influence, a personification of the still strange concept of "Indonesia".

This has been Sukarno's supreme contribution to his country. He is a silver-tongued mob orator who has unerringly projected his emotional appeal for national solidarity to the disparate millions. In his vociferous anti-colonialism, his effusive regard for Chinese Communist leaders, he appears superficially to be conniving at the Communisation of Indonesia. But while binding the Communists to his policies, he has carefully excluded them from real Ministerial power despite almost irresistible pressure.

His relationship with the huge Indonesian Communist Party is vital to both. The party needs the protection and prestige that accrue as long as it is identified with Sukarno and his nationalist policies. Sukarno needs the loyal mass support of the two-million-strong party, the most powerful political organisation in the country.

The President is an amateur ideologist who has filched bits and pieces from the ragbag of international political theory in order to stitch up something called "Indonesian Socialism".

A man who reads Engels but also listens to astrologers, Sukarno has an almost mystical approach to the problem of Indonesian unity. Born under the zodiacal sign of Gemini, he is convinced that he alone can blend all philosophies from Mohammed to Marx. He is no more a Communist than he is a democrat. He is a Sukarnoist.

The inefficiency, disunity and corruption that marked Indonesia's initial attempt to practise Western democracy confirmed Sukarno's belief in his special destiny. Intolerant of opposition himself, he visited Moscow and Peking in 1956 and with wetted lips observed monolithic systems in which liberal opposition was outlawed and rulers really ruled. By 1959 he had prepared the ground for the elimination of parliamentary democracy from Indonesia also, and in 1960, the legislature was replaced by a pyramid of purely consultative bodies with Sukarno, who has now been made President for life, at the apex.

Democracy has given way to the traditional Indonesian village principle of "gotong rojong", or mutual co-operation. The whole nation must work as one under the direction of the President, who preserves the balance between the Communist Party and the anti-Communist Army and—from the tall, tall pedestal he has assured himself—sees that whenever possible they cancel each other out.

At first glance he seems hardly the man for the job. Sukarno was born in June, 1901, in East Java, the son of a Javanese schoolteacher and a Balinese mother. After attending secondary school in Surabaya, he obtained a diploma in engineering at Bandung University.

But he is neither a simple man of the people, nor a dignified Indonesian Nehru whose very distance makes the heart grow fonder. Moving from one gleaming, over-chandeliered presidential palace to another, in Jakarta, Bogor and Bali, Sukarno is a debonair hedonist, a thrice-married Muslim with a moist eye for a neat ankle, a patron of the arts who owns one of the finest collections of paintings in Asia, a lover of the Javanese gong-like gamelan music and of Balinese dancing.

But there is more to him than this. He is possessed of a personality so magnetic that for the great crowds who listen to him with shining eyes there is only one "Bung" ("Brother") Karno. It is impossible to separate out his love of personal power, and his passionate, chauvinistic love of country. He is a Left-leaning Asian whose fervent anti-colonialism dovetails deceptively with his selfish eagerness to become leader of the world's third bloc. His nationalistic vision is paranoiac. He speaks of Indonesia as the second-biggest international Power of the future, he renames those waters of the Indian Ocean in which the islands of the republic are scattered "The Indonesian Ocean". He describes the Indonesian revolution as "greater than the American or Russian revolutions, which were only "political": in 1955, at the Bandung conference, he sponsored the formal creation of the Afro-Asian movement, an international third force of which he saw himself future fuehrer. His ambition has now led him to challenge the mandates of all existing world organisations which gainsay him, from the Olympic Games Committee to the United Nations itself.

Sukarno is no economist, has no administrative ability, is impatient of dull detail. He is accused of launching national hate campaigns—"confrontation" of the Dutch over West Irian, of the British and Malayans over Malaysia—in order to divert attention from troubles at home, for even his Government's basic economic projects for supplying clothes and food to the masses have so far failed. However, they are also designed to give Indonesians a new national coherence, an objective that will make them co-operate, work, suffer and, if necessary, fight together. They are primarily exercises in nationhood.

167

Moreover, they fulfil an even more important function : they protract the Indonesian revolution, prolong the phase of emotional heroics to which Sukarno—visionary, demagogue and revolutionary—can still be considered indispensable. For once it is over, he will simply be an embarrassing anachronism.

Sukarno has given Indonesia independence and a neutral position in international affairs. He has placated the dreaded Chinese and, fully conscious that his sprawling archipelago is the biggest strategic prize in South Asia, has made America and Russia each pay handsomely to ensure that it stays out of the hands of the other.

While millions under his care go short, he allocates precious foreign credits for white elephant projects designed to flabbergast the bourgeois rather than feed the baby—but never at the expense of national integrity. An emergent Asian country that desires quick prosperity for its people usually sacrifices something of its sovereignty and socialist principles by inviting private foreign investment. Sukarno would rather tighten his diamond-studded belt.

The President has given Indonesia a much-needed nationalistic and revolutionary impulse. But reluctantly, he is being forced more and more to put rice before reputation, to grant priority to the business of sorting out the penurious muddle that passes for Indonesian economy.

When he dies, a colourful and dramatic episode will end for Indonesia. Whatever follows, Sukarno's "guided" empire is likely to prove as ephemeral as the conquests of Alexander.

Tributes to Excellent Men

1. Jack Hobbs, Master Batsman

by John Arlott

Sir John Berry Hobbs, who has died a few days after his eighty-first birthday, was the greatest batsman and best-loved man of modern cricket. His knighthood, the first bestowed on a professional cricketer, honoured not only great technical skill, but a gracious character.

Jack Hobbs was a simple man. The idea that he, the eldest of the twelve children of a net-bowler at Fenners, was a great man always seemed to him an odd, and slightly amusing, idea which existed only in the minds of others. "But it pleases them, you know. . . ."

Jack Hobbs scored more runs (61,237) and more centuries (197) than anyone else in first-class cricket: and more than any other Englishman on the high plateau of the game, which is Test play between England and Australia.

In 1920, when a Surrey opening bowler did not arrive for a match with Warwickshire, Hobbs went on with the new ball and took five wickets for 21—and then scored 101.

He was top of the first-class bowling averages that year, which made him laugh. For nearly thirty years his speed in the pick-up and the accuracy of his whippy, low throw, made it perilous to run a single to him at cover point.

The number of his runs is the more remarkable since he did not play first-class cricket until he was twenty-two, lost four seasons to the 1914-18 war, and virtually missed two more owing to injury and illness.

When he was 51 and on the verge of retirement, he played in George Duckworth's benefit match, against Lancashire, the County Champions, and scored the only century made against them at Old Trafford that season—and 51 not out in the second innings.

When A. W. Carr fell ill during the 1926 Manchester Test against Australia, Hobbs took over the captaincy: but, in all but name, he captained England many times and with much wisdom.

On figures as well as in memory, he and Herbert Sutcliffe were the finest pair of opening batsmen Test cricket has ever known: and, for Surrey, first with his fellow Cambridge man, Tom Hayward, and then with Andrew Sandham, he shared the majority of his record number of century openings (166).

Sir Jack would never enter any discussion which compared him with W. G. Grace, though he liked to think that he inherited "The Old Man's" batting technique: by a happy coincidence, in his first match for Surrey—against the Gentlemen of England—he and W.G. were on opposing sides.

A. C. MacLaren analysed Hobbs's batting technique in a book aptly titled *The Perfect Batsman*. Neat, quizzical-looking, wiry, quick in his assessment of the bowled ball, he came without hurry to the ideal position to play any stroke: and he had them all.

Against any bowling, and even on bad wickets—where his ability lifted him above Bradman—he wore an air of ease. Often one had to observe his partner's difficulties to appreciate the sensitive skill of Hobbs.

During the 1920s it seemed as though he could make a hundred at will. Yet he gave little thought to records.

He played with enjoyment and humour: his mischief, which was completely without malice, brought laughter to many grave cricket fields.

After he sent his poignant letter of resignation to Surrey in 1935, his life changed. He devoted much time to his sports goods business in Fleet Street, which he controlled in detail, never too busy to choose a bat—and choose it with care—for a schoolboy.

He played little cricket, though the last time he picked up a bat, in 1941, he scored the last of the 47 centuries he could remember making outside the first-class game.

Until last year he played golf regularly with his old companion, Herbert Strudwick; he cherished an unfailing feeling for old friends, and a genuine consideration for those his charity could not bring him to approve of.

He settled in Hove, where for the last few years of her life he tended his sick wife with a moving gentleness.

As a player he had considered it professionally advisable not to drink or smoke. Freed from those responsibilities, he relished an occasional cigar and his own, unusual brand of fat cigarettes: he would take a hock with his dinner and given the excuse of a visit from a friend he would mildly shock himself by opening a half-bottle of champagne at mid-morning.

A shy man, he was embarrassed by public appearances, and with a single annual exception avoided speech-making: reluctantly but pleasantly, he made two sound broadcasts and one television programme.

Eventually his knighthood and the volume of his correspondence convinced him that, whatever his feelings, he would henceforth be regarded as a public figure.

Every letter he received—and hundreds came from people he had never known—was answered in his own rather painful hand: every autograph demanded of him was given, every gesture acknowledged.

Hesitantly at first, but eventually with great gusto, he consented to become the permanent guest of honour at the lunches of "The Master's Club", formed in his honour in the early fifties.

It was understood that there were no speeches at these luncheons and only the single toast of "The Master". But one year he stood up and, after his thanks "for the honour you have done me", addressed himself separately to everyone present, recalling some bygone incident to each person's credit. Thereafter, his speech was the great event of the year for the club.

On the cricket of his contemporaries he was shrewd and amusing. Of one famous bowler he said: "Ah, yes, he spun it a lot: a dangerous bowler: but, you know, he never seemed to bowl so well if you hit him over the top of extra cover two or three times in his first over."

The words used by Nyren, an earlier cricket immortal, about another, John Small, apply just as precisely to Jack Hobbs: "I can call to mind no worthier, or, in the active sense of the word, not a more 'good man'."

2. A. J. Liebling, Reporter

by Michael Davie

Every now and again a newspaper is entitled to praise someone in
the business, and the death of A. J. Liebling, the American reporter, is
such an occasion. For nearly 30 years Liebling was one of the pillars
of the *New Yorker*, and if he was less famous than, say, Thurber or
Harold Ross, he was by no means a less important reason for the
magazine's fame.

He did some of his best work as a critic of newspapers, in the
"Wayward Press" department, and he was about the only good one
there has been. He took newspapers seriously. He regarded information as a primary instrument of liberty, "the one thing most necessary to our survival as choosers of our own way." He never got over
the anomaly whereby the most important purveyors of information,
newspapers, are subject to the same rules of merchandising as
chewing-gum, and are owned in most cases by men better suited to
the chewing-gum industry.

He took a very low view of proprietors: there is a note of contempt in his prose when he writes about Colonel McCormick, the
Chicago isolationist, or Henry Luce, the publisher of *Time* and *Life*.
He disapproved, in particular, of the way rich newspaper proprietors
often try to save money by cutting down on foreign correspondents.
He was against proprietors and he was against journalistic experts,
"who write what they construe to be the meaning of what they
haven't seen."

He was in favour of reporters, who write what they see, and the
status of reporters, low as it is in the eyes of proprietors and public
alike, would be still lower but for Liebling, who considered the health
of democracy to depend on a good supply of them. He never did
figure out how to multiply the reporters while at the same time
abolishing the proprietors.

In a profession without heroes, Liebling was a hero, though no one
would have dreamed of telling him so. With one or two others, such
as Joseph Mitchell, Liebling set a standard of reporting in the *New
Yorker* which brought it within hailing distance of literature.

In his time, besides newspapers, he wrote about almost everything:
France, boxing, Second World War, New York low life, politics. But
he usually had a reason for writing, and he was always activated by
a subterranean sense of moral purpose. Even when he was writing
about con-men and gamblers, there was the unspoken assumption that
low life was superior to high life, and that the patrons of Hymie
Katz's joints were a lot more respectable than some of the people
you might run into at the Harvard Club.

171

He was not over-tall, but he was certainly overweight, with a great belly that was a memorial to a lifetime of serious eating, a legacy of unthinkable quantities of *tripe à la mode de Caen* and Massachusetts clams. He believed he was ugly, with his high bald head and thick spectacles; but he was, really, memorable, looking like someone to reckon with. His voice was a deep rumble that started its journey somewhere near the tripe, and it was often hard to know what he was saying.

He paid regular visits to England. Unlike most other American journalists who cover England, he viewed local society from the bottom upwards; it is doubtful whether he would have approved of the American television commentator, living in London now, who affects a butler. His introduction to this country was originally through the works of Pierce Egan, the historian of the old prize ring and later through servicemen, when he eventually came here in person, as a war correspondent.

He saw the country, therefore, without gloss. In 1959, when he covered the General Election for this newspaper, he began his inquiries by setting off for South London, where some old war-time pals of his lived, and he learned from them that the rumours that had reached him on Fifth Avenue about Britain being in the grip of an affluent society were over-stated.

In London, he used to stay at a small hotel off St. James's Street, but that was not because he thought it a smart quarter but because he thought it was raffish. He believed he could detect, under the surface, the old tradition of gamblers and cock-fighting layabouts. He bought a bowler hat in St. James's Street, at Lock's, and he used to wear it around New York. He told a friend not long ago that he must be becoming famous, because so many New Yorkers stared after him in the streets.

I told him once I didn't believe that his boxing acquaintances really talked the way he made them talk in his pieces, so he took me to one of his favourite places on earth, the Neutral Corner Saloon. We had scarcely bought a beer before Liebling negotiated a conversation with a young man whom he remembered as having fought one bout at Madison Square Garden, and who then disappeared. What, Liebling asked, had happened? "I was in-carcerated," the fellow replied.

When Liebling wrote about boxing, he was consciously working in an English tradition, and some pepole considered that at his best he was not far behind Hazlitt. Like Hazlitt, and unlike most others who try their hand at low life, Liebling was indifferent to distinctions of class or culture. He took his whole personality with him when he went off to strip-joints or fights, without a trace of condescension, and there is no difference in style between his boxing pieces and his pieces on, say, the Algerian war. He always took a comprehensive view, and nothing pleased him more than when he could work in a reference to Ibn Khaldun, the fourteenth-century Arab philosopher-historian, and Dr. Orlando Miller, the phoney revivalist, in the same sentence.

He had the same catholic attitude to human distinction: the greatest men he had come across in his life, he declared, were Harold Ross of the *New Yorker*; Sam Langford, who could make any opponent lead and then belt him out; Raymond Weeks, who taught Romance Philology at Columbia University; and Max Fischel, who covered New York Police Headquarters for the *Evening World*.

Visiting Day

I was on my way to the loony bin
To visit my lady, who was as queer as a coot,
When out of the radio of the taxicab
Came Bach magnificent with trumpet, fiddle and flute.
And the sanity of that proliferous German
With his umpteen kids, concertos and chorales
Went striding over the hills proclaiming again and again
The delightfulness of being sane.
So that when I walked in the asylum gardens
Among the white-robed patients lying about like tombs
And when Ruth danced her sad and portly measure
To some private rhythm out of the catacombs,
I wasn't entirely washed away:
Still had the clear dimensions of that music
In which to function, like a sunny day.

Michael Harari

From Katharine Whitehorn's Column

1. A Humble Defence of Sluts

This article is dedicated to all those who have ever changed their stockings in a taxi, brushed their hair with someone else's nailbrush or safety-pinned a hem; and those who have not had probably better not read on.

Anyone in doubt, however, can ask herself the following questions. Have you ever taken anything back out of the dirty-clothes basket because it has become, relatively, the cleaner thing? How many things are there, at this moment, in the wrong room—cups in the study, boots in the kitchen; and how many of them are on the *floor* of the wrong room?

Could you try on clothes in any shop, any time, without worrying about your underclothes? And how, if at all, do you clean your nails? Honest answers should tell you, once and for all, whether you are one of us: the miserable, optimistic, misunderstood race of sluts.

We are not ordinary human beings who have degenerated, as people think: we are born this way. Even at four you can pick us out: the little girls in the playground who have one pant-leg hanging down and no hair-slide; at 10 we are the ones who look dirty even when we are clean (unlike the goodidoodies who look unfairly clean when they are dirty): and at 15, now that black stockings are back, we betray ourselves in the changing room by legs spotted like a dalmatian's, the inevitable result of using Indian ink instead of darning wool.

People who are not sluts intolerantly assume that we must like things this way, without realising the enormous effort and inconvenience that goes into being so ineffective: the number of times we have to fill the car's radiator because we don't get it mended, the fortunes we spend on taxis going back for parcels we have left in shops, the amount of ironing occasioned by our practice of unpacking not so much when we get back from a weekend as four days later.

We acquire, it is true, certain off-beat skills: I am much better at holding a bottle of varnish between two fingers than those of my friends who do not paint their nails in the Tube, and they cannot cut their nails with a penknife, either; but nothing really makes up to us for the difficulties of our condition.

However, I am not trying to make a soggy bid for sympathy so much as to work out what we can possibly do to improve our condition. And the first thing, it seems to me, is to inscribe ABANDON HOPE ALL YE WHO ENTER HERE over the lintels of all our messy houses; for it is our optimism that is principally our undoing. We keep hoping that we will remember to wash our white collars, or find time to comb our hair on the way to the office, or slide into the building and dump our coats before anyone can see that there are three buttons missing. More it seems to me, could be done if we could only face up realistically to all the things we never will be able to do.

We can realise, for example, that no power on earth is going to make us look well turned out all, or even most, of the time. We can therefore give up right away any New Year resolutions about fashion : a second pair of little white gloves will simply result in our carrying two right hands; wigs would be a waste of money because those of us who cannot keep our real hair tidy cannot keep our toy hair tidy either. Instead, we can wear reasonably sober clothes normally, go for stacked heels because we know we won't remember to get them re-heeled before they are worn down, have only one colour of accessories, so that we cannot wear the brown shoes with the black bag.

And, having accepted that people are *not* going to say, "She's always so chic," we can concentrate every now and then on really dazzling efforts that will knock our audience sideways. Jane Austen was right when she said that no beauty accustomed to compliments ever got anything like the thrill of an ordinary looker who was told she was looking terrific *that evening*.

We can give up making good resolutions about replacing things before they run out, which is absurd, and concentrate instead on bulk buying, so that the gap between supply and supply happens much more rarely. We can also, of course, keep icing sugar, the wrong sort of rice, tea bags, spearmint toothpaste and so on specifically to tide us over when we do run out of these things. It is true that we tend not to have any money either, but as we usually spend what we have at the beginning of the month like drunken sailors anyway, we might as well spend it on vast tubs of cleansing cream, acres of Kleenex (which we have to have, since clean handkerchiefs, let's face it, are beyond us), sugar in 10 lb. bags.

Apart from this sort of grim realism, there are, I think, only two other things that can help us. The first is habit : odd as it may seem, even sluts do occasionally acquire good habits (we clean our teeth, for example, even if we sometimes have to do it with soap) and these, indeed, are all that hold us together. A slut who baths whenever she has time never baths at all: her only hope is to get up into one every morning; if she shops here and there for food there will never be any around, but a Saturday supermarket raid will settle a whole week's hash at one go.

And the second is money: for the only way a slut can really get things done is to get someone else to do them. Even the most domestic slut will find it worth earning a few pounds to pay for help in the house.

The only way to make up for missing the post is a long-distance telephone call; the only way not to have to go back to fetch things is to get them picked up by messenger. The only thing that will get a slut's carpets vacuumed daily is a daily. All sluts ought to be, or to marry, rich people: and I treasure the hope that among the really rich there may be dozens of sluts lurking undetected by the rest.

Money, low cunning and a sense of realism may help us somewhat; but it is a hard life all the same. I wrote this article two years ago, but as it was felt that it hardly came well from the pen of a fashion editor, it was never printed. So I thought I had a soft option using it now; except that, of course, I couldn't find it, and have had to write the whole blasted thing again.

2. The Rights of Spinsters

A country's single women, it often seems to me, can be an excellent index of its mental health. Scotland and Finland, for example, do a splendid line in balanced, self-reliant, cheerful spinsters; while America seems to produce quantities of women eternally defensive about being on their own, striving to remain mantraps to the end.

Unmarried women undoubtedly have a lot to put up with in this country—quite apart from any real regret they may feel at not having husbands or children. People get it all wrong, for a start, about why they are single. A society which believes that a woman should wait for Mr. Right fails to realise that the only proof that anybody does this is the women who have refused to settle for Mr. Wrong—there being few single women who have not refused an offer from some persona non-starter.

They suffer, too, from that easiest form of callousness, the assumption that anyone with problems prefers things that way: they are supposed to be "temperamentally unsuited to marriage"—a view that looks pretty silly beside the simple fact that there were a million and a half more women than men in both 1930 and 1945. Those with dependants, unlike widowers similarly placed, get no tax relief for home helps or companions—though a society was formed last summer to lobby against this; and they have an even rougher time at the hands of mortgage companies than the rest of us.

They get, too, the gummy end of the social stick: because greying single men, spoiled by their scarcity value, expect only lush young peaches to ogle across the entrée, hostesses find older single women hard to invite—though there is really no reason why people should be paired off at all unless the evening actually involves dancing or strip poker. One way and another, they get too much chat across the nursery tea-cups, not enough adult conversation in mixed company.

The great bulwark that this generation's single women have against this sort of irritation, of course, is the satisfaction of a total and uninterrupted commitment to a career. I am always struck by the contrast in one family I know between the spinsters of the last generation, both of whom trail around with no occupation (one of them simply going to bed whenever she can, sometimes for years on end) and the single teacher and single architect of this generation, who can talk of "the thrill you get when you do a good bit of work and feel 'this is what I am for'."

One would expect them to suffer most from the appalling smugness of married women who, schooled by magazines and commercials, so often think their obligations and even consciousness can begin and end with their own homes. But in fact it is the widows who, flung out of the club overnight, as it were, suffer most from this; the single seem to come to terms with it over the years, and either find their friends outside, or realistically make the best of it: a highly successful spinster said to me once: "You just have to make yourself useful to your married friends—take their children to the park and so on."

Single women may view the limitations of the housewifely attitude with amused detachment; but it is from this, none the less, that their biggest hardship comes. It is so easy for the married women to use "putting my husband and children first" as an excuse for getting out of a job she does no want to do, so far too often the single get landed with looking after dependent parents.

Yet it ought, to my mind, to be exactly the other way round. A single woman's one unquestionable advantage is her freedom—to go to the pictures at no notice, to take an exchange job, to save up or sell up and go abroad; and this she gives up absolutely if she takes on an ageing relative. A married woman has no comparable liberty to give up, quite apart from the fact that she can share the mother-sitting with her husband and children, and is cooking and coping with a household anyway.

There are advantages to family life, and advantages to single freedom; if the single woman is missing out on the love and security and bedlam that a family provides, she should not be saddled with its concomitant lack of freedom. A married woman is getting something out of family life and so has a far greater family obligation.

I know one family where two sons and two daughters, all married, simply assumed that a brilliant single headmistress would give up her job to look after their difficult old mother; and the implement they used to beat her into doing the dirty work was, of course, that gnarled old relic "family duty"—family duty which kept Beatrix Potter at her mother's bidding until she was over 40, and ensured that Florence Nightingale endured 30 years before she even saw a hospital—not to mention my Aunt Marion, who had to wait till she was over 60 to study art in Paris—*after* her mother had died.

It may have made sense, when the family unit was large, and poor relations were automatically supported, and even the dingiest of kin included in all entertainments and family councils. Its only remaining use seems to be bludgeoning the single.

From now on, though, the married are jolly well going to have to look after their parents themselves; for the ratio has changed, and there are more men in the mating season than women. Which is no doubt splendid for the women who want to get married; but it has its ominous overtones all the same. Those who misjudge the single women most are always those who do not actually know any; as the single get scarcer, and as more working married women get the best of both worlds, they are going to feel "odd women out" more than before.

Yet the single state remains what it has always been: maybe worse than a good marriage, but a whole lot better than a bad one. And the status of spinsters remains a measure of the way women as a whole are regarded. Where women are supposed to be sink-gadgets and baby-minders only, the manless are always despised; it is where it is recognised that a woman has a right to choose her own life that they are respected and understood.

3. A Vested Interest in Warmth

The heroine of last winter was unquestionably Mrs. Richard Wood, who posed in woollen bloomers in support of her husband's fuel policy: whatever the female attachments of other Ministers were putting on or taking off, this woman knew which way the wind was blowing and how to guard against it.

Her appearance provoked two reflections on underclothes in general: first, that the question of how warm you ought to be is quite irrelevant compared to the freezing question of how warm you are: and second, that the most astonishing misconceptions are entertained about underwear simply because it is unusual for the stuff to be on display to more than one person at a time.

Otherwise sophisticated people go round asserting that there is something suspicious about black lingerie, or that attractive girls never wear vests; my list of Dotty Sayings by Headmistresses about clothes is headed by the statement that people originally wore black because they did not have to wash it so often.

British buyers, after asserting for two years that the British complexion could never stand even helpful neutrals such as brown and navy, now blithely assume it can take sage green and ochre. The French, typically, are asking why the British are still wearing coloured underwear—at the same time as *Elle* is enthusiastically taking up a fashion for printed nylon tricot slips which have been around in America for more than two years. With one half of the world thinking it is unladylike to wear sexy clothes and the other half thinking it is unsexy to keep warm, the matter is fraught with confusion.

The confusion was to a large extent responsible for the sort of clothes there were to be had. On the assumption that only the staid wore vests and only the fast wore colours, there were never any vests in anything but white or shrimp pink, and no one gave any thought to their design.

Because what was available was so dreary, girls who did care what they looked like in the not-quite tended to shy off them—which in turn gave force to the legend about gay girls going vestless. I can only think it started either because astute girls removed their vests privily on the eve of battle or because the ones who, vestless, were shivering with cold were just that much more ready to abandon the freezing lamp-post for the warmth of the bachelor flat.

I speak bitterly, as one with a blood pressure of 90—blood pressure is supposed to be 100 plus your age—when I say that I have never seen any evidence (nor offered any, dash it) to suggest that there is a connection between a cold temperature and a cold temperament. I have it on good authority, what is more, that a vest and no bra is more alluring than a bra and no vest—always provided, of course, that it is the right vest.

Besides, if you do not wear any underclothes, what do you wear instead? A mink coat and no drawers—fine: but when any girl tells me disdainfully she never wears a vest I always ask for an assurance that she has never worn a duffle coat, non-matching cardigan, college scarf or pixie hood before I even start feeling envious.

Another section of the anti-underclothes brigade is to be found among those who think the state of modern clothes and houses has simply by-passed the need for them. I have even heard it said that since all (*sic*) modern clothes are lined, even a slip is unnecessary. But even apart from the fact that we are (I suppose) the only civilised country that is still *building* houses without proper heating, there is the question of mental adjustment.

Central heating is a state of mind: it implies a willingness to heat a room you are not actually in; we have all shivered in October in houses where they have the equipment but are too mean to throw the switch before the first snow.

Apart from temperature, of course, there is also history. We are easing out of a period equivalent to the Directoire, when (as every schoolmaster knows) women cast off their underclothes as a gesture of Liberty, went in for flimsy white muslin, and nearly froze to death in the interests of Mr. Laver's Time Spirit. Much the same thing happened in the twenties: no corsets, nothing-for-something brassières if any, and the only underthing a crêpe-de-chine cami-knicker. (Much of the current underwear may look, we feel, like the twenties —but it is twenties' bathing dresses we are reminded of, never the lingerie.)

And just as, after the Directoire, the petticoats and camisoles increased to the point where it must have taken an affluent woman several hours a day to dress and undress, so underclothes are coming back now. The frilly petticoats of seven years ago were auguries; bras and girdles are now definitely a fashion item, and not just a gloomy piece of engineering for people with frightful figures; and now, thanks to the cold, the habit of ski-ing, and the pressure on manufacturers to find new things to sell, the concentration is on warm, gay lingerie.

I started carrying a torch for spencers three years ago, but all I got was pitying smiles; now I am mown down by the rush to buy their more modern and charming equivalents.

They have invented a strapless vest which will be a godsend to those who frequent hunt balls and/or forget to mend their shoulder straps. There are little Victorian vests which no respectable Victorian would have dreamed of wearing, and things that look like practice tights, and a vest/cami-knicker which would overcome, I should think, the most diehard anti-vestite. And while we are on the subject, cannot some transvestite design a decent vest for men? They are all horrible.

There are other worlds left to conquer: a great many of the pretty vests are made short, on the grounds that another layer over the seat is a mistake for those who are already well-covered; but they leave a gap or a roll of wool at the waist instead.

And when it comes to under-garments, even the wildest things should be available in big sizes: the more large women wear sober top clothes the greater their longing to wear a riot beneath. But these are quibbles: minor pitfalls in the great cinerama epic of how the vest was won.

The Various Arts

Films

The Making of Cleopatra

by Roy Perrott

*Twentieth Century-Fox needed four years, 40 million dollars
and five countries to shoot in when it made its epic
Cleopatra. Roy Perrott went to New York and to Hollywood
to find out how this happened. On his return he wrote an
epic of his own from which this account of what occurred
on location has been taken.*

.　　.　　.

*Dwindling post-war cinema audiences had helped to reduce
the company's film business to an anaemic condition. Fox
executives set out to make* Cleopatra *in a mood of the utmost thrift and caution. But when their first attempt to
make it in England had come to grief through rain, fog, ice
and trade union troubles, the management was inspired to
sterner resolve. A new director, Joseph L. Mankiewicz, was
hired and told to make "the greatest". He decided that the
film so far shot would have to be scrapped and an entirely
new script created. Now read on.*

By early March, 1961, Twentieth Century-Fox was poised for a
fresh assault on *Cleopatra* after the expensive failure of the previous
autumn and winter. Though the company's desperation about its
financial state was faintly veiled by a renewed burst of executive
activity—featuring the hotfoot dash to the airport (a favourite nerve-
pacifier), the urgent planning conference, and the long-distance
phone-call—the balance sheet still loomed darkly.

Fox had now spent 16 months and $6 million (£2 million), enough
to produce three routine pictures, with nothing worth showing to
any serious-minded stockholder. After six successive years of loss on
movie-making the company was hardly making sense as a business;

and the president who had supervised the decline, Spyros Skouras, badly needed a success to steady his chair.

So, once their peeling Egypt at Pinewood was dried out, repaired and repainted, they expected to be ready for another try in early April. Then with three months' work they would be home and dry.

But in early March calamity struck again. The star, Elizabeth Taylor, fell ill with pneumonia and for several days her life hung in the balance. By the time she recovered and went off to California for several months' convalescence, the situation was drastically changed. England and the big investment in sets there would have to be written off—they could not risk the weather again. Overhead expenses would go on rising and the production would have to be that much quicker and greater to be sure of getting the money back. If "greatness" had, a few months back, looked merely desirable, it was now becoming compulsory. The more often Fox fell, the higher had to be the aim; it was an equation that went on hounding the company.

And so, while the workmen at Pinewood demolished the eight-acre Alexandria they had built at giddy speed and overtime rates only seven months before, the Fox production team flew to Hollywood to make another start. They planned to shoot all interior scenes there, then move to Italy and Egypt for outside location shots in the autumn.

By June, 1961, they had built six major sets, and down the road towards Los Angeles, on a lot once galloped over by Tom Mix, they excavated a large lake on which the naval battles could be shot in miniature.

The cement was hardly dry when new orders came from New York: the whole film was now to be shot in Italy and Egypt. The proud stoics of the scenery department again set about a demolition job. The lake, which had cost $350,000 (£125,000) was never used; a fast-moving real estate company had it under a property development before the film was finished.

Several reasons were given for the abrupt change of mind: the Hollywood stages were needed to accommodate "The Greatest Story Ever Told" (a life of Christ, which some advisers thought might gross more speedily—Biblicals were on the way up); a Mediterranean location would not only be more authentic, the point that the director insisted upon, but also cheaper; Hollywood would be too costly seeing that extras there now commanded $30 (£10) a day, and $100 a day if they spoke a line, against the $10 fee current in Italy; Miss Taylor's agent was going to demand more money if she was going to sacrifice her European tax benefits by filming in Hollywood.

In the event, none of these reasons really stood the test of time. The Biblical epic was before long indefinitely postponed when they became too dangerously immersed with Egypt to cope with anything else; the difference between Rome and Hollywood costs soon became academic; and the only "Roman" sets they shot in Rome were those built by the scenery department. But someone had worked out the figures, and at the time a move looked advisable on paper.

So, in a mood of mounting urgency, the film-makers set off for Italy. Because of the pressing need to get the picture finished and earning, Mankiewicz was given a September deadline to start shooting. This left four months to get ready from scratch, or a quarter of the time which any company in a relaxed state of mind would have thought proper for a production of this size.

They hired all available space at the big Cinecitta studios near Rome. A thousand workmen were taken on for set-building. A hundred Hollywood technicians were flown out to help and supervise—all, of course, on expense accounts. The Fox art department was busy converting its hundreds of set designs and specifications into the metric system, lire, and Italian. Shipyards in Italy, Egypt, and France were put to work building $3 million-worth of galleys, barges, and other ancient craft; and the props department went diligently to work creating authentic wrecks for the sea-battle.

Mankiewicz, having scouted the coastline from a boat, settled on the Anzio peninsula, 45 miles south of Rome, as a site for his 20-acre Alexandria set. It offered exciting camera angles, he thought. Elsewhere they started on the construction of a 12-acre Forum, rather larger than the original. They ordered 6,100 tons of cement and 26,000 gallons of paint. A shipload of 50,000 railway sleepers, salvaged from the original Pinewood set, was sailed in to provide the basis of the flooring.

The site chosen was part of a hunting preserve owned by Prince Borghese's family, and Fox rented it for $150,000 (£53,000). Before building began the contract required them to make a diagram-inventory of the extensive gardens, so that all the plants could be correctly replaced when shooting was finished. At the same time they found that the upper storey of the Prince's guesthouse got in the way of a clear shot of their Temple of Athena; they had to remove it brick by brick and put it back later.

Next, the bulldozers began stripping away layers of the foreshore to make a foundation for Alexandria—and found a war-time minefield. "Hundreds of mines and thousands of rounds of live ammo," recalls a production man who was there. Should someone have mentioned the minefield to them? Certainly, if they knew; but no one had. The building was held up for six weeks while a contractor came in to clear the mines.

This was nearly done when another hazard was reported. A Nato high-velocity gun-battery on an adjacent beach began firing seaward and, because of the risk of a short-fall of shells, the several hundred men constructing Alexandria had to abandon their rising city whenever the gunners decided they needed practice.

Representations were made to stop the gunnery—after all, Fox had its own wars to get ready for—but, to everyone's surprise, Nato would not withdraw. It became too dangerous for Cleopatra's barge to rehearse its landfall. Over the four months of building, Nato cost Fox a fortnight's delay and several hundred thousand dollars' worth of production time.

Should they have known about the gunners? Perhaps. No one told them about this either. "There just wasn't time to look around," a props-man complained.

By September, in spite of setbacks, preparations were moving impatiently to a climax. After some management doubts about their box-office potential, Rex Harrison had been engaged to play Caesar, and Richard Burton had been bought out of his current Broadway show, *Camelot*, to do Antony. Miss Taylor arrived and moved into a large villa with her husband, Eddie Fisher, her three children, several maids, five dogs and two cats. Her personal physician had been engaged to attend her at a fee of $25,000 (£9,000) for six weeks, plus expenses.

Props, home-made or imported, poured in—160 large statues, 15,000 bows and quivers, 10,000 spears, a pair of elephants, camels, jackasses, cats, numerous horses, and the asp. The art department had found that there were so many branches to look after—interior, battles (sea), battles (land)—that it wound up with eight art directors instead of the normal one or two. About 6,000 extras had been taken on; 26,000 costumes were in the making; a fleet of 40 taxis had been hired to move the technical staff about.

But one handicap remained beside which the other obstacles—the mines, the shellfire, the studio overcrowding, the strike of the taxi-drivers for more money, the handmaidens' strike for more clothes—seemed relatively slight. They still had no script.

The director had appealed for a postponement of the September starting date to enable him to work on it, but the management had demurred. Reason may well have privately suggested to them that it was going to be tricky to shoot a film when it was so uncertain who was going to say what to whom and why. But will-power, responding to the pressures of time, money and desperation, prevailed. They must start in September.

Even so—the management forcefully pointed out—this would leave them a bare minimum of four months to shoot the whole picture before the actors' contracts ran into overtime rates. These were frightening; time and a half was nowhere in it. In Miss Taylor's case overtime pay was $50,000 (£17,000) a week, in addition to her $1 million or 10 per cent of the gross which her new contract ensured. Rates for other actors were in proportion.

By late summer Mankiewicz had in his hands the basis of the screen-play, a detailed story-line, put together by two professionals,

Sidney Buchman and Randal MacDougall. But by September he had been able only intermittently to polish and fill in the dialogue because of interruptions.

There was usually a queue of people to see him: a dress-designer needing a quick decision on a batch of costumes; someone bringing along 35 cats and asking him to choose the right one for Ptolemy; helping to adjust some crisis in colleagues' relationships or escaping one in his own; hearing out messengers from production, reporting some enemy gain in the war against life and circumstance; or rehearsals; or noticing on a walk around the set that some property statue was wearing a plaster smile and having to chase up someone to put it right.

Eventually Mankiewicz held massed rallies of technical and production people so that he could ask them all at the same time, "What's holding you up?"

Some of the hold-ups were provoking to men who were trying to take a sober but stately view of their art. Once they needed a dozen figs for the queen's basket—the asp's hide-out. The director had rejected the plastic ones. So, for days, the props department was preoccupied with a fig-hunt.

The fruit were out of season in central Italy. "So we wired and phoned all round Sicily and someone sent us a load, each as big as a walnut. No good for close-ups. Then somebody said: 'Figs?—North Africa!' so we sent to Tripoli. This lot were big all right but all twisted up. A man in Rome found us a few in the end."

Ready or not, the appeals and orders from New York headquarters compelled a start. The management was desperately unhappy that $70,000 a day was slipping away in overheads before anything was being registered on film. On September 25 on one of the few sets that were ready, the cameras rolled for the first time.

Within a few days they had to move out-of-doors, but Fox's gamble with the Italian autumn did not come off. The rain came and stayed, costing them a good many blank days through that stormy winter. Some of the scenes had now grown so big, so costly and clamorous with extras (they needed many more than expected, to give the outsize sets a reasonably populated look) that it seemed to be an act of daring to bring them out on the sets at all.

When they tried to shoot the Triumphal Entry scene, after weeks of rehearsing its 6,000 extras, animals, dancers, charioteers, acrobats, a day of rain-clouds cost them $200,000 of non-film. The elephants once broke away and smashed their howdahs; but this was a bagatelle compared with the rain.

As the shooting went on in fits and starts, Mankiewicz the writer was struggling gamely to keep up with Mankiewicz the director. The shooting was a month old before he had reached half-way with his script. Occasionally he could adjust his scene-writing to the sets that were ready. But generally he was writing the story in sequence and having to shoot it that way—the most irregular and costly way to make a film since it meant that actors and extras had to be kept on the payroll indefinitely, waiting for their scenes to come up, instead of having them shot all at once.

As the days of round-the-clock working went on, with the Muse of Finance shouting in one ear and Cleopatra unravelling her dialogue in the other, the strain on Mankiewicz increased. A doctor had recommended stimulant drugs to keep him going. His daily routine at this time and for some months ahead was: rise at 6 a.m. and receive first "shot" from private nurse; day on the set rehearsing, shooting, helping with production; booster injection at lunch-time if needed, and another in the evening. Finish shooting about 5.30 p.m. Watch day's rushes until about 7 p.m.

After dinner at his hotel he would settle down to his script-writing. He was doing it all in longhand. The stress had brought on a penicillin allergy which affected the skin of his hands, so he had to work in white cotton gloves. Between 1 and 2 a.m. he used to turn in with a sedative for four or five hours' sleep.

While the production team found the immediate present difficult enough, the lack of a script made the future impossibly obscure. Until Mankiewicz could settle down to write a scene, who knew when, or whether, they were going to need a set, a few thousand extras, or a 64-dollar basket of figs?

The director tried to make it clear, whenever the question came up, that he was not handling the production side; but since no one cared—or perhaps had the nerve or the time—to veto any part of the director's slowly unfolding drama, in case it should be some vital screw holding the whole thing together, expenditure inevitably followed his pen.

No one could make an advance budget. By the time the accountants had worked out what something was going to cost, the moviemakers, hustled along by management, had already spent it. Headquarters could only fix an absolute, positive maximum which it was a matter of life and death not to exceed; and when this had been overtaken, fix another.

Once a special emissary was sent from New York to insist that total costs should not exceed $10 million, "But we've already spent much more than that!" he was told. "Never mind," the visiting economist replied, "that's the chief's firm decision."

As the winter came in, so did new sources of tension and alarm. The costs of the production were running at about $500,000 a week with the film barely half-finished. They had $9,500,000 on loan from banks at high rates of interest, another $25 million from insurance companies at long-term rates, and other cash drawn from company funds. The interest was mounting up.

There was a growing unease among many of Fox's 15,000 stock-holders. Relatively few of them had big holdings; it was a stock widely spread among the American public—parcels of a few score or hundreds of shares owned by California lawyers, grocers in Illinois, old ladies in Wichita Falls who liked, the brokers say, to have a sensible financial stake in the romance of the motion-picture—"to have Gary or Marilyn working for them."

They had seen the value of their shares, normally very static, fluc-tuate with the fortunes of *Cleopatra*, usually downward, with inter-mittent recoveries. On one day in 1961 12,000 Fox shares changed hands on the Exchange, a fairly large shift for such stock. A good part of it was speculative trading by knowing brokers; but a propor-tion of the sales came from stockholders wanting to get out, feeling they had gone far enough in Egypt. Late in 1961 the stock reached a low of $15\frac{5}{8}$ against a "normal" of about $40 per share.

There were murmurings from some stockholders of possible legal action against Fox for negligent management. Some members of the board, representing big investment-house holdings, were insisting that all decisions on *Cleopatra* should now come from the board's executive committee. This had no practical effect except, perhaps, to increase the confusing number of field-commanders.

The simple but alarming fact was that the film had developed a momentum of its own. Fox executives were in a state of vigorously determined helplessness.

They flew, they argued, they phoned, they cabled. Management energy, which was prodigious, had to have some outlet or it would have exploded. The seven or eight top executives spent a good part of their time in the air. The studio chief, Peter Levathes, made 51 flights between Hollywood and New York in 20 months for *Cleopatra* talks and, over a year, a trip a month to Rome.

Occasionally, in this mood, they could be too fast on the draw. One executive recalled that a technician whom he urgently wanted to see had, without his knowing, been recalled to New York by someone else. He calculated that they must have passed each other over the Atlantic at 1,200 m.p.h.

The board members were now becoming most sensitive to the way things were going. They demanded cuts. Mankiewicz said he'd be glad to help—but how could he cut scenes he hadn't even written? The board tried again. Couldn't he immediately, this week, shoot Cleopatra's death scene and get the ruinously expensive star off the pay-roll? What, before she'd even *met* Antony? Out of the question, said Mankiewicz, and stalked off to another midnight session with his notebooks, his white gloves, his Plutarch, and his sleeping-pills.

By early 1962 things were moving rapidly to a conclusion, one way or the other. Fox had a half-finished picture, but they had already spent about $25 million on it, or nearly the equivalent of a third of

187

the total net assets of the company. They were alarmingly aware that few completed films in Hollywood history had ever grossed that amount.

Some of the board gravely doubted whether they could ever get their money back at the box-office; it could be that every new dollar spent on *Cleopatra* was cash down the drain. Meanwhile, over in Rome, their unnervingly confident director, Joe Mankiewicz, was slogging himself into artistic exhaustion in his quest for the "real" and the "authentic"—territories which some doubted were worth a visit at the price.

But what could board or management do? They could not sell a half-finished picture; it was already a Hollywood "blockbuster" and no one had invented a word beyond that. The trade papers' accolades for truly great box-office stuff—"socko", "boffo", or "wham", on *Variety's* calculated yardstick—had been left well behind. The movie-makers had to be allowed to go on. There had turned out to be no practicable way of cutting the scale of the picture, though the board went on trying. There was no obvious way of reducing the $500,000 a week in outgoings on the production.

There were broadly two alternatives. The first was to finish the picture as quickly and cheaply as possible, then get out of movie-making for ever. Significantly, two of the most influential stock-holders represented on the board had been working out what they would get back if the company were liquidated. The second was to soldier on as they had been doing with appeals and orders for economy.

In the event—Fox was hardly in a position to make clear-cut choices—it got a little of both. The company soldiered on, still half-believing in other people's optimism about finishing dates, but in a continual state of apprehension that something disastrous would be forced upon it.

There was one particular disaster that it feared: that Cleopatra might have another long illness. "A touch of the sniffles from Liz and the whole board would have had heart failure," recalls a production man.

Fox had managed to insure Miss Taylor's life for $10 million at about treble the normal premium, a risk and profit shared by a consortium of fifteen of America's biggest insurance companies; but since her serious London illness in 1961 no company would insure her health or the production against loss on that account.

Yet it was not the star's health exactly that, in January, 1962, raised the apprehension of board and management to a new peak. It came out that Antony and Cleopatra had been continuing their attachment off-screen. Life had begun to imitate art, and the management was deeply stricken by the unfairness of it.

Fox up to then had been in the habit of financing trips to Rome by Hollywood columnists who wanted to see the outfit at work. Now, unbidden and unsponsored, reporters and photographers flooded in. The *paparazzi*, the fanatically aggressive cameramen from the Via Veneto, invaded the studios with or without disguise; with telephoto lenses, they swarmed in the trees round the stars' villas. Studio guards were hired, but even a fine-meshed security screening did not reassure Fox that even policemen might not carry cameras. "Scum!" growled Mankiewicz at the prying lenses and groped for concentration and sanity.

In the end, the invaders got more or less what they wanted, when the couple were photographed eating oranges together at a seaside resort. This photograph was regarded as somehow decisively intimate, and it was syndicated for a fortune round the world. Some of Miss Taylor's servants began to sell their memoirs at fancy prices. The Hollywood gossip-writers, indefatigable when it comes to helping out old pals, bounced in again, at their own expense this time, and publicly advised their close friends Liz, Dick and Eddie, how they should sort it all out.

The episode put the various Press agents involved, some attached to the individual stars, some to Fox, in a dilemma. It certainly got Cleopatra in the papers; but was it good box-office? Some cried, "Sell it!"; weaker spirits cried, "Deny it!". From time to time they did both. The board and top management, almost out of habit now, inclined towards deep anxiety. They foresaw dangerous emotional crises; or else the takings might be affected in puritan areas. In the end, exhaustion supervened and there were other things to think about—finishing the shooting, for example.

Once again a gamble with the weather had been lost. Winter gales had knocked about the Alexandria set on the Anzio peninsula, and big repairs were needed. The most spectacular scene, Cleopatra's triumphal entry into Rome, had now to be set up again, and the dancers, acrobats, charioteers, horses, elephants and several thousand extras taking part put back into training. Since the cast were now on overtime rates—that $50,000 a week in Miss Taylor's case—any delay was doubly mortifying. When clouds or wind spoiled a big scene it could cost $200,000 with nothing to show.

The budget supervisors were doing what they could. They found that the bill for bottled mineral water, which the American staff insisted upon as a safer alternative to foreign tap-water, now amounted to about $80,000. It seemed that several thousand extras had joined in unauthorised drinking. With only a few weeks to go a budget man suggested that everyone should do their bit by buying their own mineral water. "And," he is reported to have added, "for Pete's sake fellers, take it easy with the paper cups."

On May 15, Skouras went into the stockholders' meeting in New York prepared to defend himself against the worst. He had no *Cleopatra* to show (his ships and legions were still being assembled for the critical naval battle) and he had to report losses of more than $22 million for 1961.

But his misgivings were premature. Only 200 of the 15,000 stockholders were present, and the sniping from the floor was less than deadly. One stockholder complained that a switch from cash to stock dividends had watered the value of shares. A woman songwriter proposed Miss Taylor for a directorship as the only way to get some of her salary re-invested in Fox.

Skouras countered these mild signs of rebellion with a statement that all salaries above $500 a week had been cut (his own from $139,000 a year to $90,000), adding an assurance that *Cleopatra* would be on the market by February, 1963, and would gross $150 million, "the greatest of all time".

Warm applause greeted this. The president was re-elected. After refreshments and a trailer showing other coming releases (it had generally escaped attention that there were any others) the stockholders amiably dispersed. A few days later one paper reported ASP BITES LIZ—WORST NOW OVER. But, of course, it wasn't.

For the board's mood was less genial than that of the stockholders. If it was reassured by the promise of $150 million sweeping back to engulf them, it did not show it. Judge Rosenman, the chairman, and his executive committee now sent a delegation of three senior Fox executives, the toughest triumvirate available, to Rome. They had written orders to tell the producer, Walter Wanger, that he was removed and would get no more salary or expenses; that Cleopatra herself must be off the pay-roll within nine days; and that all shooting must finish within one month—the production had cost $32 million (£11 million) by this point.

The reaction was furious. Wanger felt that he was being made a scapegoat. Mankiewicz, supported by his cast, pointed out that the time allowed was impossible: the players would be reacting on film to battles that had not been fought. Compromises were eventually reached. Wanger said he would stay anyway. Mankiewicz was given until mid-July to have the whole thing completed: six weeks to pitch camp and shoot in two new locations. But the board was now looking so steely-eyed that the movie-makers got the impression they would be lucky to get their return fares paid if they overran the time limit.

At the end of May, with even more than habitual haste, the whole company moved to the island of Ischia, off Naples, to shoot the naval battle of Actium in which Octavius Caesar routs the combined forces of Antony and Cleopatra. The director's insistence on "shooting for real" (that is, not by trick-photography in a bath) involved a logistics effort rather greater than Octavius had put into the original. An assembly of war galleys, a fire-tender, camera-barges and a hospital ship (no one knew where realism might lead) moved to Ischia. In their wake, by various free-lance methods, followed a battalion or so of Rome extras, chasing their $10 (£3 12s.) a day to the bitter end.

The Ischian period severely tested everyone's last reserves of stamina. Each day they spent long hours at sea under a glaring sun. The queen's barge, 250 feet long, covered with gold linoleum, veritably burned on the water. "We had to give the hand-maidens damp cloths to stop them getting blisters. What the hell did they do in olden time?" This was the second queen's barge they had built. The first was still marooned up the Nile. At the time they needed it, floods had prevented them from getting it under the bridges and out to sea.

For a director with an all-indoors, parlour-wit reputation, Mankiewicz entered into the spirit of the open-air spectacular with startling vigour. "The spears, arrows and fiery missiles were flying around all right," recalled the art director not long ago. "You just picked up a shield and hoped for the best. It's the first time I remember the technical staff taking cover."

Ashore, production men were bargaining with the residents of a small Ischian port about dressing up their houses to represent the old waterfront at Tarsus. The residents, aware of their monopoly position, pitched their prices high.

Optimists in the unit had supposed that on Ischia they would be briefly islanded from headquarters pressure. But by a triumph of the Ischian postal and telegraph services, communications remained excellent. Urgent insistent voices from New York or Hollywood were there at all hours of the day and night. How much they shoot today? What the rushes like? What doing tomorrow? How's Liz?

The movie-makers sweated away from dawn to dusk. There was no sign of sympathy from any quarter. Back home in Hollywood people in motion-picture circles had been gulping down news of the outfit's disasters and financial troubles with a sort of cheerful amazement. Jokes about it monopolised the talk at Hollywood parties. "So there's all these slave-girls jumping in and out of the Nile, see? In and out all day. Not a minute's peace because they're all in such a goddam rush. So one slave-girl says to another: 'Say who d'ya have to sleep with to get *outa* this picture?'"

In New York, the company was shaping up to its own Actium. The board had to some extent restrained its large store of impatience partly out of fear of rocking the boat during a crisis, partly out of helplessness. Now, with the end nearly in sight, a number of directors were hot for a showdown.

The drain of money on the epic had persuaded most of the twelve-man board that a change of president was urgently necessary; but they were undecided about what sort of man should replace Skouras — a financial wizard or a showman. The most determined candidate was Darryl F. Zanuck, a major stockholder, formerly the company's studio chief, and now an independent producer. By July, Zanuck had rallied enough support to get himself appointed president with Skouras as chairman of the board; three directors resigned.

Zanuck was every inch a movie-maker. He had written scripts for the first of the wonder-dogs, Rin Tin Tin; helped with the birth of the talkies; got gangster pictures going; struck a tuning-fork for the musical extravaganzas; helped to push social significance on to the screen with *Grapes of Wrath*. He was credited with being a good showman in every waking minute. He liked to think of himself as a person of reckless informality—no tie, casual cigar, wind-on-the-heath, wind-in-the-hair; the laughing cavalier of motion pictures.

At script conferences he used to stride round the table swinging a polo mallet, acting all the parts in turn, actresses' too. He took a pride in keeping four secretaries going at once with dictation. He was, in short, essential and basic Hollywood Man.

The effect on the company of his appointment was instantaneous. Zanuck men poured into jobs at all levels at headquarters and overseas. Staff and salaries were cut. All films except *Cleopatra* were suspended for a year.

While this palace revolution was proceeding, the momentarily forgotten movie-makers were moving doggedly on to their last location. Octavius Caesar had put the enemy navies to flight, and now all they needed was a desert where the rival armies could confront each other.

The director's prescription, with the wide screen in mind, was a desert of rolling sand-dunes going on and on out of sight. Old Foreign Legion pictures, someone recalled, had always been shot a cab-ride from Hollywood; but that was too far away, and around the Mediterranean, for some reason, the right terrain proved curiously hard to find.

Eight or nine desert-hunting expeditions were mounted. "We tried Morocco, but didn't go for the political situation," recalled one explorer. "Then Spain, then Libya. No good either. Finally we ended up in Egypt." One reason for settling there was a hint from President Nasser that several thousand Egyptian troops would be available as extras at $1 (7s. 4d.) a day, a bargain not to be missed. When the team got there, they found the army rates had rocketed and it was just as cheap to rent civilians. The Queen of Egypt wasn't allowed in : they refused a visa because she had helped Israeli causes.

The movie-makers pitched their tents in suitably rolling sandscape near Edkou, twenty miles from Alexandria, surrounded by electric fly-catchers. The props-men set about learning ancient techniques with sand sledges to move heavy equipment and set a close guard on their props, having found that the *fellahin* of the villages, in their chronic need for firewood or simply things to possess, would seize anything they could.

About 3,000 extras were mustered, a large group from Alexandria, the remainder from the villages. No one quite knows what went wrong. Perhaps it was rural resentment at having their dollar area invaded by city men: possibly some obscure vendetta of Arab politics. The dismal fact was that fighting broke out among the extras before they had time to get their screen armour on.

"There was hardly a day without a stabbing incident. The wardrobe men who were handing out the weapons were terrified," recalls one veteran of the campaign. Wasn't this the way the Roman Empire went down—trouble on the periphery and dissension at home? For once, the board was too preoccupied with its own revolt to have time to register anguish in a cable. Finally the movie-makers tamed the extras, and got them into their armour. In a day or two, the last part of the picture was all shot and finished. Or so it looked.

The next thing that happened was that Zanuck, the new president, discharged Mankiewicz. He, Zanuck, would do the final editing in person. Mankiewicz was indignant—almost, but not quite, beyond words. "They can cut it up for toothpicks if they want to," he said; but the don't-care attitude was not convincing. He did not want his "authentic" child of nature dolled up into something else.

The true bulldog growl came out when the first samples of publicity material came his way, and he wrote back (for example): "The vastness of the Roman Empire *is not the subject of our film* . . ."; and "Caesar and Cleopatra are *never* passionately in love . . ."; and "PLEASE do not refer to Mark Antony as 'Caesar's most trusted warrior'. This type of phraseology conjures up all the worn-out corn we have tried desperately to avoid."

The Zanuck-Mankiewicz tussle lasted months, the essence of the argument being that the president wanted to see more "showmanship" in the picture, while the director's more subtle theatrical spirit cowered at the prospect. Reconciliation came at last; and in February, 1963, Mankiewicz found himself standing on a windy hill in southern Spain, with $2 million more to spend, directing large battle-scenes which the previous management had vetoed.

Props-men who had hired everything from asps to elephants in Rome and house-fronts in Ischia, now prowled the paddy-fields near Almeria looking for forty teams of oxen at $40 a day. They took on 1,000 horses, with Gipsies to ride them, built a couple of miles of canvas stabling and hired 3,000 Spanish extras—the fifth nationality to don the imperial armour. Between sandstorms and horse-stampedes, Caesar defeated Pompey. Then a final fortnight in London to dovetail Burton, on a patch of artificial sand, into the desert-scene (he was in another picture by then) and it was all over bar the cutting.

For the next two months the film shuttled to and fro between Mankiewicz in Hollywood and Zanuck in New York, sharing the editing process as a sort of needle tennis match. Episodes which had cost much toil and money to film were either reduced to a flicker of screen-time or expunged altogether. So it reached Broadway and, the other day, London.

But the wrangle about who was to take the blame if the film was a catastrophe or, alternatively, who was to get the credit if it succeeded, went on. Walter Wanger brought a suit for damages against Twentieth Century-Fox, Zanuck and Spyros Skouras, and Skouras sued Wanger for $700,000 damages for libel.

It seemed that the baleful influence of the serpent of old Nile had proved as timeless as clairvoyant historians had suspected. The whole experience may have aged *Them*. It didn't seem to have withered *Her*.

Antony with Cleopatra

Certainly our fields were planted
With lilac and poppies
When there was need of cotton and wheat.
So toward the end of summer
We began our walks on the outskirts of the city
To watch for the coming of strangers.

We were not young—but excellent.
What a long way from Italy,
The Nile never seemed so deep;
It was the very brim of summer,
Still the best time of the year for love,
Roman soldiers dived arch-backed into the sea.

Across the Mediterranean came Caesar and ships,
His spikes and axes multiplying the sun,
His sails full silver;
Our sheets still warm and wrinkled,
Cleopatra pretending sleep,
Antony still naked beneath his armour.

                                        STANLEY MOSS

The English Capacity for Pain

by Penelope Gilliatt

Lindsay Anderson's *This Sporting Life* is a stupendous film. It has a blow like a fist. I've never seen an English picture that gives such expression to the violence and the capacity for pain that there is in the English character. It is there in Shakespeare, in Marlowe, in Lawrence and Orwell and Hogarth, but not in our cinema like this before.

This Sporting Life is hard to write about because everything important about it is really sub-verbal. Perhaps it is best to begin, like the film, with the physical facts. Frank Machin, the hero, magnificently played by Richard Harris, must weigh fourteen stone. On the football field he has the power of a tank. His instinct in any situation is to get his head down and push; you see him first in a Rugby League scrum and then working in the mines in the same fierce stance, chewing gum as though his mouth were a treadmill. He looks as proud as a legendary animal; when his front teeth are smashed in a scrum the stumps are like the broken horns of a bull.

Lindsay Anderson's films before this have been documentaries, but his first feature certainly isn't a documentary about Rugby League. Nor is it a sociological study of a kind of contemporary man. Frank Machin could have lived at any time, and he is not anyone's representative; the film is about a unique man who suffers an absolutely personal kind of pain. The events almost seem to be happening to him in the dark. Half of them are told while he is under dentist's gas, in flashback, which is a clumsy device if one is telling a story but the natural method if one is searching around a character.

The first time you see him with his landlady—Rachel Roberts— you wonder what on earth the pressure is between them. This is the way it happens in life (and in Ibsen's plays), but hardly ever in cinema; their lines carry a terrific charge of the past. In a conventional narrative film it would be because he had made a pass at her or hadn't paid the rent, but here it comes out of character.

There is something about her put-upon Englishwoman's silences that makes him behave like a pig, and he could boot her for the way she droops over the memory of her dead husband; but at the same time there is a kind of purity about her withdrawal that somehow consoles him, although he does everything to wreck it. When he has sold himself for £1,000 to the North Country businessmen who run the team, he puts the cheque in front of her like a dog laying a putrid bone on a pillow.

The relationship thickens with hostility. Sometimes love-making works, but she generally manages to make him feel that he has assaulted her. They begin to have a gruelling power over each other, but it is a power only to give pain; they make demands of each other that are cruel because they can't be met, can't be communicated, can't even be defined to themselves.

Part of the quality of David Storey's script, from his own novel, is that the characters never offer explanations. Often what they say is not what they mean at all, which is one of the things that give the film its agonising tension between a rich instinctive life and a poverty-stricken expressive life. There is a very good scene when Frank unwraps a fur coat for her before taking her out on a spree. The cramped kitchen suddenly freezes over with the classic English repressiveness, and the neighbour who has come in to baby-sit behaves as though the place had turned into a brothel.

But when Mrs. Hammond pitches into a row after his best friend's wedding, her grievances about what the neighbours are saying are not really the root of her misery: they are simply the easiest reason to find for it. The difficulty isn't that they aren't married, it is that he disturbs her. In their last fight, which brings on a brain haemorrhage, all she can do is to yell that she wants peace.

The football game after her death is like the awful scene in a bull-ring when a Spanish audience whistles scorn at a matador because they suspect him of cowardice. His supporters are suddenly booing, and they are booing his pain. Something primitive and tragic is happening. One can't forget the way the game looked in a dream earlier on, a slow-motion sequence like a picture of boiling lava in the middle of the earth.

The black subjective spirit of the film is overpowering. It floods the sound-track, which often has a peculiar resonance as though it were happening inside one's own head; Roberto Gerhard's score is one of the best I have ever heard. Technically *This Sporting Life* is like a rock. For one thing, it has obviously been made with a clear idea of how it was to be edited, which is rarer than it sounds. For another, the actors rehearsed for ten days first, and the scenes between Richard Harris and Rachel Roberts were done roughly in continuity; how else can serious actors work and how often does the cinema bother about it?

The tension between the two of them is suffocating. There is also a remarkable performance by Colin Blakely as Frank's friend, who is his ear at the end for his one helpless attempt to understand himself. Like the classical tragic hero, Frank has no power to change his life because he has no insight into it; all he has is a final stab of knowledge about how he looks to other people. "She called me a great ape on a football field," he says about his mistress. And about the football crowds: "They want someone to act big for them." This is what heroic art is about.

How Far Out is the Avant-Garde?

by Peter Heyworth

*Our music critic reported these findings from the Festival
of Contemporary Music at Palermo.*

First the facts, in so far as I have been able to grasp them during
a gruelling week of very advanced music indeed at Palermo.

The structuralism of the fifties is out. Today, no self-respecting
composer would be caught dead with a series that is rigorously applied
to all the elements of music (rhythm, duration and dynamics as well
as pitch), and mere mention of works that are serially determined
in this way now draws derisive comment from tongues remarkably
similar to those that once proclaimed such edifices as new pinnacles
of human achievement. How, they ask, could anyone ever have
supposed that just because there are twelve notes in a chromatic
scale, the figure twelve has any special relevance to the other elements
of music? How indeed?

But the burden of perfect freedom is hard to bear, and it is not
surprising that a majority of the 30-odd composers represented at
Palermo have had to find some new shelter from the strain it imposes.
The latest encampment (one cannot speak of permanent buildings in
an area so fluid as that of advance-guard music) now flies a banner
bearing the strange device "aleatoric".

My researches reveal this to be a scientific term, used to describe
a situation that is fixed and determined in the main, but in which
there are small areas that remain undetermined. Unfortunately the
very work that heralded the whole movement, Stockhausen's Piano
Pieces XI (1956), proceeded to stand the word on its head. The element of freedom here lies in the order in which the pieces are played.
The result is something determined in detail rather than in the
whole.

In fact aleatoric has come to be used of almost any music that offers
possibilities of choice (or chance) to the performer. It can cover a very
modest element of freedom, as in Maxwell Davies's String Quartet. Or
it can embrace the reading of the evening paper's headlines to
determine (but how?) the "articulation" (whatever that may be) of
Donatoni's Quartetto IV. But in all cases it implies a score that can
materialise in various guises.

At Palermo this Donatoni piece had two performances, one quite
different in character from the other. In Germany, where they go

into these things more thoroughly, a quartet recently devoted a three-hour concert to exploring some of its further possibilities. And lest the reader suppose that I have malevolently chosen an extreme case, let me add that this quartet was in fact among the more musical (and the more conventional) works to be performed.

That composers should have felt the need to escape the straitjacket of structuralism is understandable, even if the spectacle of so many solid, middle-aged citizens hastily stampeding from a world in which everything is determined to one that is "free", is comic rather than edifying. But utterly opposed to an all-embracing serialism though the aleatoric flux may seem, the two schools do in fact have one essential in common: they both offer the composer refuge from the agony of creative decision.

In a totally serial structure the composer can wind up his machine like a clockwork mouse and then unloose it without incurring too much responsibility for the details of the scenery through which its serial springs may take it. In an aleatoric work he is similarly relieved of the burden of deciding precisely which of the paths his score may take is best.

Of course there must *be* a best, and almost any composer's sketchbook represents a struggle to determine which it is. Indeed this is the very crux of creative labour. But on what principles are composers who have rejected both tonality and serialism to base their decision? No wonder so many of them prefer to evade it.

In fact they have landed themselves in a position curiously similar to that which confronted Schoenberg after the first rupture of tonality and before the emergence of the serial method. A few of the composers at Palermo have had the courage to confront this fact, and it is no coincidence that, for example, the prism of slowly changing colours in Clementi's organ-like "Informel 3" should strikingly recall the *Klangfarbenmelodie* movement from Schoenberg's "Five Orchestral Pieces" of 1909. There was also a most evocative and beautifully controlled exercise in orchestral virtuosity by Ligeti, called, with unusual accuracy, "Atmosphères". But there are limitations to mood music, and that is maybe one reason why Ligeti has since (I am told) written a work for massed metronomes.

It is, of course, despair of the possibility of any rational musical order that lies behind an experiment of this sort, just as it is despair in the very possibility of musical communication that has pushed another group that has been well represented at Palermo into the orbit of John Cage's neo-Dada pranks, and into using musical resources for any purpose other than musical expression.

Kagel's "Antithese", in which a white-coated technician desperately tries to stem a barrage of electronic eruptions from a battery of old gramophones and radios, may be thought a good Chaplinesque joke but badly lacks a Chaplinesque sense of timing. Castaldi's "Anfrage" is a collage of snippets from nineteenth century and advanced piano music, organised, no doubt, on aleatory principles. Up to a point some of its juxtapositions are quite funny, and with a good deal of cutting (for all these jokes are fearfully long-winded) it might well appeal to the audiences of Hoffnung concerts, and so no doubt would the electric fan that figures prominently in Evangelisti's "Random Or Not Random".

But what is one to say of a work such as Dieter Schnebel's "Glossolalie", in which the singers grunt, snore, whistle, utter strange words and finally leave the conductor to continue the recitation; or of Chiari's "Per arco", in which a 'cellist sits slumped, like a spastic moron, over his instrument, and during some fifteen minutes does nothing but make an occasional unsuccessful attempt to draw his bow across the strings of his instrument?

This work was described by an admirer as "tragic". And so indeed it is, for it represents the total abdication of the artist in the face of his task of communication. No amount of ingenious theorising about "a continuum between what is heard and what is seen", about "audiences integrated with the performer by acts of aggression committed against them", or "a musical theatre that finds its dramatic material in its own performance" (these neo-Cageian concepts were offered at Palermo with a bewitchingly bland air of reason by Heinz-Klaus Metzger, the movement's main theorist), can disguise the fact that works such as these quite literally represent the end of music as we have known it. Indeed, the composers themselves seem to be the first to rejoice in that fact.

One evening as I came away from a concert my headlights picked out rats scurrying among the refuse strewn about the Via Di Lampedusa. Do they already sense decomposition in the air?

A single work may appear arbitrary. But a whole movement (and what is taking place in music has its all too clear equivalents in "happenings" in the other arts) is never so irrelevant to the society that gives it birth as may appear at the time. Signor Chiari's 'cellist may not fiddle, but if art is still exercising its usual prophetic functions, then fasten your seat belts, for this time a great deal more than Rome may burn.

Let me, however, pay tribute to our executioners; to the two Palermitan orchestras that laboured heroically under the fluent direction of Daniele Paris to produce performances more coherent than is usually the case when so much music of this sort is given in a single week: to the exceptionally fine piano playing of Frederic Rzewski; to Liliana Poli, who, unlike most sopranos who specialise in this field, has a voice with colour in it and timbre, and who, together with that superb singer-*diseuse*, Cathy Berberian, almost managed to impart momentary significance to an hour-long charade by Bussotti entitled "Torso".

And I must also mention Berio's "Tempi Concertati". In substance this may amount to little more than a divertimento. Yet here at any rate musical ideas are still fashioned into a comprehensible sequence by a mind that has not yet abandoned all attempts at coherence. But then it was written aeons ago in 1958. Heaven knows what Berio is up to now.

"My Best Work"

by Jules Feiffer

Mother and Daughter of Revolt

by Alexander Bland

Martha Graham is not only the mother of revolt; she is also a true daughter of the revolution. She has all the virtues and vices of the pioneer. She is stern, moral and muscular. She has no time for fripperies and would probably not appreciate Wilde's view that only shallow people despise superficiality. She likes men to be men, and women to be the next best thing. To her, as to the ancient Greeks, moonlight means just bad shooting conditions. She will not faint at the sight of blood and has an open-air attitude to exercise and sex. She believes in things being done right.

The nineteenth century made dancers airborne. Skirts got shorter, jumps higher, steps faster. The emphasis was on lightness and softness and speed. This trend has continued until there was a danger of the whole thing floating up into a misty sky of unreality. Graham put ballast in ballet. She has taught her dancers to exploit gravity instead of defying it, to make pain and strain, which the classical dancer conceals, a means of expression. Her choreography does not glitter or twinkle. By eliminating classical ballet's virtuoso effects—spins, beats, extended line—she has slowed everything down, like a musician who scorns the semi-quaver. This leaves large areas out of her reach, but it makes easy what classical style (c.f. Cranko's *Antigone*) finds most difficult, solemnity and majesty. She has found, in fact, a modern equivalent of the old big-scale epic as carried on by the Bolshoi—a company with which hers has a curious affinity.

In an age groping for new theatrical forms this is important. If some total theatre emerges, incorporating speech, song and dance, Graham will surely be an ingredient, in the same way that her non-narrative approach to her themes is in tune with the Brechtian angle currently so influential. Her slow tempo also enables her to use the stage and to furnish it in a new way. Her solid rhythms are those of sculpture, an art much more important than painting to dancers and choreographers, but not always equally studied.

The movements of Graham's dancers are not, incidentally, much more "natural" than those of a classical dancer. A child at play would no more jerk her stomach than twirl on one foot, and under a ceremonial robe a bare big toe is as exiguous as a pink point-shoe.

The tone of her theatrical voice is odd. It is puritan, yet obsessed with sex; lust, not love, is her principal theme. It is sinewy and masculine, yet not without a titillatory sensationalism. It is modern and austere; yet a strong thread of lush *fin-de-siècle* romanticism runs, all purple and gold, through the sumptuous tangles of doom into which she transforms Sophocles or the Old Testament.

She began, in fact, as a straight romantic. An understandable revulsion against classical ballet's too easy lapses into sentiment and charm led her into a knotted, tensed-up manner which is weak where that style is strong and strong where it is weak. Perhaps naturally, where Ashton, Balanchine or Fokine explore the femininity of girls, Graham concentrates on the masculinity of men. She writes most and best for her male dancers; her girls tend always towards athleticism and the—to European eyes—assertiveness of "the American woman".

This is amply demonstrated in her new ballet *Circe* in which Ulysses is tempted by animal lust, represented by Circe and her band. As voluptuousness is portrayed by four near-naked men and one well-clad girl, the affair often skirts perilously near to a male striptease act, especially as the part of the seductress is short and rather weakly and drily conceived. But there are recurring moments of wonderful poses and piled-up groups which marry Epstein to Michelangelo and it is a good vehicle for two of the talented company's best dancers, Richard Gain and Robert Powell.

Graham is, artistically, an unregenerate egoist (both she and all her company dance the whole time as if they were alone). She started as a soloist and the roles of creator and interpreter are still closely interwoven in her. As a performer she has necessarily less and less to give and it will be exciting to see this inimitable teacher and moulder shaping a successor in the roles which she must obviously soon relinquish.

In the long view Graham's approach and particular idiom of movement will be absorbed into theatrical history. Take her or leave her, her little bare footprint will not be erased from the stage. At this particular moment in our local history she has made two vital contributions. She has redressed the balance in an art too often thought fit to record only the sunshine hours; and she has achieved the apparently impossible feat of summoning up a new audience, an audience open to dance experiment and new forms. The problem now is to nourish and so conserve it.

Drama

The National Theatre's First Night

by Bamber Gascoigne

The danger, of course, was that the great inaugural production of the National Theatre, eagerly awaited for over a half-century, might seem just one more Shakespeare at the Old Vic. I'm happy to say it didn't.

To start with, the building itself has had a very necessary face-lift. The corridors are now lined with a bright saffron hessian (this has something of the desperate quality of thick rouge on a very old face but is certainly far from dull) and the auditorium is a pleasant green. The stage has a simple and attractive new wood-panelled proscenium. And for the occasion it was ideal to select the world's most famous play, our own bard's most surefire tragedy, *Hamlet*.

Sir Laurence Olivier's production started off rather shakily, with signs of undigested pieces of business and carefully planned moments which still looked like carefully planned moments. But this was probably only nerves (we were nervous, too) and by half-way through the evening it was clear that we were seeing an efficient and at times a most imaginative version. Olivier is not trying to prove anything new about the play, but he has approached each scene with considerable freshness of vision.

The "nunnery" scene, for example, is often played on one note of anguish and distrust. Olivier opens it with a most effective jolt—Hamlet and Ophelia fly eagerly into each other's arms—and he then presents us with what is unmistakably a love-scene. The delight of sexual play keeps bubbling up near the surface, helped there by Ophelia's desires and half-welcomed by Hamlet. One feels that this meeting (and it is the first time we see the two together) could well have been entirely delightful but for the rottenness of Elsinore and Hamlet's own predicament. Never before have I so fully believed that the two actually love each other.

Another superb example is the fight in Ophelia's grave. In most productions the sacrilege of this event is almost academic—we don't feel the trampling on a corpse. But Olivier interprets literally Laertes' statement that he will take his sister once more in his arms. This Laertes gathers up the body and hugs it to him, and when Hamlet leaps into the grave Ophelia is still visibly there, lolling buffeted between them. The effect is horrifying and entirely true to the scene.

At moments like this Peter O'Toole's Hamlet is splendid. This is a Hamlet of action, convincing and at ease when there is something for him to do, whether jesting with the gravedigger, mocking Osric, stage-managing the players, duelling with Laertes or even reacting, against his will, to the charms of Ophelia. The trouble with this is that one begins to feel there is nothing but the plot to stop him murdering his uncle, particularly since O'Toole is much less convincing in the dark scenes of quiet and doubt. I never felt the brooding, wounded introvert, even though the outward signs were there. O'Toole seemed to wear his melancholy like a mask, lengthening his face and staring at us with sad unfocused eyes when grief was in the air. Too often this was a clown of sorrow, a huge blond Marcel Marceau.

The supporting cast is, as indeed it should be, quite exceptional. Michael Redgrave plays Claudius with a subtle mixture of sly charm and genuine courage; Diana Wynyard gives a good picture of ageing lasciviousness; Robert Stephens is the most convincing Horatio I have ever seen, playing him as an ordinary and even rather tentative person instead of the usual head prefect; Rosemary Harris's Ophelia is extremely touching, with a matter-of-fact and very successful version of the mad scene, done without a trace of balletic wispiness; Derek Jacobi makes a quite excellent Laertes and Max Adrian is predictably enjoyable as Polonius, though hampered by a ridiculous mock-Tudor balaclava through which his ears elfishly peep.

Sean Kenny's set consists of a huge curving structure, which at rest spans the centuries between Stonehenge and a Marples ridgeway, and between the scenes writhes and flexes like a dinosaur. Olivier puts it to a wide variety of uses and its shape makes a good frame for the action, but I found its texture ugly and disconcerting.

In general, this makes a very promising opening to the National Theatre. Most important of all, there is already the nucleus of an extremely strong company; and if the progress from Chichester eighteen months ago to the Old Vic can be continued from the Old Vic to the opening of the theatre on the South Bank, then that really will be an impressive first night.

Littlewood's Lovely War

by Kenneth Tynan

It seems to me quite likely that when the annals of our theatre in the middle years of the twentieth century come to be written, one name will lead all the rest: that of Joan Littlewood. Others write plays, direct them or act in them: Miss Littlewood alone "makes theatre".

She has come back to Theatre Workshop, after two years' lamented absence, with a triumph unimaginable anywhere but on a stage; it belongs uniquely to its birthplace—the bare boards that are Littlewood's home ground, filled with the passion of Littlewood's home team.

According to the programme, *Oh What a Lovely War* was "written by Charles Chilton and the Members of the Cast"; it is further described as a "group production under the direction of Joan Littlewood"; but I must risk the lady's fury by insisting that it is essentially a one-woman show. The big, tough, purposeful heart that beats throughout the evening belongs only to Joan. You feel that her actors have a common attitude towards more than acting, a shared vision that extends to life in general; it is thus, rather than by any rehearsal method or technique of staging, that true theatrical style is born.

The plot is history: nothing less than the First World War. The cast is decked out in the ruffs and white satin suits of a seaside pierrot show. We are to witness (the compère brightly confides) that famous extravaganza, "the War Game", enacted by the entire company with musical interludes drawn from songs of the period. The proscenium sparkles with fairy lights; and a terrible counterpoint is soon set up between the romanticism of the lyrics, all gaiety and patriotic gusto, and the facts of carnage in France, illustrated by stills of the trenches and the news reports flickering across an electrified ribbon screen.

Between songs, and with minor costume adjustments—the addition of a tunic, a helmet, a Sam Browne belt—the cast perform a montage of brisk, laconic sketches, rooted in improvisation but stripped of all irrelevant detail. We glimpse a bayonet practice, conducted in lightning gibberish; a military ball, rippling with intrigue; a shooting party of international tycoons, blazing away at wildfowl while debating the relative merits of various neutral trade routes for exporting arms to the enemy; and the Christmas truce on the Western Front, while Miss Littlewood handles with utter disdain for sentimentality —the Tommies recoil with nausea from a gift of German cheese, and respond by lobbing an inedible Christmas pudding into the opposite trenches.

Meanwhile the songs grow more bitter; the lunatic Haig has taken command, and the dead are rotting in mountains, monuments to his unswerving conceit. And still, indestructibly if not always suddenly, everyone bursts out singing.

In the second half the show tends to repeat itself, as the war so tragically did; but by then Miss Littlewood's passion has invaded one's bloodstream, and after the final scene, in which a line of reluctant heroes advances on the audience, bleating like sheep in a slaughterhouse, one is ready to storm Buckingham Palace and burn down Knightsbridge Barracks. The production brings off a double *coup*: it is revolutionary alike in content and form. And even those who mistrust revolution can hardly deny that it has the most memorable score in London.

The cast (an ensemble from which I invidiously select the names of Ann Beach, Murray Melvin, Victor Spinetti and Brian Murphy) behaves with the same relaxed audacity that Miss Littlewood captured on film in *Sparrows Can't Sing*. I hope success will not doom her present troupe to the fate that immobilised its predecessors: indefinite incarceration in the dreaded West End.

Books

When the French Refused to Fight

by A. J. P. Taylor

Reviewing Dare Call It Treason *by Richard M. Watt, which deals with one of the episodes featured in Joan Littlewood's production.*

That rational creature Man does some strange irrational things. None stranger than that he puts up with war. War is all right in the abstract. It provides perorations for politicians and fills the history books with heroic passages. Real war means being killed in a horrible way. Yet men have gone on fighting throughout the centuries.

Some no doubt have enjoyed it. Many have been ready to sacrifice life itself for their political or religious beliefs. The great mass of men have fought because they were told to. Why? Perhaps in earlier times because they were deliberately brutalised and incapable of seeing even the nearest future. This could not work for the great armies of the twentieth century. Loyalty and habit sent them forward. Then a vague hope of survival kept them in line.

At any rate, for whatever reason, only one modern army has ever downed tools while the war was on. Armies have disintegrated after defeat, as the Austro-Hungarian army did in 1918, or after a political revolution in the capital, as the Russian army did in 1917. Even British soldiers mutinied in 1919, in order to go home faster. Only the French army mutinied in the face of the enemy.

This unique episode was concealed at the time and has remained obscure ever since. Mr. Watt reveals the full story for the first time. He has pieced together the details with scholarly ingenuity. His tests of credibility are a model on which historians should meditate. He writes attractively, and the book deserves the praise which Captain Cyril Falls gives it in the introduction: "Good, erudite and lively."

We learn for the first time what really happened to the French army in May and June of 1917. The men did not mutiny in the strict sense. There were few attacks on officers and surprisingly little desertion. The soldiers continued to hold the front line. They refused to take part in further offensive operations or to enter the trenches for obviously offensive purpose. Some of them seized trains and set off to Paris with a crude idea of overthrowing the Government. None of these trains arrived at its destination. The men lost interest and drifted back to their duty after a few days of disobedience.

The mutinies had a simple cause. The French army had lost faith in their leaders. The soldiers believed that the offensives could not succeed and that the generals did not understand modern war. Both beliefs were justified. Pétain restored discipline when he showed that he cared for his men and intended to keep on the defensive. Of course, Pétain also had many of the ringleaders shot. This is the darkest point of the story and will never be illuminated. No one will ever know how many French, dead for the country, were killed by Frenchmen —some hundreds, perhaps some thousands.

Mr. Watt's book is faultless while it sticks to the mutinies. Unfortunately, even his research can stretch these to cover only half the book. Mr. Watt has strayed into general history, and here his touch is less sure. Here are three examples in ascending order of importance. There were not twenty-two assassins waiting for Franz Ferdinand at Sarajevo, only six. Nivelle did not convert Lloyd George to an offensive in a railway carriage; this is a legend invented by John Buchan. Pétain did not ask Haig to launch the Flanders offensive in order to take the strain off the mutinous French army; this is an excuse invented by Haig in 1927, as even Haig's champion, Mr. Terraine, recognises.

Some of the background chapters make sense. The prolonged and futile offensives from August, 1914, to April, 1917, explain why the French soldiers reached breaking-point. Our only complaint is that they have been described fully and effectively by many previous writers, and they spoil our appetite for the new stuff which comes later. Mr. Watt ranges further back. He discusses once more the political troubles provoked by the army of the Third Republic from Boulanger to Dreyfus. Perhaps these ought to have broken the faith of the soldiers in their leaders. There is little evidence that they did so. Instead Mr. Watt might profitably have considered whether there was something peculiarly at fault either with the French commanders or with the junior officers. Mr. Barnett recently did much better here.

Mr. Watt's most serious weakness is that he has listened too much to the French generals. He slips over into implying that the mutinies were caused by pacifist propaganda—an easy cover for military incompetence at all times. He goes further and accepts as pacifists those who wanted a negotiated peace. Despite his title, he comes near to describing them as traitors.

This is an almost inevitable attitude nowadays, when we have all been schooled to march under the banner of national union, first against Hitler and now against Soviet Russia. Those who preach war are always patriots even when they are leading their country to ruin. Those who oppose war are always pacifists and traitors. It all depends on the point of view. I have heard stalwart fire-eaters regretting that there was no negotiated peace in 1917. Mr. Watt himself remarks that, if Caillaux had made peace with the Germans, "perhaps today he would be regarded as a great statesman, the 'first European', and a man of peace. Treason, after all, is a transitory crime." Yet Mr. Watt presents Clemenceau's accession to power as a glorious triumph and even rejoices at the trial of Caillaux on trumped-up charges.

I doubt whether a historian should take sides in these old quarrels. The French moderates of 1917 were not traitors, and the French generals, not the French pacifists, caused the great mutinies. Though not enthusiastic for capital punishment, I am for shooting generals, not the lambs whom they led to the slaughter.

Mutiny in 1917

A Letter to the Editor

Sir.—I was interested to read Mr. A. J. P. Taylor's review of Richard M. Watt's book *Dare Call it Treason* in your issue of January 26 in which he mentions the mutinies of British soldiers in 1919.

I remember them well as I took an active part in them. But what he doesn't mention was the mutiny of British troops in 1917. Strangely enough, I have heard very little about the so-called Bull Ring Mutiny and have met only one man in recent years who was actively connected with it.

The first I heard of it was in the summer of 1917 when I was corporal in charge of two Lewis guns in the Durham Light Infantry in the 50th Division. Several of my men who had been wounded returned to the unit with wounds that were far from being healed.

When I asked why they had returned in that condition they invariably replied: "To get away from the Bull Ring." At first I took little or no notice of this; then one day a man returned and, after three days' rest, I ordered him to do something. He asked me if I could let him off the duty. When I demanded why, he stripped off his tunic and exposed a wound that was not only raw, but gaping. He gave the same excuse for returning, namely, the Bull Ring. Knowing him to be an honest and truthful person I asked him to tell me about it.

According to him G.H.Q. gave orders that no wounded man had

to be sent to Blighty unless his wounds were really serious. Otherwise he had to be treated and returned to his unit as quickly as possible.

When they were thought to be fit enough they were sent to a so-called convalescence camp near Calais. The day after they arrived an instructor would advise them that they would have to be strengthened up for their return to their units. After they had been dished out with rifles which had to be cleaned and inspected they would be given a short march with their rifles slung.

On their return their rifles would be inspected. As the march was across sand-dunes sand would cover the rifle breeches and the instructor would rant and rave and give the worst offenders two hours' marching with full pack. From that moment every instructor was on the look-out for faults, real or imaginary, and the men were for ever on extra duties or undergoing punishment.

According to my gunner the instructors were the worst in the Army—some, I was told, were brought from the glasshouse at Aldershot. They made the lives of these men so miserable, they begged to be returned to their units. It was a savage way of dealing with men who deserved better.

The M.O. returned this man to hospital. Some time later another of my men came back. When I asked if he had come from the Bull Ring he laughed and told me it was no more. It was he who described the mutiny and I had no reason to doubt his word.

One morning an instructor was taking a squad on aiming practice. Armed with a small metal disc upon which was painted a target, the instructor would stare through the hole in the middle of the disc along the sights of the rifle and order the man to aim and fire. If the gun wavered the slightest fraction of a millimetre the instructor would shout and curse at the culprit and give him extra duties or punishment.

This particular morning, one of his squad, who was little more than a boy, inserted a live round in the breech of his rifle. When ordered to fire he blew out the instructor's brains. Almost at the same instant another instructor was shot near the gate of the camp. Instantly the mutiny was ablaze. Within an hour another nine instructors died. The remainder fled along with the officers.

The mutineers appointed officers and N.C.O.s who organised a siege. The men were armed, trenches were dug and manned, machine-gun posts were set up and the men settled down to take anything that might come. They were ordered to surrender and refused.

Troops were brought up and, under darkness, surrounded the mutineers' lines. Among them was a battalion of Australians who, when they heard they were to open fire upon the mutineers if they did not surrender within a given time, went over to the mutineers to a man. The numbers of the besieged grew until they were estimated to be around 5,000.

G.H.Q. were in a flap. It so happened that Horatio Bottomley was lecturing over there at that time and he offered to mediate between the men and H.Q. His offer was accepted and it was agreed that the Bull Ring would be disbanded. Men would not be discharged from hospital until their wounds were healed and there would be no victimisation.

Liss.   J. HAYS

The Pleasures of Sex

by Marghanita Laski

In November the police seized copies of an eighteenth-century book called Fanny Hill *by John Cleland and later the Bow Street magistrate declared it obscene. Our critic anticipated the court's verdict with another of her own.*

Till now, all the post-Chatterley books about sex have had, whatever their intentions, the effect of putting one off it. *Fanny Hill*, a story of some literary merit that refreshingly makes no claim to be actually about religion or somesuch, does not. I enjoyed it very much.

Shockingly, this first overt edition in England since the first tells us nothing of the author and nothing of the book's history, not even the date of first publication beyond "over 200 years ago". The Dictionary of National Biography fills the gap. John Cleland (1709-89) was educated at Westminster School, entered the East India Company, left after a quarrel and wandered destitute round Europe. In 1748 he published the first part and in 1749 the second part of *Fanny Hill*. For its indecency he was summoned before the Privy Council where he successfully pleaded poverty as his excuse. Later he became an inept philologist, intent to retrieve the primitive language of Europe. For *Fanny Hill* he received 20 guineas; the publisher is said to have made £10,000.

Fanny Hill is an epistolary novel, told in the first person by the titular heroine. The innocent orphan comes up to London and falls in with a bawd who seeks to exploit her virginity. Fanny runs away with and loses it to a charming youth, soon rudely snatched from her. After a time in other keeping, she joins the small stable of an amiable governess who caters only for the *ton* and keeps an eye on proceedings by undisclosed means—one suspects a double mirror. Eventually a well-dowered and retired Fanny marries her first love, and the book ends with the eldest son just introduced to London vice as the best possible incitement to future virtue.

The book's first merit is that it tells a gay and enjoyable story. Cleland enters into his female *persona* at least as well as Defoe can, and of Defoe we are, at least in the clean bits, often reminded. But of course the important part of the book is the sex, several dozen copulations or related activities being fully described.

The great thing about the sex in this book is that it is true to life, in feeling and in fact, as in no other pornographic book I have read. Leaving aside, for the moment, the story circumstances of each act, what takes place is sex as we all know (or believe) it to be, and, which I found especially pleasing, with a full acceptance of women's equal desire and pleasure. "How often, when the rage and tumult of my senses had subsided . . . have I asked myself . . . if it was in nature for any of its creatures to be so happy as I was?" Many writers have tried to describe a woman's sexual feelings; this one succeeds.

No detail is burked. The language is of a flowery and euphuistic kind (no four-letter words), at its best immensely effective and even pretty, at its worst (alas, when dealing with True Love at the end) Amanda Ros-ish. Of course the book is pornographic in that it rouses feelings of sexual desire, but it does so directly and straightforwardly, without any possibility of confusing these feelings with others, and usually without any after-taste of disgust.

People vary of course in what they find disgusting. I was disgusted by an episode with an idiot, bored by a flagellation episode, apparently unavoidable in an English book of this kind, shocked by the author's censoriousness to male homo-sexuality.

As to whether the book is immoral: yes, it is immoral in that all the episodes take place in extra-marital contexts. Sadly we have to accept that, in literature at least, sex is not considered as exciting in marriage as outside it. But if we are to condemn books for sanctioning extra-marital sex, then the issue of pornography is irrelevant and we have no more or less reason to condemn *Fanny Hill* on this point than, say, *Saturday Night and Sunday Morning* or *Bel Ami* or *Moll Flanders*.

The question is rather whether to describe sexual activities in detail is immoral, and for my part I would decide on what activities and how described, and by the latter I do not refer to literary merit but rather to honest reporting, which this book undoubtedly shows. As to the activities themselves, the author by intention describes a substantially varied range but, on the whole, keeping well within what would usually be accepted as normal and pleasing, whether in marriage or outside it; and where people do choose to practise sex is each person's own moral decision. That Cleland also describes episodes less pleasing, such as the fumblings of impotence or female December with male May does not seem to me to condemn his book in that such episodes, which we all know to occur, are fairly and realistically described.

But with a cheap paperback edition we do have to ask what we feel about it in the hands of the young. There is a lot to be said for self-denial, and I do feel that on the whole young people are as well-advised not to read about sex, beyond essential physiological information, before they encounter it, as they are not to look at photographs of Venice before they go. But, as we all know from our own experience, we have to reckon with prurient curiosity and self-denial is improbable. What effect is this book likely to have?

In any normal person it will rouse sexual desire. But it is already normal for sexual desire to be easily aroused in young people, whether corruptly, as I see it, by many advertisements, films, songs, comics, or directly by say, spring or the opposite sex, and because *Fanny Hill's* appeal is direct, not furtive or covert, I would not call it harmful on this ground. Then, because what it has to say about the practices of sex is realistic and true, it could, I think, be helpful rather than harmful.

People have got to learn about sex from somewhere and, as Marriage Guidance Councils sadly report, experience is often insufficient. People who read *Fanny Hill* will learn a wide range of normal sexual practices and normal responses to them, and also the useful lesson, too seldom taught, that uncontrollable sexual desire may be roused in both sexes by propinquity or by pursuing sexual curiosity, even though rational inclination preferred chastity.

I am inclined to think that *Fanny Hill*, with its emphasis on sex as thoroughly enjoyable, might well be a better, healthier guide than the self-conscious, self-righteous, painfully frank instruction manuals of our own time. The likely harm will not be from the practices described but from the apparent delights of the extra-marital contexts and for this, as I have said, we cannot condemn *Fanny Hill* alone or even books alone.

We must separate content and context. For content *Fanny Hill* is the most enjoyable and realistic pornographic book I have read and I don't believe it harmful. Context must be each individual's own moral decision. But some people should avoid this book: those who cannot or may not or would rather not satisfy the desire it rouses; and those who find sex disgusting.

Painting

Yeats and the Painted Cloths

by Nigel Gosling

Enjoyment, truth, vision, technique—these are four powerful things, and Jack Yeats had them all. The impact of his retrospective show at the Waddington Gallery is electric. If any 40 paintings can persuade us to remove him from the local team into the international one, these are they.

They are easy pictures, accessible to anyone, but they contain a variety of appeals. To begin with, Yeats is an out-and-out romantic, which means that his own personality is given a free rein. He must have been an extraordinary character. Son of a competent portrait painter, and brother to the famous poet, he was born in Soho and brought up in Sligo. There, in his crucial boyhood years, he absorbed the Irish scene, which was to remain his stamping-ground for life—green fields, the sea, horses, rope-haired girls, tinkers at a fair with arms flung up in rage or wild triumph against what he called "the weather rolling about the sky". The wind got into his paint. He had drama in his bones and poetry ran out of his brush.

Yeats came back to London as a student and attended an art school. At 20 he visited Venice—his only European trip—and married. Two years later he was back in Ireland. Apart from a voyage or two to England and America he never left it again until his death in 1957 at 86. The European revolution in art passed him by.

In the first quarter of this exhibition it is Yeats's feeling with, and relish for, his fellow men which emerges. The language is still stilted, resulting in rather magazine-illustration paintings like "Morning After Rain". But when he reached 50 a new element crept in. The texture of his work suddenly loosens and an extraordinary gush of lyrical energy is released.

Look at the painting from 1919. "Before the Start". A jockey sits sideways on a great black horse talking to the trainer. Beyond, another horseman waits for him. Behind that the fields and woods lie banked against a heavy sky. The whole scene, caught with an instant click of apprehension, is swept over the canvas in one dazzling stream of rippling colour. The horse's arched head, the tweedy crook of the trainer's elbow, the sheen on the racing blouse and the lean, proud, melancholy face of the rider are all dissolved in a web of nervous strokes which has rightly made Beckett compare Yeats with Watteau. It is unlikely that a better racing picture will be painted.

This is the time when Yeats seems most surely to have touched

213

the crock of gold—a moment when vision was held beneath reality by the thinnest shell. His little bare-back galloping urchin in "The Jockey Act" is wild and resonant as a Delacroix; the lighterman's gesture in "The Breaker-out" has a slow un-moral solemnity echoed in the dark water; the sundown view of O'Connell Bridge in unexpected monochrome finds and fixes the Wordsworthian richness of an urban river.

Later come the purely visionary paintings, where he leaves Ireland behind. These are, at their best, more splendidly unusual (Turner and Kokoschka come to mind) but also less even. The childlike wonder of his imagination is something to be savoured—who, before Nolan, could paint a man stretched in the grass (drunk, no doubt) apostrophising a singing thrush?

But Yeats is venturing here into dangerous altitudes. There are occasional patches of inspired emptiness. The baroque theatricality of his vision in a painting like "Discovery" or "Leaving the Raft" is sustained only by an instinct for pumping life into every centimetre of canvas by sheer manipulation of pigment.

His colour-sense, always good, has now become spectacular. The dazzle of blue spread over and into the dark foreground figures of his magic-lantern scene "Singing, 'It was the schooner Hesperus'", and the delicate pink traceries which indicate the walls round the "Man in a Room Thinking", are bits of painting as pure as anything from contemporary Paris or New York. They are markings as clear, indefinable, beautiful and useful as the spots on a rainbow trout.

Yeats was working in the tributary of a stream which had taken a new turn and he never won real fame. His wife died; he lived on in Dublin with only his dreams. But the cloths he has painted for us are just those his poet brother coveted, to spread beneath the feet of his mistress—"enwrought with golden and silver light, the blue and the dim and the dark cloths of night and light and half-light"; and they too may be trodden on softly.

Architecture

The Hilton on London's Skyline

by Michael Manser

A good deal of sentimental nonsense has been talked about London's skyline by critics of the Hilton Hotel and the new skyscrapers.

The truth is that London is a monotonously even spread of second-rate building, and hasn't had a skyline since the times when Westminster Abbey rose head and shoulders above Whitehall or Wren's churches dominated the city. Apart from vistas down the lake in St. James's park to the Foreign Office and down the Serpentine to Big Ben, only the profile of St. Paul's really deserves its sky-space.

Elsewhere the skyline is yet to be made. Soho, Victoria, Paddington, Notting Hill, Oxford Circus and Marylebone have gained immeasurably from towers. They re-identify lost neighbourhoods and contribute variety and drama to the form of the city if grouped in clusters at chosen local centres. Even Earl's Court has gained identity from the splendid crudity of Empress State House.

On this basis, there seems very little reason for the site of the new Hilton Hotel, and cogent reasons against it. It represents no focal point in the urban arrangement and has no relationship to Hyde Park Corner, to Shepherd Market, Piccadilly or anywhere else. So it stands lost, a monument to the disconnected end of Park Lane.

It overlooks the Royal Parks and damages the privacy of Buckingham Palace. These two facts are not, to my mind, faults in themselves. You should surely expect to see buildings through the foliage of city parks, and high towers allow more building-bound people to see trees —which is the purpose of the parks. As for Buckingham Palace, this lost its privacy with the first double-deck bus, and nowadays Windsor and Sandringham are better hideaways.

What is so wrong on this score is that a much better tower, New Zealand House, in the Haymarket, was cut short at conception, to its detriment, by the Royal Fine Arts Commission, for precisely these royal reasons. Surely if New Zealand House is not fit to be seen from the parks or its civil servants to overlook the Queen, there is even less justification for the Hilton and its tourists.

These failings could be excused if it were an exceptional building, if it had the zip and grace of the Pirelli building in Milan, or even the simple form and detail of the Vickers tower on Millbank; if it at least made up for being in the wrong place by justifying its prominent position with superlative architecture.

But it doesn't. It has the cardinal sins of tall buildings—an indefinite profile, fussy detail and an unbalanced proportion of tower to podium. In a curious way the Hilton seems to strike an architectural affinity with the neighbouring Dorchester Hotel, which in its time was good commercial architecture. But little balconies and curves and bits of metal don't extrude well in 1963.

There is persistent confusion of balance between horizontals and verticals. Verticality is sought with columns of white stone or continuous vertical windows, then contradicted by heavily emphasised horizontal balcony elements. The leading elevation to the park, with its ladder of balconies surmounted by a penthouse window like the lamp on a miner's hat, seems to bear no relation to its flank elevations in a kind of pseudo curtain-walling. The tower hits its base without apparent articulation, and there is no sense of location—in that it could have arrived at any other point on the podium.

Compared with the frills in the tower, the base block and main entrance where the eye could appreciate detail is unexpectedly bare, and fails to conjure the impression of luxury and excitement appropriate to a monster hotel.

TV

As I Saw It

by Maurice Richardson

Extracts from our TV critic's weekly column.

Boozy confessions:

"Twelve to fifteen pints, who knows?" . . . "Seven pints and fifteen scotches" . . . "Four and a half pints and four scotches" . . . "Eight doubles" . . . "Whisky, beer, gin, the lot, but don't forget, old boy, I'm an advanced motorist." . . .

The boozy confessions of the saloon bar-fly motorists, interviewed by *This Week* on New Year's Eve, all cheerfully confident about driving home, came pouring out in a stream of blokey euphoria. Sober they may have thought they were, but there didn't seem to be one who wouldn't have bust the breathalyser. No wonder poor Marples, coming on afterwards to wind up, looked like Joey the Parrot used to look in *Rainbow* after he had had his feathers plucked by Jacko the Monkey and his pals.

This, with its close-ups of corpses and bereaved families, may have been a somewhat *Daily Mirror*-ish treatment of the road death story but it was sensationalism in a good cause. It was certainly a brilliant piece of TV journalism. As a contender for the Thersites award for 1964, which goes to the programme that can show the subtopian hominid live in his most alarming guise, it should take some beating.

Proxy climbing:

Vicarious vertigo is a pleasing hearthrug sensation. It gives you a mild diluted thrill without the dread—something like smoking a filter-tipped reefer, perhaps. Last week's *Adventure*, about climbing an impossibly vertical peak in the Andes, was an excellent specimen of this genre. The camera couldn't be there for the final stage, but we got enough human-fly pictures *en route* to justify the bated breath of Christopher Bonnington's precise, model-illustrated commentary.

The method of fixing in advance pitons for short ladders and rope holds may be frowned on in strictest mountaineering circles, but it makes for sensational viewing. Some of the close-ups—though I could never be certain whether Don was smoking a cigarette or chewing a piton—of the penultimate 300 ft., which took eight hours, were terrific. I suppose if you have enough pitons you can, in theory, climb any imaginable rock face, even if it includes a mile or more of horizontal overhang. Perhaps James Bond might be induced to try one, preferably with a moll on his back instead of a pack.

The Mau Mau General:
It's always difficult, when watching an important piece of news coverage, to gauge the value of a huge feat of screen-stealing. The appearance, in *Panorama's* Kenya on the eve of independence, of the Mau Mau General Mwariama, could hardly fail to produce recurrent total recall all through the week, if not, indeed, hearthrug materialisation.

Forest fresh, with mud-ropy plaited mane, profile of a faun very late in the afternoon, and a technique of eyeball rolling entirely new to television, he was preposterously arresting. But even if he got visually, so to speak, a trifle out of hand, Kenyatta's stage management of him was a clever piece of public relations calculated to reassure everybody. It presented the new Mau Mau image as a harmless ghost with savagery, tide-washed by nationalist aspirations, fulfilled.

Various semi-fantastic historical analogies suggested themselves. It was as if an African De Valera was chaperoning a bog-shaggy I.R.A. gunman at a garden party. Judging by the confidence in Kenyatta expressed later in the programme by Lord Delamere and others, it was a genuinely significant turn, that summed up a whole trend in a few moments' showmanship.

On nuclear war:
Even now, crisis-hardened though our eyeballs have become, there are few programmes that can hook them so firmly as a nuclear weapons documentary—provided it seems detailed and authoritative enough. The first instalment of the B.B.C.'s *Overkill* certainly did that.

The pattern was not unfamiliar, of course. There were visits to the Pentagon, to the Operations Room of S.A.C. in Omaha, to the conning-tower of a Polaris submarine. There were reassuring interviews with high ranking United States officers, laced with American global strategic prose. My favourite was General Power's: "If man resorts to nuclear war he will have reached the highest plateau of stupidity." I wasn't quite so pleased with his other aphorism: "Survival is always morally justifiable."

New, to me anyway, was the Minuteman Missile Base in (I think) the foothills of the Rockies. The motto here is "Peace is our Profession." They specialise in intensive psychological indoctrination of academically highly qualified personnel. The system of checking is indescribably elaborate; the possibility of collusion between two—and more—genocidal maniacs is taken into account.

Also new was the prospect which emerged in the interview with the ever-genial Admiral Rayborn that Polaris missiles may shortly be planted in the sea bottom. On the European situation, French and West German representatives were typically equivocal. The finale was a warning about weapons in orbit and danger from the moon.

Next Tuesday, as a softener for Easter Week, and Aldermaston, we get the second instalment, "The Balance of Hope," on prospects of ending the Arms Race. I hope it will be more encouraging than the Pneumatic Glove, guaranteed to solve the boxing problem by reducing the power of all punches by at least 50 per cent, which was being discussed on *Sportsview*.

Alexandra's wedding day:
A Royal Wedding every week would be too much strain on the national talent resources. Relatively infrequent, as they are bound to be, these rites make superlative television and there is enough variation for old Abbey hands to compare and contrast to their hearts' content. All agreed that this year's cast was unusually strong.

I much enjoy these communication experiments once I have settled in, but find them disorienting afterwards. For some time I am not sure where I am: leviated high above the nave; back on my own hearthrug; or trapped in Dimbleby's waistcoat pocket unable to find out whether he is at the reception or talking ecstatically to himself.

Following all those cameras I become a disembodied spirit, especially during the early stages when people are taking their seats. I zoom down on to the Prime Minister's beautifully tailored lap. I pause for a second above Lord Attlee's neat little cranium. (Who is the African lady by his side? Not even Dimbleby can tell me that.)

During the service I begin not only to think I can lip-read but also to hear individual voices. I am positive I can catch guttural accents singing the hymn "Love Divine"—Loff Diffine. Must be some of those foreign princes. The minor royalties, as Dimbleby calls them with a note of patriotic disdain. Dear Dimbleby! As usual he is in fizzing form, relaxedly correcting himself when he fluffs but getting nearly everything all pat, including the names of the carriage horses. This is his day as well as theirs. He is so much with it that he even draws attention to the bride's suppressed giggling fit on the way out. The I.T.V. commentators are woefully ill at ease, not on terms at all.

What, in fact, was the televisual high spot? Afterwards in the local pub, which was in its customary state of loyal hyperaesthesia, I retrieved my reputation—tainted with cynicism for being too fond of that horrid TWTWTW—by remarking on the uninhibited performance of the chief bridesmaid. After the signing of the register she was obviously telling the bride and bridegroom to hold hands before they set off down the aisle. Other observers claimed that she also pointed to herself and said: "Me next!" but by this time my Crawfie vein had run out.

Footnotes on Food and Drink

1. Chips and the Class War

by Syllabub*

The turn of the century was greatly enlivened by the teasing Lord Randolph Churchill used to give Mr. Gladstone. He seemed to think the old gentleman a humbug.

In one celebrated attack he asked what goods Mr. Gladstone in fact delivered after his promises of wonderful legislation, great prosperity and universal peace. Lord Randolph's reply was chips. "Nothing but chips. Chips to the faithful allies in Afghanistan, chips to the trusting native races of South Africa, chips to the British farmer, chips to the Egyptian fellah, chips to the manufacturer and the artisan, chips to the agricultural labourer and chips to the House of Commons itself."

Was Gladstone plotting to hold the Empire together with fried potatoes? The idea might not have been a bad one and in some senses may even seem to be a matter of established fact today.

In truth, the attack was crueller. Gladstone had carefully arranged to receive a delegation from the labouring classes of the "pure and immaculate borough of Chester" in the glades of his castle at Hawarden and there, amid fallen oaks and with chopper in hand and sweat on brow, he so surprised and mesmerised his visitors that they accepted, not golden sovereigns, not mugs of beer, but handfuls of oaken chips as a memorial to the occasion.

The fish-and-chips age was to arrive much later as a first and permanent instalment of affluence to come. And chips (unsung by Mrs. Beeton) when they did come at once established themselves as a class food with an impenetrable barrier between those restaurants in which every item listed is "with chips" and those in which the word chips never appears, the article being disguised as *pommes frites*.

In all the history of world food this seems to be the first invention of a class name in the kitchen. Today oysters will be eaten from barrows in the open air and in costly restaurants, and both establishments will call them oysters. Tomorrow partridge will arrive, but they will be exclusively for wealthy tables unshared by the masses

* *Syllabub (Aidan Philip) died in February, 1964.*

under a different name. But yesterday, and for an endless future of tomorrows, chips and *pommes frites* will make a certain division in an England that prides itself on becoming progressively classless.

Possibly we have an inner necessity to make these distinctions whenever some excellent and homely food is organised on a national scale. Perhaps when vegetable oil refiners and the manufacturers of oil boiling vats made excellent fried potatoes available thoughout the kingdom the word "chips" had to be invented.

2. What Beerbohm Drank at Teatime

by Cyril Ray

Ever since I found that Max Beerbohm took a glass of Bardolino at what a lesser man would have called his teatime, I have had an especial regard for this light, dry, red wine from the hills above the south-eastern shores of Lake Garda—a wine easy enough, anyway, to be fond of for its own sake.

So I was delighted to find myself in the charmingly unsophisticated little lakeside town that gives the wine its name and, by a happy chance, on the day appointed to celebrate the vintage. Not, alas, that there is much this year to celebrate. Rain and hail have done as much damage in the North Italian vineyards as in France, and the Bertani firm here in Verona, which is the actual grower of most of the excellent Valpolicella, Bardolino and Soave it ships to England (through Giordano of Soho), tells me that the 1963 crop will be only half as big—in some areas a third—as last year's.

All the same, the peasant wine-growers trooped happily into Bardolino to sell their fresh, crisp 1962 wine at the tasting-booths—threepence for an eighth of a litre—along with salami sandwiches and crisply-fried fresh-water sardines straight from the waters of Garda. A young priest officiated at the microphone, waxing more and more eloquent as they went on filling his glass.

As more and more foreigners visit Italy and when they get back home ask for Italian wines, so demand increases—there seems no end to the German thirst for Valpolicella. This alone would send prices up. In addition, 1963 has been a bad year, especially as the lower-lying slopes—producing the cheaper wines—have suffered most during the rains, being more easily waterlogged than the hillside vineyards, which grow the dearer wines. Nor can much more Bardolino be grown, for the best slopes are already covered with vineyards. Valpolicella is a bigger area, and new vineyards are being planted—when they come into production in a few years' time they may help to stabilise prices. That's if we don't get too many summers like that of 1963.

The Sporting Year

The Racing Scene

by Jack Leach

1. The Crusaders Backed a Winner

Those of us who have been in racing all our lives naturally tend
to take the whole strange and wonderful set-up for granted. But
people are forever asking me about the deepest origins of the
thoroughbred, about where and how it all began. It is a story worth
telling, so here it is.

A thoroughbred is a horse registered in the stud book and to be
registered he has to be descended from horses already in the book.
That came about in this way.

England first met the desert horse in the Crusades. The male
knights of the crusades in full armour and with all accoutrements
weighed well over 20 stone and they had to ride heavy and powerful
horses. They couldn't stay in the same parish as those lightly armed
Saracens on fleet and hardy desert-bred Arabs.

If the Crusader could bring the Saracens to grips he could bowl
them over like ninepins but the Saracens wouldn't come to grips.
Instead they ripped into the baggage trains and food supplies and
made communication lines almost impossible by disrupting them.
They were in, out and gone before the English could get their ponderous battle wagons into a gallop.

England remembered the desert horse and began to bring in what
she could get. The Arab, the Barb and the Turk were all close varia-
tions of the same breed and England imported all three types. Henry
VIII founded a royal stud and Queen Elizabeth I bred horses. These
were not bred for racing, although there was racing even then. The
idea was to produce horses for war.

They wanted to develop horses that could carry soldiers rather
than jockeys and for a while there was a royal edict that races could
not be run with the horses carrying less than about 15 stone. There
was also a law prohibiting the use of stallions under a certain size,
for the Arabian, although speedy and possessing great stamina, was
still a trifle small for heavy use.

Exactly how these early horses were bred nobody seems to know. We know that England imported all the Eastern horses she could and must have crossed them with the native stock, getting, I suppose, a sort of country-bred. So the blood of the thoroughbred isn't pure from the start. Everything available went into him with the idea of producing a horse suited by size, speed and toughness to carry a soldier into battle.

But when you get fast horses you get racing. When the racing of these Eastern-bred horses began isn't exactly known, but Oliver Cromwell imposed the first ban on racing in 1654 because racecourses were Cavalier meeting places. Somewhere about this time racing became big enough for men to start breeding horses with the racecourse in mind. More than 100 years were to pass before the production of an official stud book. Records were kept privately and some naturally were lost.

Still, this is where the thoroughbred became a definite and distinct breed. By the test of the racecourse three horses began to stand out. The earliest of these was a Turkish horse supposed to have been captured at Belgrade and ridden by a Captain Byerly in the Irish wars. He got to England about 1680.

The Godolphin Arabian is the subject of several more or less fantastic legends but he certainly arrived in England shortly after 1730. The Darley Arabian was bought in Aleppo and imported in 1704. He was really the only one of the three about which much is known. However, these three were so successful as stallions that now every thoroughbred in the world goes back in straight male line to one of them.

The origins of the mares from which the thoroughbred came are even cloudier—two or three were imported, the others apparently came from a mixture of Eastern and native blood. But by the time the stud book was started in England in 1791 enough had been bred out to leave only about 50 tap-root mares.

This, then, is the thoroughbred—a horse descended from Arabian stock which has been tested and selected for speed and stamina, generation by generation, for 300 years.

He's grown a bit, too. Thanks to the selection of stock and possibly a more temperate climate and more plentiful and better food, the modern thoroughbred is about four or five inches taller than the Arabian stock from which he sprang.

2. Squeezing Them Home on a Silken Rein

Australian jockeys—who, incidentally, won five out of six races at Sandown on Eclipse Day—are again having a wonderful season over here.

They are fine riders, but even so I think one or two of them would do even better if they gave their horses an inch or two more rein. I am certain that Scobie Breasley does not grab them quite as short as he did when he first came to this country, although when I spoke to him about it he seemed a bit uncertain and said: "I don't know, but maybe I have given them a little more rein on some of the English courses without thinking about it."

I think I know the courses he means. Some of them in this country have quite a bit of ridge and furrow—not enough to be noticeable from the stands, but it's there just the same, and horses bob up and down a little when they meet it. Anyone who has ridden hunting across Leicestershire will know what I mean.

Talking about horses bobbing up and down, it is very noticeable that the Australian jockeys, especially Breasley and Hutchinson, bob up and down when they are cantering to the start, and even in the early stages of a long race.

This is just a habit or a gimmick. It doesn't mean a thing. When the serious business of the race develops they forget about the bobbing and sit still as mice, until it comes to driving the horse home at the finish. I imagine this bobbing business started when the crack jockey in Australia used to do it, and Breasley copied him. Now other jockeys copy Breasley.

Bougoure, who rode Khalkis when he nailed Miralgo in the very last stride in the Eclipse, gives his horses much more rein now than when I first saw him ride.

Williamson has still got a hold on Miralgo, about 9 in. from the bit. Khalkis is racing with his head down and stretched out, while Miralgo's head is slightly in the air. This is not altogether Williamson's fault, as Miralgo has a habit of carrying his head rather high, but I have seen great jockeys like Gordon Richards throw everything at horses in the last few strides to give them a chance to stretch their necks and drop their heads practically on the winning-post. A horse will always race a few strides without getting unbalanced, even with a loose rein, and nobody knew this better than Gordon. He snatched many a race out of the fire by this method.

The old-time jockey Sam Chifney says in his book, *Genius Genuine*, that "a horse should be ridden as if you had a silken rein as fine as a hair and you are afraid of breaking it—this is the true way a horse should be held fast in his running". *Genius Genuine* was published in 1804, and what Sam Chifney wrote well over 150 years ago is still worth thinking about.

Two brilliant Australian jockeys, Frank Bullock and Brownie Carslake, who were riding over here in the 1920s, told me that they gave their horses quite a few inches more rein in England as our courses were nearly all undulating and not perfectly flat as they are in Australia. I think Steve Donoghue rode with the most delicate touch on a horse's mouth of anybody I ever saw. I'll bet Steve never read *Genius Genuine* because he never bothered to read anything except a race card, but he was a natural, and even old Sam Chifney would have envied his hands.

For me to try to teach the crack jockeys of today how to ride is like teaching your grandmother how to suck eggs. But every really great jockey I have known always admitted that he never stopped learning.

3. Eccentric Horses

Horses are like people—most of them are fairly normal. But I have known and heard about some that have had quite a few idiosyncrasies. Take High Trees, for instance. He's a very good horse when he wants to be, but he's a comedian, a sort of clown who loves hamming it up. He won't do any more than he has to, and would race with a donkey. When the opposition is moderate he only just finishes in front and sort of leers at them while he is doing it.

In the Ascot Stakes this year, running with a big field of good horses, he got a bump just before the first turn and didn't think it at all funny—the others were playing rough and he was too much of a gentleman to join in—and so wouldn't go a yard after that, and ran badly.

When he won the Middlethorpe Stakes at York last year he stuck his toes in just one stride past the winning-post, shot Joe Mercer over his head, stood and looked at him for a few seconds and then swaggered off into the paddock. Incidentally this was one of the nine races he won during the 1962 season.

Carbine was the greatest horse ever bred in Australia and sire of our Derby winner Spearmint. He often won two races in one day and neither weight nor distance seemed to bother him. His only peculiarity was that he hated rain on his ears, and one day his trainer had to lead him down to the start holding an umbrella over his head.

Many years after Carbine, my brother Chub had a top-class sprinter called Doch and Doris who had the same peculiarity. When it rained Chub ran him in a nightcap.

Years ago I used to ride an old plater called Ramboda who wouldn't do his best unless you pretended he was running away with you. I also remember a horse called Hope Deferred, who hated cats, and would step on them in the stable yard if he got the chance. But I never believed Fred Astaire's story of the horse that liked to sit down on little dogs—and fish.

4. What Makes a Good Mudder

Speaking of heavy going, most racegoers think that horses with big feet have the bulge on the others when these conditions arise. I do not subscribe to this opinion, especially as it cost me a lot of money some years ago. I was stalled off backing a winner at a very long price when it was pointed out to me that the filly I fancied had little donkey feet and no chance in the extra deep going that day. She trotted up and I learned my lesson.

My opinion is that it is action, not feet, that constitutes a good mudder. A good mover with plenty of liberty generally acts well in any going and much better than most of the others when it is really heavy. The best mudders I can think of offhand were By Thunder, Charmant, Nothing Venture and, of course, Sovrango, who is certainly the best mud runner on the tracks at the moment.

By Thunder and Charmant had big feet but they were both very big horses. Nothing Venture had small feet and Sovrango's are medium-sized. All were beautiful movers, except perhaps Sovrango, who is not brilliant, but steals along with an economy of effort which has the same effect.

I talked to Jack Jarvis about the question of feet and heavy going and he agrees that it is the action that makes the difference and told me that he had a wonderful win on Firmament in the Manchester November Handicap many years ago. This filly had very small feet and won very easily when the going was almost up to their earholes and they were practically swimming. It is a good idea to watch every runner canter down to the start when it comes up mud.

Defeat for the World's Best Three

by Bob Ferrier

When Bob Charles won the Open Golf Championship in July he was the first New Zealander and the first left-hander ever to do so. How the three favourites felt as their hopes waned is described here.

It was a marvellous first day. Six players had rounds in the sixties, but oddly not one of the "big three" of Palmer, Player and Nicklaus made any impact on the championship. Palmer's opening 76 was as critical as any round scored, for it laid upon him a crippling burden and restored to the rest of the field the thought that the defending champion was after all a member of the human race.

All three men had scored well in practice. All three came up to the championship fit and ready, although Palmer was sniffling off the last of a heavy weekend cold. You could almost believe this was psychosomatic. Last year at Troon he had inexplicable back trouble.

Palmer was first of the three to start at 11·44, by which time Haliburton had turned in 29 and all but posted his 68. It was an early target.

Palmer played badly. On the second tee he stepped back from his ball as a diesel train brayed past on the Blackpool-Kirkham line, but he said it wasn't nerves, just a precaution. He missed from a yard at the 4th, going five on the par 4 hole, and looked bleak and black.

After the round (76) he went straight to Eddie Musty's shop and clamped his driver in the vice and filed at the face. Then he hammered the heads of some of his irons. It looked nothing more than a count-to-ten exercise and when I got to him I don't think he was angry. He said: "I drove it badly, putted it badly, played my irons badly."

After he expended his tension on the clubs he went straight to the practice ground. He thought the weather was "O.K.—a couple of showers, but it was pretty good out there. I wouldn't think the wind was too bad." Winnie, his wife, looked a little melancholy.

Gary Player was on the tee at 1.20. Instead of his usual black he wore dark grey. Someone said the course had made him "turn grey overnight". He started badly, finished badly. At the 2nd, 170 yards from the green, he hit a 7 iron. It went 15 yards over the green. At the 3rd, 190 yards out, he hit a 6 iron and only a bunker stopped it from going 20 yards through.

Player looked affronted. The small ball, downwind, was posing problems. He had driven the ball badly in practice, but drove it well in this first round. His iron play went sour. The problems of championship play were bearing down on the big three. But Player still had some eager philosophy to spare after his 75.

"In the U.S. Open I went out to make very low scores on the last two rounds when in fact 272 would have won it. This one isn't over yet and I can still win with three 68s."

By this time Rodgers was in with a 67. Nicklaus went off at 2.16 with warmer temperatures and a mellow wind drying the course. He tackled the first four holes conservatively, keeping it on the fairway. He played well, putted well, but didn't make them drop and had 35 putts in his 71.

He said: "I decided 280 would be a good score and I was shooting with that in mind. I don't think about the others or whom I have to beat and when I turned in 32 I was good and relaxed. But 14 and 15 (he scored 5, 6 on the holes) killed the round. I just can't hit that 14th fairway. Everything goes into the right rough, even if I aim off 45 degrees to the left. Tomorrow I guess I'll pitch a 5 iron from the tee."

Thomson came in late with a 67 and all three men were impressed by the good scoring on the day. Palmer spent a lot of the afternoon on the practice ground before he and Winnie went back to their hotel, the Clifton Arms at Lytham, two miles from the course. The Players and the Nicklauses ate together at their place, the Majestic at St. Anne's, half a mile away.

After dinner, Nicklaus expounded on practice, saying that practice rounds and tournament play were two different sports. "We all get tensed up," he said. "Even Arnold. But don't fool yourself. Palmer is still the favourite here now, tonight, even with 76. With this small ball he really is some player."

THURSDAY: WEATHER—CALM, WARM, SUNNY.

Player was first off at 9.20 and got in with a 70, in these conditions no more than a strict par round. He summed it up by saying: "Well, it's better than packing and going home tonight like some fellows." Nicklaus teed off at 10.16, played no better than yesterday, but this time the putts went in and he had a 67, the kind of score that thrusts a man right back into the championship and which was eluding the other two.

Nicklaus said: "I had the round going so good that on 14 I changed my mind. I took the driver and hit it smack right in the middle of the fairway."

Palmer's start was scheduled for 3.44, last but one out. Before the round he still couldn't explain yesterday's 76. It wasn't rational, just one of those things, but in the face of the scoring he allowed that this second round would be "critical" and he would need a "real good low round and better than three 68s to be near at the finish." He didn't seem tense or preoccupied with it.

He made a good start but his birdie putt at the 6th "disappeared in the hole—and came out again, don't ask me how". At the 7th (553 yards) he hit prodigiously, drive and one iron 15 ft. from the stick. Then he made a rank bad putt, the ball swinging wide below the hole, and he missed the next one back.

"On the 8th tee I'm pretty hot with myself and gouge it a little with a 3 wood into the left rough. I get a good 5 iron out a foot from the green, only five yards from the hole. So now I figure I'll chip it straight into the hole for the birdie, and I knock it three feet past and miss the putt—score five.

"The hell with it, I thought, why worry about it, why bother to qualify, let it go, let's Winnie and me get out of here tonight. A plane flew over. I got to thinking I should be in one, headed for Dallas to prepare for the P.G.A. championship next week. So I tell myself to swing easy at the ball and just knock it around the rest of the way.

But I can't do that. Every time I stand up to the ball I have to care. It has to be important. I have to hit it like I want every shot to go right in the hole."

At the end of the round Palmer went back to the file and the bench in the pro shop. Then he practised some putting. The time was 8.30. Winnie in tangerine slacks and sweater was perplexed and mused, "Maybe we got here too soon, maybe he is over his peak. He doesn't seem to hold his peak so long now. The same thing happened at the Masters this year. His concentration doesn't seem right any more. He broke the insert on his driver at the Duke of Edinburgh's exhibition last Friday. The new one is perfectly all right, but perhaps he's thinking a little about that. Or perhaps we're just clutching at straws."

Palmer said later he was as tired as if he had played three rounds. All he hoped for was a damned good score next day.

FRIDAY: WEATHER—CALM, WARM, SUNNY.

Now our three men faced one of sport's greatest tests of nerve and courage—36 holes of solitary gruelling effort. Palmer's pride drove him again to go for at least one good round . . . "and I had it going good until I got mad". That happened at the 11th when his second shot was jammed in a footprint in a bunker. He took six and began to think of aeroplanes again. From that moment he really didn't care. He scored 71, 76 on the day.

Player scored 72, 70, good if never inspired play. At the lunch break he was mellow but still busy with his public relations. "I want you to know I've enjoyed it. It's been like a vacation. The pace of life here is about one-quarter of the States. Everyone has been real nice. Ronnie White, George Gibson, so many people, came up to say they'd read my article and that I'm imagining things about popularity, you know?"

Of our "big three", Jack Nicklaus was the one who had the championship by the throat, who ran a fantastic gamut of the emotions over the last five holes of the last round. After a fine birdie at the 14th and a superb iron to the 15th green he was sure he was winning, sure he was leading Rodgers and Charles playing behind him. He three-putted that green and was in trouble again.

He got a birdie at the 16th and at that moment he was convinced again he was Open champion. "At the 17th I was in the same position from my drive, under the same conditions of wind as I was on the morning round. I hit exactly the same second shot, but this time the ball went 10 yards farther over the back of the green. How do you explain that? It cost me five. So I'm in trouble again.

"On the last tee I lingered. Charles and Rodgers were on 16 and I waited for the crowd to roar if either birdied it. Nothing happened. I figured I had a four to win.

"My drive at 18 hooked. I wasn't over-nervous. I hit it well. But it nooked into a bunker, the only tee shot of all the 72 that hooked. How do you explain that? I scored 5 on the hole, but when I walked off I was sure Charles and Rodgers had to finish 4, 4 to tie me. When I heard that in fact they had both birdied 16, when I heard the true situation I was sick, sick, sick about the whole thing. I still am. Maybe I always will be."

Sweet Swansong for Worrell

by Alan Ross

Our cricket correspondent here looks back on the year's incredible Test series between the West Indies and England, the last in a brilliant career for Worrell, the West Indies captain.

.   .   .

What happened : *1st Test at Old Trafford: West Indies won by 10 wickets.*

2nd Test at Lord's: Match drawn—but with a finish of agonising excitement. When Cowdrey went in with his left arm in plaster (his wrist had been cracked the day before) there was one wicket to go and England needed 6 to win. As The Times put it: "The crowd could scarcely cast their eyes upon the scene".

3rd Test at Birmingham: England won by 217 runs.
4th Test at Leeds: West Indies won by 221 runs.
5th Test at the Oval: West Indies won by 8 wickets.

Frank Worrell's swansong had, after all, a final sweetness of melody. No one could have wished it otherwise, for the side he so unobtrusively led here this summer enriched the common idiom of the game. West Indies gave, even as they got, enormous pleasure, transforming our staid cricket grounds and making of a damp, ignoble summer something romantic and memorable.

They brought back Test cricket, long the private property of the connoisseur, to the public consciousness. They added to spontaneity and individual virtuosity a sense of purpose and style. This is not the moment to analyse weaknesses—though except on the greenest of wickets they had precious few—but to record gratitude.

Worrell this summer allowed himself few words; but his smile, more expressive in its lazy geniality than any film star's, was ample.

Much of the time he displayed a non-committal sleepiness, detached almost to the point of indifference. Victory and defeat, his shrugging demeanour suggested, were much the same thing, quickly forgotten.

His own epic feats were behind him; nostalgia, it seemed, a more powerful agent than ambition. He confessed himself "a mediocre all-rounder". Perhaps he really did not care, for himself anyway. But his presence on or off the field was as pervasive as the most lingering of scents. It might have appeared to the undiscerning, judging only by the casualness of his approach, that he was merely a kindly father-figure, dispensing soothing advice. Nothing could have been further from the truth.

On the field, as a captain, he kept gesture to a minimum, but his control, authority and tactical astuteness were never in doubt. He played to win and he won. In this, his own performances were decep-tive. Hampered by strains and undergoing constant treatment, he nevertheless, whenever it was relevant, produced the goods. It was rather that he kept his gifts in cold storage, offering others the limelight.

Few modern sides have been better equipped all round than this one. They could, as at Edgbaston, play well below themselves, but generally speaking England were not strong enough to extend them. England needed a lot in the wicket to make a match of it and West Indies, in the three Tests they won, did so by huge margins. The simple difference was that they had the batsmen to reap the rewards of a good wicket and the bowlers to appear hostile on an easy one.

On the only pitch that took spin, Old Trafford, Gibbs came into his own. On the others Griffith and Sobers got lift and swing of a kind that had England perpetually struggling. They had always, one felt, resources unexploited while England's were stretched to the ut-most. We lacked real pace, top-class spinners, and commanding bats-men. West Indies had all three. Over and above this, they were a team, only one position, that of an opening partner for Hunte, ever in doubt.

England kept only four of the side that toured Australia, and only three of these—Dexter, Trueman and Barrington—played in every Test. We began without an opening pair and we finished without one. We found neither a leg-spinner nor a left-arm bowler. The early batting was brittle, the tail mere cardboard.

In between, our solitary gain from the series, was Sharpe. Trueman sustained the bowling, in the aggressive sense, almost single-handed, though Dexter at Edgbaston and Shackleton at Lord's played useful parts. Our spinners were rarely called on and when they were had little to offer.

With Cowdrey missing, the lack of class in the batting was cruelly exposed. None of those who went in first had either the defensive technique or the range of strokes to give the innings momentum.

Barrington, scarcely recognisable as the limpet he was in Australia, walked an unending tight-rope. Dexter had everything except the knack of staying in.

Close and Parks earned their keep, perhaps rather more than that. Close averaged 31, Parks 23, and against bowling any less menacing have the methods to score freely. Australia next summer are unlikely to mount an attack anywhere approaching this West Indian one in either pace or variety, and England's whole batting set-up could look quite different.

What was dispiriting this summer was not just the fact of failure, but the poverty of technique shown by English batsmen generally. Far from seeming overcoached and inhibited by too slavish adherence to principles, county batsmen as a race play flagrantly across the line, the bottom hand in control. The drive has been replaced by the nudge.

In bowling, too, the number of fast bowlers with a tolerable action can be counted on the fingers of one hand. It may be that wickets are to blame, the preponderance of inswing bowlers at medium pace, but whatever the cause the result is disastrous. In consequence, county cricket, despite the excitements of the knock-out and the closeness of the championship, is more often than not a dreary spectacle.

If we have learned anything from the West Indies, it should be that success requires initiative, and that without imagination there can be no spectacle. Complacency and pawkiness of outlook are the besetting sins of county cricket and until a proper sense of adventure is restored on every level we shall be following, not leading. It is not enough always to be hanging on by the eyebrows.

The Hawk of the Forward Line

by Hugh McIlvanney

Jimmy Greaves, who will not be 24 until February [1964], is established beyond all legitimate doubt as the greatest finisher, the most efficient scorer of goals, British football has ever seen.

They tell him that the next League goal he takes for Tottenham Hotspur will be his 200th in the competition, but he is no more excited by the statistic than a Test batsman who sees 20 go on the board. It is not that he affects detachment from the business of scoring records. He is politely grateful to those who keep count, and he admits that he personally could not argue if someone told him he had not got beyond 160.

It is simply that he cannot see this as anything like an appropriate time for reckoning and assessment. When he says, "It's just another stage on the way to 300, 400 or 500" this seems neither a conventional shrug of phoney modesty nor a statement of extreme dedication.

He is just speaking as a footballer of 23 who believes deeply and naturally that the best is yet to come and that it should keep coming at least until he is 30. More elaborately, he is speaking as the prodigy who has matured into a master and will be happy to be judged by the achievements of his prime, unaided by sentimental echoes from the astonishing successes of his teens.

That Greaves should still have youth's wholehearted commitment to the present, enthusiasm for the future and only perfunctory interest in the past is slightly remarkable, for he can already look back on more years of prominence in first-class football than many very good players can at the end of their careers.

"I cannot remember when I wasn't in the game," he admits. "It gives me a weird feeling at times. I mean, I meet up with somebody like Don Revie now and he is firmly set up and fixed in people's minds as a manager. But then I remember: 'I played against this fellow.'

"I feel I've been around a long, long time and I suppose other people must feel that, too. I reckon when I'm about 26 they'll be telling me to pack up and make way for a young man."

Being a legend before he was a man brought more serious disadvantages. People tend to forget that in football even legends run on legs and lungs and that even the most gifted boy has no substitute for a man's strength.

"When I was with Chelsea, people often accused me of not keeping in the game," Greaves recalls. "They thought the goals I scored were fine but they complained that I played in bursts and took rests in between.

"Of course I played in bursts. I just wasn't strong enough at 17 or 18 to keep pace for an hour-and-a-half with the fully developed men I was against. It's only quite recently that I've felt myself getting the full strength of a man."

Physical maturity for him means a height of 5 ft. 8 in. and a weight of around 10 st. 10 lb., much of it concentrated in freakishly strong thighs, and a body that is light but unobtrusively muscular and easily kept fit regardless of what or how much he eats.

On the field he is one of the most readily recognised of footballers and this is not entirely due to characteristics of movement like his outstandingly fast leg action. He has a distinctive head, with a long jaw, and the back of the skull does not curve inward greatly as it goes down on to a strong neck.

These features go with a pale complexion and a slightly drawn expression, so that, whereas the faces of other players often appear on the far side of the pitch as little more than blurred blobs of good health, Greaves's looks are somehow defined with strange clarity even at a distance. In fact, everything about his play has a sharpness of definition that lifts him out of the hectic swirl of a match as if he is the only man who is really in focus.

This impression is, of course, connected with the fact that he is so often concerned in climaxes, mainly in the fundamental climax of the game—the scoring of goals. Exactly why this should be or what equipment makes it possible is not easy to analyse.

His goal scoring, he says, may look easy but it never feels easy. Predictably, he thinks that it is based on an amalgam of highly refined instincts. Balance, quick reflexes, timing in the actual strike, a sense of anticipation and positioning, instant acceleration and an overall animal alertness—these are the attributes he knows to be vital and he is justifiably satisfied that he has them in substantial measure.

He does not equivocate about the priorities he has in mind when he goes on the field. There is no nonsense about taking the goals if they come along. He acknowledges that he goes out knowing that everything he does must be relevant to getting them.

"It's one theory that great players always give the impression of having plenty of time to do what they want to do, but I know it does not look that way with me very often. Fellows like John White and Johnny Haynes always appear to have much more time to spare than I have and to play with a much more smooth and fluid style. But I think I know why that is.

"It is because the patterns of their game are unrestricted, allowing practically any kind of flow. As long as they can see that the end will be positively creative. John and Johnny are quite happy to swerve and carry in almost any direction. With their talents they get marvellous results from that method.

"But the way I'm made I have always got to be forcing myself round to head directly for goal. That may make my play look jerky at times, but it really kills me to have to turn away from goal. I don't feel really right until I'm moving forward with the ball, aware of the blur of the goalposts ahead of me—you never have time to see things in clear outline in a match. Once I've got that situation it does not matter how many opponents are between me and the goal because, whether I get through or not, at least I know I'm doing the thing I'm fitted to do."

One flaw that he has removed is the weakness of his right foot, which was once only for standing on but is now probably more accurate if not as strong as his left. Yet he retains an anxiety to justify one-footed players, suggesting that Puskas might never have been as great if he had tried to develop his right.

He sees Puskas as the highest realisation of his kind of inside-forward play. Certainly, there is no exact contemporary equivalent anywhere, and if Greaves is to be overshadowed in the goal-scoring lore of the sixties it can only be by Law, a player who is all things to all occasions.

For many of us, in any case, Greaves will remain one of the great unique football phenomena of our time. Other inside-forwards will excite with their wheeling, gliding grace, but we may remember best of all the man who hovers and swoops with the killing economy of a hawk.

Hounds and Heavies under Butter Crag

by Geoffrey Nicholson

The Grasmere Sports—a crowded day of running, leaping, wrestling and hound-trailing—date back certainly to 1852 and probably beyond.

Grasmere on the morning of the Sports was full of foreign girls in anoraks, Kendal mint cake, locally thrown ashtrays, schoolteachers looking for Wordsworth's grave, dripping eaves and leaves, and white fluorescent mist. A Lakeland scene.

The mist overflowed the mere and hid the top of Butter Crag where later the fell guides and trail hounds would race. It soaked the arena where the lilywhite Cumberland and Westmorland wrestlers would fall, and made life hard for the professional athletes who would, in the local term, be leaping and running. Flags and spirits drooped. The new pavilion had still to be paid for.

Before noon, though, it brightened a little. The ground began to fill, and not so much with tourists as with leathery men in navy suits, brown caps and gumboots. After more than a century they still provide the hard core of support. By mid-afternoon, though drizzle fitfully returned ("The sun is shining eight miles to the north," the announcer said), there was a crowd of 7,000.

It's an old-fashioned set-up. The competitors come from the farms and the shops, the organisers from the gentry. Even now that the sports are run by a limited company, with any profits ploughed back, the committee remains squirarchical—with some overlapping, a brigadier, a colonel, four majors, a captain R.N., three J.P.s, an M.F.H. and an earl.

When the last, the Earl of Lonsdale, started the hound trail by dropping a flag, he was reminded, almost reproachfully, that his uncle always used to do it with an enormous white handkerchief.

In these rural circumstances it was taken hard that a gas fitter won the main event, the guides' race—a 996 ft. climb over rough pasture and bracken to a rocky spur, from which the cloud miraculously lifted, and back down over slippery moorland grass. He wasn't any gas fitter; he was Bob Morton, winner of the Powderhall mile; but the bookmakers in their enclosure, perhaps with a sense of the fitness of things, had given him only a 6—1 chance.

At evens was Reg Harrison, a farmworker and an unbeaten fell runner this season; and the most fancied outsider was Bill Teasdale who, though 38, had won the race eight times in the past and bounded about the hill every day as a shepherd.

Harrison fell several times, and tried a desperate short cut over fences which lost him ground; the craggy Teasdale was burned off; and Morton was full of talkative confidence after winning his £20, though he thought he'd stick to miling for a while since the money was better.

All but the children's races were professional, and bossed by the handicapper, W. Twentyman, a master builder and himself a famous pro miler and half-miler in his long day, which lasted from 1920 to 1937. Now, no one knows how, he keeps track of the form of nearly 600 athletes, sees through the deceptions of self-effacing entry forms and sub-standard performances, and tries for 99 per cent success in producing even races. "His rule is law—we permit no interference," the secretary said of him magisterially.

When the scratch man, J. Tinnion, won a close mile after giving one runner 295 yards, Mr. Twentyman might be said to have had a 100 per cent success.

All the while, in a continuous side-show before the stand, the Cumberland wrestlers embraced in strangely formal bouts that rarely lasted more than a minute. Richardson put Hayton down with a buttock "invented by a Church of England minister" and then a cross-buttock to win the lightweight prize. And so it went on through the classes, all the wrestlers dressed in white tights and vests and velvet trunks, often elaborately embroidered with silk and pearls.

Thomas Hodgson, a chubby 14-year-old, won the junior prize for the neatest costume with a rich butterfly design, all his mother's work, and looked half-pleased, half-embarrassed about it.

The band of the Royal Signals played; stalls sold Lakeland delicacies and Grasmere crafts; the bookies shouted the odds for runners on two legs and four.

Then the bizarre excitement of the hound trail began. At 2.30 a man trailing a bunch of rags soaked in paraffin, aniseed and crude oil, appeared through a gap in the arena. The hounds, soft, lolloping, friendly dogs until then, howled and bayed as though they would tear him to pieces, but when slipped from their leashes, burst past him to follow the stinking trail for 10 miles across the fells.

Nothing for 25 minutes; then a man in a riding mack began shouting "It's trail!" If any hound had appeared before that, it must have meant he'd taken a short cut. Now everyone looked up at Butter Crag. A tiny white oblong figure was sighted below the skyline. And all hell let loose.

Men whistled with whistles and through their fingers. A woman set up a high-pitched Hoo! Hoo! Someone waved a handkerchief. Another rattled a food tin. A child gave a repeated primitive scream. Tourists laughed uncomfortably about it, but the handlers were oblivious of anything until their hounds came to them, playful and affectionate once more, all their aggression spent.

Jackpot won. Lured by the "Hi-jack! Hi-jack!" of its owner, Robert Rodgers, it ran up to beat Dido and the favourite, Dairyman. Unlike Dairyman, fed on egg and sherry, Jackpot is teetotal; but Rodgers is a butcher and sees he gets the best chicken and meat.

Rodgers wasn't saying anything about Jackpot's parentage—"It's a wise dog who knows his own father"—but will put him to stud next year at £15 a time. This win had guaranteed him a pampered retirement.

A Shiny Night

by Colin Willock

After a lifetime of largely detected crime (29 convictions for poaching and allied offences up to 1956, when he at last decided to go legit), Mackenzie Thorpe, the greatest of Lincolnshire poachers, wildfowlers, and wildfowling guides, has sold the private wildfowl trust that he keeps in the back garden of his Sutton Bridge council house and now threatens to migrate to America.

Kenzie talks of leaving about the time his familiars, the pink-footed geese, fly north in the spring. Unlike them, he would not be returning to the beloved Wash saltings—or so he now says.

It's probably a tragedy for everyone, except one or two farmers and the pinkfeet who will now find a good deal less lead flying about in the night sky over Lincolnshire. To mark this strange turning-point in his life—Kenzie is now 54—he recently suggested that we should make a moonlight foray together after the geese.

It started normally enough at eight in the evening with a three-mile slog along the sea wall. The grass was already turned into fingers of sugared angelica by the frost. We took post in the bottom of a dyke behind the sea bank, confident that 1,000 geese who had been roosting out on the sands would flight in to feed in a huge potato field half a mile inland just as soon as the moon rose high enough.

By midnight one lone goose had come in from the sea. Kenzie had somehow picked it up far off on his own personal radar and had honked at it. The goose had honked back like an airliner answering ground control and had gone into a cautious orbit round us while keeping up a continuous gabble. Normally you need cloud over the moon to see anything of an air-borne goose, but the moon was so bright that we could see every feather.

The pink, I dare say, could spot the end of the cartridges in our guns by looking straight down the barrels. He circled derisively three gunshots high and then the other 999 geese on the potato field picked up his, and Kenzie's signals and began to call deafeningly and in chorus. The straggler swung on to course now, realising where his real friends were. Somehow, somewhere, the whole 1,000 had by-passed us and were now gorging themselves on rotten spuds.

Kenzie declared that we would stalk this goose pack. Naturally this would mean crossing someone else's land. Kenzie's recently found legitimacy as a shooter allows itself a fair degree of latitude. There would, he emphasised, be no loosing off at moonlit pheasants, however tempting. The idea was to crawl up to the geese unseen, put them off and then flight them as they came back.

Kenzie led off at a smacking pace along the bottom of the intricate trench system that divides the fields of Lincolnshire. He never once hesitated at a turning or junction. Cock pheasants, disturbed where they had been jugging in the open stubble and not realising the cause of the disturbance, rocketed over the parapet like low-flying shells. One ducked involuntarily as they whistled over. The whole caper had an uncanny resemblance to one of those First World War cartoons by Bruce Bairnsfather.

We did a good two miles like this with Kenzie mounting the fire-step every 100 yards or so to look up, sniff and listen like an old labrador catching air scent. Once when I tried a peep over the top, I found myself practically nose to beak with a wild duck that had been busy cleaning up the frozen stubble. She took off with an outraged quacking.

We kept going for two hours without coming above ground level, but always the geese seemed to be at least a field further on. At one point Kenzie whispered that we had reached a dead end and would have to climb up into the open before meeting the next trench. He made it sound as if the gap was likely to be swept with machine gun fire or at least by the beady eye of a somnambulant keeper. We clambered up to find our bodies cut off from the knees downward by a shallow, level carpet of mist. Ahead was a small pond and round it a perfect little pheasant cover. The next few seconds were among the most surrealist I remember.

The landscape was given a dimension of unreality by the mist and moonlight. But everything that moved against it was believable and crystal clear. First, 100 mallard rose from the pond as we rose from our trench. Their quacking alerted as many teal, who wheeled around us like demented bats. The commotion awoke the pheasants roosting in the little wood, who roared out from the frosty treetops, passing so close over our heads that you could see white neck-ring, red eye-wattle, bronze sheen of neck feather. This eruption of pheasants in turn detonated a cloud of dozing pigeons.

Kenzie had sat down on his empty goose bag and was laughing with tears that threatened to freeze solid on his cheeks. "That's about the lot," he said at last. But he was wrong. There were still three tawny owls to come out of the wood.

I don't know exactly the distance we covered along those frozen communication trenches. At one point I estimated we were not far from Fosdyke, and that's a long way from where we started. We got back to the sea wall at six a.m. with two stray geese we had caught flighting seawards as the moon sank. We never did come up with the other 998. When we reached the car at last the door was frozen into its frame.

Now there will be no more shiny nights for Kenzie Thorpe. The gigantic bird explosion by the little pond and covert told me better than anything why he has kept it up in all weathers all these years.

Kenzie's married daughter lives in the States and his wife wants to make her home there. But a thousand and one nights like this one cannot be denied. I have yet to hear of a wild goose being pulled by a migrational urge across the Atlantic from west to east. Kenzie Thorpe, who is as near to a grey goose as it is possible to get without sprouting feathers, may be that exception.

Places

Leningrad

by Nigel Gosling

Imagine a great classical (say Regent's Park) façade at seven o'clock on a Sunday morning, the streets washed clean and hardly a car in sight. Imagine an area stretching from St. Paul's to the Albert Hall laid out in this style, punctuated by palaces and churches, theatres and enormous squares.

Lace it with canals and place it on the edge of the sea. Wash it with colour. Prick it with gold spires and domes in a silvery sunshine. You are inside a Canaletto or an eighteenth-century print. You are in Leningrad.

Neglected between the wars, Leningrad is emerging now in fresh paint and new plaster. Within a year or two it will be one of the wonders of the tourist world, with only Venice as its rival.

Moscow is just a big city but Leningrad is a dream. It is big, too— 3,370,000 inhabitants, the second industrial centre in Russia. The present is strong. It would need a heart of stone to listen unmoved to the stories of siege, starvation, and 900 days' defiance only twenty years old; and on the periphery there is a confusion of cranes and bulldozers and loveless lumps of housing. But the centre is still and spacious, harmonious, noble, rich. The ghosts of tsars and empresses, of Raskolnikov hurrying over a bridge with an axe under his coat, of Lenin jutting his angry chin above a shouting multitude, are contained in a pale stillness which has a kind of warmth.

Leningrad is the Brasilia of the eighteenth century. It was created virtually at a stroke, virtually from nothing, at Peter the Great's whim. From 1703, the whole building energy of Russia was beamed on it; nowhere else in the whole country might a single stonemason be employed.

With dreams of Holland and, surely, England in his mind (Greenwich, where he stayed would fit comfortably in a corner) Peter opened his "window into Europe" wide upon the estuary islands of the Neva River. His architects were Italian and French, their materials mainly stucco-plastered brick. The scale is Russian and the style severe and martial, with pillars ranged like sentries and windows in long, drilled ranks. The water-courses are granite-edged and bridged with modesty. The orderly seemliness, falling easily on the English eye, skirts triumphantly the very edge of monotony, for Peter's building ordinances stretched far. The wide three-storey block is ubiquitous. It is hard to tell whether it houses a municipal office, a big store (plate-glass windows are here a rarity), a ballet school, a cinema, or a conglomeration of overcrowded apartments.

Extremes of rectilinear geometry might make a grim town were it not for the master-stroke of colour. Leningrad is the vindication of polychrome architecture. Washes of pale green or blue or yellow make the immense buildings float instead of squat. The low, red-tiled roof-line allows gold spire or onion to spark against the sky.

Things seen: Metal watercarts labelled "Kvas" (a sort of cider made from bread).

A woman having her shoes cleaned by a bootblack. Enormous drainpipes on every building to carry away melting snow. Men's bright-blue suits. Few caps. No bicycles. No horses. More mysterious still, in a town apparently starved of vegetables, no allotments. . . .

The biggest treasure in this handsome treasure-house is the Hermitage Museum. This is surely the most magnificent art-display in the world. Rastrelli's vast green-and-white structure (formerly the Winter Palace), with its subtle charcoal mouldings and statuary, is an architectural masterpiece on a superb quayside site. From the moment you climb the dramatic flight of indoor marble stairs, steep and pillared like a Bakst décor, you are kept gasping alternately at the setting and the contents. This was an imperial show-piece, and princely splendour reigns. Seventeen miles of inlaid floor, of damask and tapestry, mirrors and silk and chandeliers, gold and polished walnut, painted ceilings and polished wood. It is Buckingham Palace and the National Gallery and the V. and A. and the British Museum thrown into one. There is art from Greece and Rome, from the Far East, from India and Egypt and Mexico. There are pottery and porcelain and furniture, ivory and textiles, prints and drawings, weapons and *objets d'art*. There are Scythian gold treasures of breath-taking delicacy and pre-historic remains of incalculable age. There is a Pushkin corner and a room containing portraits of 300 generals. There is the throne of Peter the Great, and a map of Russia as big as a flag with the cities marked by emeralds and rubies.

But the glory of the gallery is its collection of paintings. Built up by Catherine the Great and added to by her successors this assembly of 4,000 pictures (not all hung) is one of the most splendid in the world. The monumental compassion of Rembrandt's "Prodigal Son" or his cavernous "Danae" (two out of thirty-eight by this painter), the noble calm of a Fra Angelico fresco or Giorgione's "Judith" are feasts in themselves. From the "Benois" Virgin and Child by Leonardo (discovered a hundred years ago on a barge on the Volga) the eye is drawn away through the window across the wide lagoon of the Neva to the prison where Dostoevsky lay awaiting execution, to the battleship which fired the signal for the Revolution or to the spire of the fortress church where the Tsars of Russia lie in dark, half-disgraceful splendour.

Upstairs, in rooms whose austerity borders on bleakness, the Western visitor will get a shock. For here are displays not only of Cézanne and Van Gogh, Gauguin and Degas and Renoir, but whole rooms of early Matisse and Picasso, part of the hoard of two great private collectors. Matisse's huge red-and-blue "Dance" and "Music" are skied above the stairway, but the rest are generously, if not temptingly, displayed.

The gallery teems with crowds, mostly in the wake of free guides. There is a tiny entrance fee; women must wear felt overshoes; photographing is allowed. Postcard reproductions are minimal and sold in packets only, mostly mixed. Cézanne comes under "Fruit and Flowers".

Everywhere those white ruched curtains we associate with posh sweet-shops, even in the Underground booking office. Standardised stoneware urns for rubbish by the dozen, meticulously used even for fag-ends. Streets washed daily, right out into the suburbs, and spotlessly clean. Not much smoking (cigarettes 1s. 6d. for 20).

In theatres, champagne by the glass (expensive) and caviare sandwiches (ditto), freely patronised. Plenty of cafés—non-alcoholic, no pubs or bars. No gulls. No fishermen, fishing-boats or fish shops. No feel of being a port. Over the empty waterways light, graceful, incredibly speedy hydrofoil water-buses (why not in Venice or London?). In the night, it seems, the great bridges over the Neva rise up together and let the river shipping slide through.

Fifteen miles out from Leningrad lies Peter the Great's answer to Versailles, Peterhof. Like its rival, it stretches a great façade across a hill and from the terrace runs a vertiginous perspective of waterway and fountains. But Peterhof has the advantage; the vista opens up dramatically into the Gulf of Finland.

To right and left gold-leafed classical statuary spout rainbow spray against oak and maple. A little pavilion sits on the water's edge offering a sweet, melancholy view of bays where grass and trees run down into the tideless sea. Monarchic humour breaks out in false bushes and paving which spurt water in surprise pulses.

New paint, shining gold, shrubs mounded with manure—this is no place for nostalgia, but a great mouthful of green-and-white refreshment. Families amble slowly through the woods; a soldier stands behind a majestic nude eyeing a girl; two gigantic priests, all white beard and black soutane, pose on the steps as if they were going to break into an aria.

Hotel bedrooms huge and Edwardian. Bed blankets sandwiched inside a sheet with a big hole to show their design. Hidden under the chair of the lift girl, two jars of pickled onions.

From Leningrad to Moscow is as flat as a pancake; walk up two floors and you have a panorama. Famous for its lofty, healthy air, a little hummock a few miles out of the town attracted the Tsars to build a palace there, Tsarkoe Selo. Now it is rechristened Pushkin and feels like a Russian Hampton Court—quiet, and rather refined.

The quietly baroque palace—vast as usual and designed, like the Winter Palace, by Rastrelli—is a miracle of balance between monumentality and elegance, achieved again by colour. Here is Rastrelli's favourite bright china blue, set off by white and charcoal. Running the eye upwards from the green lawn to the azure panels to a gold dome against a peacock sky gives a visual chord of Stravinskian plangency.

Like Peterhof, this was occupied by the Nazis. Before retreating they pillaged it (the contents must still be buried somewhere in Germany) and set fire to the building. With staggering skill, expense and taste the decorations have been restored, fabrics copied, floors relaid. Walking round the lake in the English-style garden, past the statues and the little theatre where Nijinsky and Karsavina used to entertain imperial parties in the summer, an English visitor will feel oddly at home; particularly when he enters the graceful Adam-ish wing which the Scottish architect Cameron built at Catherine's special order.

Things heard. An Uzbekistan jazz-group serving Palladium-style music in reefer jackets. The vocalist sings a torch-song, "Tashkent! Tashkent!", another croons a spiritual, "My soul belongs to the company store", in lowered lights and an Uzbek-Mississippi accent. All the girl dancers look like Margot Fonteyn.

The famous Maryinsky Theatre, now named the Kirov after a post-revolutionary cultural benefactor, is an enormous domed building in apple green and white. Its ballet-school—the nursery, genetically speaking, of our own company—is a little way off, occupying one side of a dignified yellow-and-white street of arches and pillars. Inside the modest door through which Pavlova, Nijinsky, Diaghilev and Karsavina used to hurry, incongruity reaches a peak.

On the left is a bust of Lenin. On the narrow stairs are noticeboards

of admonition and congratulation. Soviet-style photographs of virtuous pupils decorate the walls. But in the passage you are met with
a cluster of pigtailed girls in goffered pinafores who bob a curtsey
and drop their eyes as you pass; tiny boys as slim as pencils in grey
button-up uniforms with belts bow stiffly. Two ages seem gummed
together, not quite fused.

Passages and studios stretch over several storeys. In one in which
the floor is sloped at the same angle as the stage, a vigorous woman
is taking a class of nine exquisite thin blonde girls, honey-pale and
sweating in little chiffon skirts. Upstairs a teacher in a sweater drives
nine wiry boys through a session of fiery *enchainements*. "It's hard
to find good boys," he sighs as they pause for a moment, panting.
Through the wall comes the sound of *Les Sylphides*.

Tradition here is something you can almost touch. On the walls
are photographs of stars of past and present—almost indistinguish-
able in feature, costume, pose and photographic style. There is a
library and a museum stuffed with records of the past, names familiar
only to experts. There are pictures of Pavlova and Ulanova, Fokine
and Balanchine, even Stravinsky, whose connection with the school
seems mysterious. Nothing of Diaghilev.

*Three or four buses and lorries to every private car; empty squares;
five cars parked together a rarity; streets as quiet as a road. You become aware that it is the car, blocking what was meant to be empty,
bustling along stretches designed for peace, dividing structures intended as a unit, which is the principal obstacle between us and architecture of the past. Except in the summer garden the trees are mostly
new-planted—and monotonous, all of the same small-leafed green.*

The Leningrad-Moscow road covers 500 miles like an arrow. The
seven-mile Moscow Boulevard drives through the giant housing
schemes, imposing in scale if not in imaginative planning, out into
a flat forest of small trees, stretching interminably. The traffic is
mainly small lorries, rather slow. At frequent intervals are hamlets of
twenty or thirty log chalets strung out in rows, each within a
palinged garden. The windows tend to have lace curtains (only) and
are surrounded by beautiful little carved frames, usually finished
in bright paint. The log ends are sometimes painted too to give an
odd lozenge design. No visible centre to the community, no church
or square, though sometimes one house is labelled "Club".

A hundred miles down the road is one of the cradles of Russian
culture, a little town called Novgorod. Almost totally razed by the
Nazis, it is now a pleasant, quiet, suburban-feeling place. But it sits
beside its past. In the tenth century it was perhaps the chief city in
Russia, and the warm red crenellated wall of its citadel still stands.
Within is a museum with some of the finest icons in the country (in

Russia an icon is not one of those tiny objects you find in posh flats in Paris, but a large painting of effulgent colour), a cathedral with a massive bronze door from Magdeburg and white plaster walls, forming courtyards which catch the light from green turf and poplar trees and great grey onion-domes from which the jackdaws tumble.

In one corner of the town is a whole cluster of those tiny, tall, onion-topped churches, which is what Russia made out of Byzantium. They are mostly bare now, and under strenuous restoration, though in one a narrow stair leads to a precious fresco by the father of Russian religious art, Theophanes the Greek. The thick-pillared upward-soaring buildings give a feeling of claustrophobia. But step through the gate of the battlement and suddenly before you is spread one of those dizzy perspectives which make you think of an Eisenstein film.

Beyond the wall the ground drops away to a river, broad and still as a lake, reflecting an astonishing spread of egg-shell air on its surface. The flatness seems to spread over the banks into flat pale lawn and flat green shaven meadow. Pinned on the horizon is a fairytale cluster of towers and domes, small and bright as in a medieval illumination. Beyond it the globe curves down out of sight. The sky seems to swoop away over it into the distance, out into the heart of Russia, to Moscow.

From the waiting coach, lonely in the huge Russian evening, comes a small cosy sound of singing—Elvis Presley on the Leningrad radio.

The Tomb of a Drinking Man

by Cyril Ray

They say the Lion and the Lizard
    keep
The Courts where Jamshyd gloried
    and drank deep

I don't know about that, but at the top, or smarter, end of Tehran, where the other day the Shahanshah himself declared the new Hilton Hotel open (and a pretty cosy caravanserai it is), there is a supermarket and a Miami nightclub, one restaurant called Barbecue and another called The Hot Shoppe.

Down in the centre of the city, too, where the red double-decker buses ply, the bazaar will have to exoticise itself somewhat if the tourists from the Hilton are going to be able to boast back home of what they picked up there. In a Persian Market, for a song. When I strolled last week among the stalls offering plastic-handled, nylon-bristled toothbrushes; cotton rugs from India featuring dear little pussies; Kleenex; Carr's biscuits and genuine Texas jeans, virtually the only echo from the Arabian Nights that reached my wistful ear was the trade-mark on the paraffin stoves for sale: Aladdin.

Yet only an hour by air from the tall tower that is the Hilton are the domes and minarets of Isfahan—once, to the marvelling eyes of Elizabethan Englishmen, the most splendid capital in the world, and still distilling a magic compounded partly of blue-and-gold tiles reflected in ornamental water, partly of the crowded clamour of the vast bazaar and the bustle of the streets.

All the same, and even in the gardens of Isfahan, I was thinking of a remoter garden still, and a voice farther away in time than those now proclaiming in organised and amplified spontaneity their enthusiasm for the Government's new measure of land reform: how could I visit Persia without making pilgrimage to the tomb of old Khayyám?

And so I took the Golden Road to Samarkand—those 600 miles of it, at any rate, that run from Tehran almost to the Soviet frontier; and I took them the easiest way: two hours by air to Meshed, and another couple by road, back on my tracks to Naishapur, rather than spend twenty-four hours in the train, or a couple of days in a car.

The desert and the mountains, which press closely in on Meshed, press closer still on Naishapur. But at the edge of the little town, after a dusty jolting over seventy miles of made but unsurfaced road, we suddenly turned off over smooth tarmac, skirting as primitive a mud village as any you would see in Afghanistan—not all that far beyond Meshed—and great gates set in brave new brick opened on to the blue-domed shrine of the holy man, Muhammed Mahruq, in the garden of which Omar lies buried.

Even the tarmac, with its sodium-vapour lamps, the new wall and the fancy gates, hadn't prepared me. Over-topping and outfacing all is a modernistic, latticed, elongated dome, more than sixty feet high, of concrete and coloured tiles, fenced in by massive cones of concrete that would look like a tank trap if it weren't for the floodlights set in them.

My interpreter gestured grandly, and I protested, "No, no: there must be some mistake! Omar's is a *little* tomb, close to the wall of the shrine. . . ." And I added, lamely, that I had read as much, for I had never set foot in Naishapur before, though I could have cried out loud that Omar *couldn't* lie under this gimmicky erection from a World's Fair. Not Omar. Not at rest.

Alas, there was no mistake. We walked under the tall lamp standards that line the path to the tomb, all aluminium paint and cubist panes of glass, while the cooing doves deposited their own art criticisms on the top of the new memorial, and my interpreter explained.

It had been finished only a month or so, he said, but the local unco' guid had long been agitating for the move: the shrine was a holy man's, whereas Omar had been a drinking man, and not fit to lie so close—hence the removal of his remains 100 yards or so from the wall of the shrine. It was like keeping a decent distance between Robert Burns's remains and those of John Knox.

"After all," the boy went on, at the look on my face, "we *are* Muslims, and Meshed and Naishapur are places of pilgrimage."

"So you don't drink wine," I said, "in Naishapur and Meshed?"—knowing well that there were vineyards hard by, and that I had drunk good Iranian wine in Tehran and Isfahan, and perfectly horrible Iranian wine in Meshed, to say nothing of Iranian Grande Champagne Cognac Impériale, made by a company called Ararat, and smelling of chocolate creams.

"Oh, yes," he said, "and especially on Saturday nights. But even those who do, don't expect to lay their bones by a holy man's, and they don't think Omar should, either."

We had reached the wall of the shrine, where the tomb used to be, "And *you actually moved his bones.*" I cried, "from here to there!" Not, I was told, until they had been sent first to Tehran to be, as my interpreter put it, "analysed". And by this time he must have been enjoying my incredulous disapproval, for he added, gratuitously, that the modest white memorial stone, too small to be appropriately accommodated under the vast new monument, had been moved to a square in the town—just by the Khayyám Cinema.

It was another poet, under later and greyer skies, who pleaded:

> Good frend for Jesus sake forbeare,
> To digg the dust encloased heare.
> Blese be ye man yt spares thes stones.
> And curst be he yt moves my bones.

and, in spite of all temptations, and letters to *The Times*, we have dutifully forborne. Poor Omar, though, less lucky in his countrymen, prophesied all too truly, eight centuries ago:

> Ah, Moon of my delight who know'st no wane,
> The Moon of Heav'n is rising once again:
>   How oft hereafter rising shall she look
>   Through this same Garden after me—in vain!

Back in Meshed, the British Council man said that he didn't believe it was because Omar was a drinking man: the Iranians had just got around to his being a tourist attraction, and the removal of his bones was only incidental to tarting up the tomb. In Tehran, a man from the Ministry of Propaganda said yes, they *had* wanted to give Omar a more resplendent memorial, to please the visitors, but it was true, too, that it wouldn't have pleased the pious if it had been too near the holy man's.

Whatever the reason, I reached for my Iranian Grande Champagne Cognac Impériale, drank deep and, mindful of the old gentleman's last words, turned down an empty glass.

A Sacred Muddle

by Patrick O'Donovan

The Holy Places almost invariably distress Anglo-Saxon non-believers. They tend to be of debatable attribution, of poor design, to be small and poverty-stricken, to be filled with trinkets and to offer a long history of most un-Christian rivalry and violence.

But a pilgrim's eye, or the eye of a man not disciplined by the stern and unemotional decorum of the north, will find them over-whelmingly satisfying. Their humility is right. The ugly inter-sect rivalry that surrounds them is at least evidence of living faith. Their muddle is the encrustation of history.

Their attribution is usually approximately correct and they have been uniquely hallowed by centuries of prayers and awe. There is something exotic about them; they are not English Lady Chapels: on the contrary, they are, what is historically quite proper, Levantine.

They stand now in both Jordan and Israel. The greatest are in Jordan, and the most magnificent is Bethlehem. Bethlehem is a poor, bare town high up among naked hills. But hunched down among the four-square Arab houses on its hilltop is a great basilica. It was started by Constantine, completed by Justinian, changed by the Crusaders.

It is a great, solemn, empty hall with two long rows of columns on each side. The saints painted on them include King Canute. The high altar is Greek and the side altar Armenian. The Latins have a church pressed against its shoulder; a poor, slum parish church after the great male magnificence of the basilica, where the worst liturgical excesses of the south meet and mingle with the Irish taste in statues.

But below the basilica is a cave. It is shaped like an irregular Y. There are four ways into it, down dark and narrow stairways, through antechambers and chapels. It is revered as the cave of the Nativity. It has been enlarged by pious chisels. It has that famous silver star (one of the public causes of the Crimea War) beneath an altar to mark the birthplace.

It is a hot, low-ceilinged, primitive place. Canvas hangings conceal the bare rock, but the rock breaks through and bulges under altars, in passages, and the ceiling is rock turned black with soot. If places have any significance in religion, this is among the greatest.

Jerusalem itself has dozens of holy places. The old city, from a way off a tiled, walled, medieval town, a miniature from a missal, bulging with towers and domes and heaped-up houses, is in Jordan. The places occur without drama in a street of shops or on one side of a haphazard courtyard. They are often hardly bigger than booths. They are seldom beautiful. They can be as emotive as the greatest cathedral in the West.

The centre of it all, for Christians, is the Holy Sepulchre. The very name rings great bells in European history. Time has sunk this church, too, among its neighbours. It is small and muddled. It is a rotunda to which annexes, chapels, crypts, galleries and penthouses have been added.

It is a sacred, dark muddle. The real trouble is that the old rounded rock on which Christ was probably crucified was treated by the Emperor Constantine like a piece of cheese. With dreadful vulgarity he whittled it away to suit his plans for a church, so that no sense of place is left.

In addition, five religions have their altars in the church, the Orthodox, the Latins, the Copts, the Armenians and the Syrians. The Abyssinians have a shrine on the roof and considerately conduct their mysteries in gym shoes.

Each detail of the church, down to the last flickering lamp, has been apportioned among them. And since they cannot agree, the church is in grave danger of collapse. The Orthodox Patriarch, when he mounts his throne, sits wedged and hidden behind a gigantic scaffolding beam.

And yet it remains the most moving church in Christendom. Its imperfections are symbolic. Its holiness survives the foolishness of the sects. There is an English knight, one of the signatories of the Magna Carta, buried outside its door. So much history, so much prayer and yearning, its unique place in the heart and mind of Christianity has left a mark on it.

The whole of what was central Palestine is strewn with these places, guarded by a few Franciscans, or a lonely Greek priest, or some ageing Russian nun. There is an air of desertion about most of them. The local Christians are few; the visitors are mostly tourists. The places survive as an end in themselves.

One of them is almost certainly authentic. This is a great worn pavement in the basement of a convent in Jerusalem. It is the Lithostrotos, the pavement of the courtyard of the Antonia, which was the Roman garrison fort dominating the Temple area. Here Pilate pronounced his judgment and the soldiers played their rude games. But absolute authenticity seems an unnecessary thing in this country. It is the idea that overwhelms.

Minor Capitals of Communism

by Mark Frankland

They say that pre-war Budapest was a great favourite with the Duke of Windsor when Prince of Wales. Even after a war, a dozen years of Stalinist rule and a revolution you can still understand why. Prague would probably have been too Germanic for his taste. I don't know if he ever went to Warsaw. I find it hard to believe that it existed before the war. Its rebuilt palaces and old quarters remind me not of the pre-war city but of the war ruins and Polish patriotism.

Bucharest is another matter altogether. If the Prince did go there he had the choice of two very suitable hotels, both of which still exist. The Athené Palace is the senior, refreshingly dark in the hot summer and with a small vine-shaded courtyard as a dining-room. Or he could have gone to the Lido, which has a swimming bath that makes artificial waves and must have been very smart indeed in those days. You can still have a princely dinner at a restaurant which the Prince would have known as Capsa's and is now called the Bucharest.

Capsa's plays an important part in the best Marxist-historical novel I have read, *The Boyars*. Written by a Rumanian called Dumitriu, it takes you through Rumanian history from the nineteenth century to the Second World War. Selfishness, sex and senility are among the sub-themes (his old men have faces like "sweating cheese"). If Dumitriu was right, and there is no reason to believe he was not, Capsa's was about the only thing that deserved preserving from the old days.

The first time I went to Bucharest the first drink I was offered was a gin-fizz—quite a shock because I had come from Moscow. Experience has confirmed that it is a drink that Bucharest barmen like to suggest. I think they enjoy making it.

It is not, however, the Rumanian national drink. Out towards the airport, past the imposing Council of Ministers' building with its Ministerial Mercedes parked outside, there is an excellent museum of old peasant houses that have been collected from all over the country. In one is a simple still for turning plums into tuica (pronounced tsweeka). Rumanians drink it cold, as an aperitif.

Prague is one of the great beauties of Europe. Like Budapest, it is built on two sides of a river, with the old city climbing up a steep hill. At the top are the tall, smooth walls of the Presidential palace and, growing right out of the middle of the palace like angry cactus plants, the prickly Gothic spires of St. Vitus's Cathedral.

Curiously, my most persistent memory of Prague is not visual: it is of the city's smell. It is partly beer, not so much hops as the half smell, half taste you get drinking draught Czech beer. But it is also a compound of autumn smoke, incense and dust. It is the smell of a vast old church.

Getting back to the Prince of Wales for a moment, there is no doubt he would still prefer Budapest to the other East European capitals. More than all the rest, it is a city of public pleasures. It has good food and good wine. Its night life ranges from the time-honoured large blondes sitting patiently at a bar to sophisticated piano-playing in a small, dark room. It is also possible to eat dinner surrounded by Gipsy violinists: at some of the hotels with a good foreign trade it is rather difficult not to.

In other East European capitals you sometimes get the impression that the night life, such as it is, is there to keep the foreign visitors out of harm's way. It does not always work out like that. In a Bucharest night spot called the Melody Bar I came across a group of Russian tourists listening glumly to the best modern jazz I have heard in the Balkans. The ambience was clearly not their idea of Socialism, and luckily they left before the floor show. But in Budapest the night clubs are for Hungarians just as much as for foreigners.

Warsaw is the real phoenix of Eastern Europe, but it is surprising that Budapest—remembering 1956 and the terrible demoralisation that followed—should now be the most prosperous, most relaxed, of the East European capitals. Hungarian officials enjoy the astonishment of foreigners who have just discovered this, but one suspects that they are still a bit surprised themselves.

Warsaw is the reverse of relaxed, nor is it very prosperous at the moment. In spite of all the rebuilding the city still somehow suggests war and shortages.

But the Poles look more intelligent and have more chic than most other Europeans, East or West. In Warsaw the girls are now going in for Titian hair and rather heavy make-up. They also wear hats, which is rare for East Europe. The present favourite is not unlike a converted jockey's cap, but it looks all right on a Warsaw girl.

The Poles do not call one another Comrade (they use the equivalent of the French Monsieur and Madame), and the men are great hand-kissers. A small, middle-aged man in a beret and an Italian-style rain-coat bending over the hand of a slender girl whom you can see to be beautiful and feel sure is also wise and sad: I saw that once in Warsaw, at least I think I did. What the Prince would have made of it I do not know. But because he liked Budapest he would probably at least have agreed that all these cities have been forgotten by the British for far too long.

Milan to Calais: Sleepless

by Paul Jennings

After years on aeroplanes, had almost forgotten that secret of Continental (Milan-Calais) train journey is to relax. At start (5.30 p.m.) no one in right compartment, corridors swarming with opera Chorus of Brigands, Village Women, Cigarette Workers, Soldiers, Parties of Scottish Youth, all clambering blindly over each other like ants, loaded with great bags and bundles (eggs?). Peevish English voice reiterates endlessly, "*But this one IS 32*". Official who organises *couchettes* doesn't even get on train till Lugano (or Lucerne, say some. Or Basle, say others).

Relax, be old travellers, go to dining car. Sure enough, after great vealy meal, walk back through empty corridors. Where all Brigands, etc., *gone*? Train has stopped once or twice at small stations in high, remote, windy part of Switzerland, they can't all have got out here? (Burghers in night-caps roused by shouting and wailing in streets, emergency clocken-glockenbell signals, blankets, soup, army cots in Town Hall. . . .)

Find *couchette* man (why he's French, already! It's the railway that dissolves frontiers, not the aeroplane, which is really just a Bath Road cocktail bar that happens to be able to do 500 m.p.h., leaving you totally unprepared for mad foreign soldiers and money). Find own *couchette*, relieved to find other couple not Brigands, but like us, got children, late cheap holiday, don't like go in same aeroplane. He jolly smiling Italian antique dealer.

Settle down, wives in lower bunks, men in upper. Antique dealer goes out to corridors, reappears magically thirty seconds later wearing pyjamas; have feeling he just pulled ripcord and joke suit fell off. All settle down, lights out. Well, if he pyjamas, me too. Terrible contortions under blanket (silly really, since dark anyway). Sit cross-legged trying to make place on rack for shoes. What hell this, ah yes, great bottle mineral water (remembered last time in *couchette*, waking with fearful thirst). Just shove it up a bi— —*thub!* Bottle falls on tender inside of kneecap. Rub ferociously to relieve both pain and frustration at not being able to utter dreadful curses above whisper.

Not five minutes since lights out, yet antique dealer already snoring; regular, business-like snoring of man who means to snore for ten hours. He has lots of hangers, even his shirt on a hanger (mine stuffed between shoes and string bag out of which great bottle fell). Hour after hour he snores, hangars clink gently as train rush round bends so it can have long stop where snoring even more inescapable.

Why? What they *doing*? Driver having great French soup, bread, wine, veal, in engine shed, while loudspeakers on windy platform appear to address political meeting (during nightwork porters' lunch hour, as it were), till railway gendarmerie break it up, charging with armoured trolleys. Tremendous door-slamming, shouts, *pheep-pheeps*. Then absolute silence. Except for damned antique dealer, *hornk*, *oik*, *hornk*, *oik*.

Why I only one kept awake by him (wives both asleep long ago)? What good his fool hangers, elegant luggage, what good if he have *trouser-press*, if he snore like Brigand? If he rich antique dealer, bought all these shirts and hangers, why not anti-snore operation, removal adenoids or something: Why he so *peaceful* about it? Snorers encountered in Army, etc., have always worked to crescendo ending in paroxysm, they wake up just in time to stop their entire mouth and tongue falling down into their lungs, then mumblegroan to comparative silence in which can try to get to sleep before they start again. But antique dealer's snoring *is* his breathing, not a blemish on it.

Read somewhere that short, sharp sound, e.g., whistle, will stop snorer. Whistle has open-air sound, like calling taxi, sounds mad in hot dark snore-thundering compartment. Rapid interrogative Italian from antique dealer's wife. He just go on snoring. Lie utterly still, till she asleep again.

Will train ever start again? All gone away now, driver too. Mind wanders. Going to be here for ever. Man isn't snoring really (else wives would surely be awake too?), it is noise in own head. What Italian for *snore*? French? *Ronfler*, *gonfler*, please snore my tyres. Rhonchus, bronchus, man has rhonchitis. Roncesvalles, Valley Of Snoring, awful rail limbo, we here for ever. Stertor (Greek hero, dragon?).

Suddenly, unheralded, train lurches off again. Ha, idea. Use coat as pillow, press *couchette* pillow over ear. By pressing really hard and humming to self can shut out sound of snore; but woken from light quarter-sleep by feeling *couchette* pillow falling off the moment pressure relaxed. Snatch at it, in doing so dislodge one, possibly two, of those hangers. Lie utterly rigid again, imagining soft clothy rain of shirts, trousers, etc., floating down in darkness on to antique dealer's wife, lights on, questions (at least it would wake snorer)— but no sound. I only person awake in whole train. Going mad in dark. Lunatic ornamentation of original idea, will *tie* pillow and coat on either side of head, like enormous cloth headphones, with luggage strap; *must* shut out snoring with which hot dark claustrophobic universe now filled. Scrabble in rack for strap, pull it off bag, wrench, tug, *thub!* Blasted bottle falls on identical place, inside of kneecap. Dreadful pain, kneecap now centre of dark universe, bright painburst

with rays shooting out. Read somewhere damage to kneecap dangerous; probably lame, huge spreading bruise, water on knee. *Mineral*
water on knee, mirthless joke in mad darkness. . . .

Morning, nodding and smiling over coffee at antique dealer and
wife, *couchettes* folded up, perfectly normal train journey past many
French brickworks and thin little woods. He asks if I slept well, is
obviously nice man. But next time will try either to share with
Brigands or go in two aeroplanes.

Clouds over Gleneagles

by Anthony Sampson

On the edge of the Highlands, miles away from anything except
a railway station, stands the grey square palace that is the pride of
the Scottish tourist industry—the Gleneagles Hotel.

All over Scotland now, new roads, new bridges and new caravan
sites are springing up to develop the tourist traffic, to replace the old
railway trade and to take cars and coaches farther and faster to the
north.

Scottish tourism is having a difficult time. With sunnier, gayer
places becoming much more accessible, the appeal of rainswept moors
is less compelling. Last year, while visitors to Italy increased by twelve
per cent, there were actually fewer visitors to Scotland. Big hotels can
no longer be confident of long bookings, made months ahead; more
and more they are catering for two- or three-day visitors, on their
way to somewhere else.

But Gleneagles remains a monument to an older, grander age of
tourism, before cars and jets began to interrupt the old, stately progress of railways, servants and trunks. And Gleneagles is a symbol
of Scotland's problem.

Its huge shape sticks out from the empty Scottish moorland like a
liner aground: and, like a liner, it has its own complex, quaint way
of life, its own careful mythology, completely cut off from the land.
You drive up from the station, along a rhododendroned avenue, past
a golf course, round a floral roundabout, and there is the long façade
of Gleneagles, with its 350 rooms, its 700 acres, its three golf courses,
its swimming pool, cinema, squash-courts.

Once inside, you need never come out again, provided you have
enough money. There are a bank, Post Office, barber, shops and
beauty salons along the broad corridors. There is Miss Helen R. Ward,
who has been engaged as hostess for the season and who "will be
happy to arrange bridge fours, partners for tennis, golf, squash or

croquet, or to assist guests in any other way required". Above all, Gleneagles is the Temple of Golf.

Gleneagles marks a chapter in railway history. It was begun, before the First World War, by the old Caledonian Railway, to outbid all other railway hotels in splendour; but it was not finished until 1925, by the L.M.S. (into which the Caledonian had then been merged). It provided a spectacular escape for Englishmen, who could leave London on a night train after dinner and arrive in the midst of Scotland for breakfast. It had tamed Scotland, and made it habitable for the most fastidious traveller, protecting him from all alarming experiences.

Now Gleneagles is part of British Railways, but it still generates a special and stately way of life, as if the First World War had never happened. Troops of servants appear and disappear down long corridors and through high doors. The tariff anounces that a suite for two people costs from £18 a day. A special rate of 48s. 6d. is charged for visitors' servants, and the servants' quarters are quite full—not (as a hotel man explained) with the servants of rich Americans, Frenchmen or Spaniards, but with the chauffeurs and maids of the English gentry.

The clientele has certainly changed with the years: all kinds of people from all over the world fly in to play golf, and Americans without ties can be seen swinging clubs in the bar. Scandinavians (who do not seem to notice the cold) are streaming into Scotland. Most guests nowadays arrive not by train but by air or by car. The main customers are still the English—old, solid Englishmen—and one of the most faithful guests is Harold Macmillan, who comes up for golf every year and inhabits a special suite wired for a scrambler telephone.

But Gleneagles, with all its grandeur, is not altogether confident; and now, at the height of the season, it is only half full.

The hotel has its problems. In the first place, most of its guests are undeniably old and (as one of its staff pointed out) old people are apt to die off. Younger people, it seems, are not quite so attracted to baronial Scotland. A more hopeful substitute is the convention business, which keeps the hotel busy in spring and autumn; industrial executives, car salesmen or whisky dealers converge on Gleneagles to have pep talks in the morning, golf in the afternoon, and togetherness in the evening.

But the greater and more permanent snag is weather. One big semi-circular room is hopefully called Le Restaurant du Soleil: but the sun is not often present. For Gleneagles, as for most of the Scottish tourist industry, the absence of sun is the overriding embarrassment. Nowadays cheap jet flights can whisk pale tourists to Italy, Spain, and almost certain sun; but Scotland must still offer the less exotic, more spartan pleasures of walking and stalking and golf in the rain.

Drizzle and mist may have attracted the older, more Puritan travellers, but they seem to have lost their special fascination for the younger. Macmillan and Butler may favour Gleneagles and Mull, but Maudling prefers the Mediterranean.

Betweens

To hear a dripping water tap in a house
That has no tap in it, in the dead of night.
To hear footsteps come naturally to the door
And stop there forever. In bed in an empty room
To hear a voice on the pillow whisper, "Hello".

A wheatstalk dances lasciviously in the fire.
My hand drags its plough across this white field.
My head from a sort of radiance watches a chair
Continually completing its meaning. A picture
Tries to plunge from its nail to the centre of the earth.

Immense tides wash through everything. My knuckles
Are tiny whirlpools in it. I stream sideways.
The room's roots are straining. Sounds of the fire
Unmuffle themselves from black coal, are a theatre.
My foot rocks because my heart says so.

How could things stop? And three plump cheers for
    distance . . .
To shake a hand, and be left with it. To see
Sight cramming itself into an eye and wheat
A harrow of fire; and all a correspondence
Shielding the truth and giving birth to it.

NORMAN MACCAIG

Driving to Florida

Driving down the great highway, fast but
within limits, he's the big one now.
Mother sits by him, with her eyes shut;
he is moved beyond words to see how

vulnerable she looks—wrinkled face
and such small tight hands. The car is snug
with love. . . . It was another Christmas
that, a young mother dressed out of Vogue,

she drove him south. He tries to regain
the charm of that past trip. All at once
—authentic, abrupt evocation—
he re-enters an adolescence

whole and lucid as a ship in glass.
He is fourteen again, trapped in time
by a rage of puberty, helpless.

But a word from Mother recalls him.

She expands to fill out the whole car,
her senses quick as an animal's
to protect him from that rough hunger:
a conspiracy of tentacles!

Vulnerable? It is not her hand
sweats on the wheel. She's the big one now.
He drives on, stifling in her love, and
hankers after New York's trodden snow.

THOM GUNN